Making Sense of Your World

A Biblical Worldview

W. Gary Phillips & William E. Brown

Bryan College

Sheffield Publishing Company

Salem, Wisconsin

For information about this book, write or call:
      Sheffield Publishing Company
      P.O. Box 359
      Salem, Wisconsin 53168
      (414) 843-2281

To our parents
Bill and Mildred Phillips
Joe and DeLois Brown
who first gave us our worldview
which we have at various times over the years
embraced, questioned, rejected, reexamined, and
now eagerly explore

William E. Brown earned his B.A. (honors) in Mathematics from the University of South Florida, and his Th.M. and Ph.D. (honors) from Dallas Theological Seminary. He is Professor of Bible at Bryan College, where he has served as Academic Vice President and Provost. In 1992 he became the sixth President of Bryan College.

Dr. Brown regularly speaks at conferences and lectures to teachers and officials in the former Soviet Union. He has written or contributed to several books and journals. He is a member of the Society of Christian Philosophers, the Evangelical Philosophical Society, the Evangelical Theological Society, and the Executive Board of the Appalachian College Association. He has been chosen "Teacher of the Year" by the Bryan College students. Bill and his wife Lynne have two children: April and Alex.

W. Gary Phillips earned his B.A. from Vanderbilt University (Math, Philosophy, English), his Th.M. from Dallas Theological Seminary, and his Th.D. from Grace Theological Seminary. He is Professor of Bible and Philosophy and is Chair of the Division of Biblical Studies at Bryan College.

Dr. Phillips speaks at conferences, has written or contributed to several books and journals, and has been chosen "Teacher of the Year" at Bryan College. He is a member of the Society of Christian Philosophers, the Evangelical Philosophical Society, and serves as an officer in the Evangelical Theological Society. Gary is a medical ethics consultant, and is Pastor of Signal Mountain Bible Church in Chattanooga, Tennessee. He and his wife Betsy have three children: David, Beth, and Rebecca.

CONTENTS

INDEX OF GRAPHICS

FOREWORD

Instead of viewing Christianity as a collection of theological bits and pieces to be believed or debated, Christians should see their faith as a total world- and lifeview. Once they understand that both Christianity and its competitors are worldviews, they will be in a better position to judge Christianity's strengths with respect to other systems.

A worldview is a conceptual scheme by which we, consciously or unconsciously, place or fit everything we believe. We use our worldview to interpret and judge reality. Unfortunately, many people have little or no idea what a worldview is, or even that they have one. One of the more important things a good education can do for students is to help them realize what a worldview is, assist them in achieving a better understanding of their own worldview, and aid them in improving their worldview. From an informed Christian perspective, this education in worldviews will best be done in the setting of a Christian education.

The right eyeglasses can put the world into clearer focus. The correct worldview can function in much the same way. When someone looks at the world through the wrong worldview, the world will not make much sense, or what the person thinks makes sense will be wrong in important respects. Viewing the world through the correct worldview can have important repercussions for the rest of a person's belief.

The case for or against Christianity should be evaluated in terms of total systems. The reason many people reject Christianity is not because of problems with one or two isolated issues. Instead, they reject it simply because their anti-Christian worldview leads them to reject information and arguments that provide believers with important support for the Christian worldview.

The first modern Christian thinker to utilize a worldview approach to his defense of the Chrisitian faith—as far as I know—was the Scottish theologian James Orr in his book *The Christian View of God and the World.*[1] I can still remember my first philosophy professor, Cariton Gregory of Barrington College, expressing the hope that someone might someday update Orr's work. Several decades after Orr's death, in the late 1930s, Gordon H. Clark began to develop his own worldview approach in his philosophy and apologetics classes at Wheaton College.[2] It is no coincidence that Clark gave one of his early books the title *A Christian View of Men and Things.*[3]

In their own works, two of Clark's undergraduate students at Wheaton College, Carl Henry and Edward John Carnell, utilized the worldview approach they had learned frm Clark. Even though Carnell's *An Introduction to Christian Apologetics*[4] was published a few years before Clark's *Christian View of Men and Things*, it should not obscure the fact that Carnell borrowed important elements of his approach from his teacher.[5] Henry's indebtedness and continued respect for Clark is apparent in many of his writings.

As most readers of this book will know, the great popularizer of the worldview approach to Christianity was Francis Schaeffer. Schaeffer did more than use a worldview approach to defend the Christian faith. He utilized it effectively in developing and promoting a Christian approach to culture.

Given all that I learned over the years from the likes of Orr, Clark, Henry, Schaeffer, and others, no one should be surprised to find a major emphasis on worldviews in my own work. Whenever I have taught beginning courses in philosophy over the past twenty-nine years at Western Kentucky University, I have always tried to impress upon my students the importance of this approach and the urgency of their getting clear about their own worldview. When it finally came time for me to write my own book on apologetics and the philosophy of religion, the first four chapters

1. James Orr, *The Christian View of God and the World*, 7th ed. (New York: Scribner's, 1904).
2. For an interesting account of Clark's days at Wheaton and his influence on Carl Henry's later work, see Henry's autobiography, *Confessions of a Theologian* (Waco, Tex.: Word, 1986), chap. 5. See also Henry's fine tribute to Clark in *The Philosophy of Gordon H. Clark,* ed. Ronald Nash (Philadelphia: Presby. and Ref., 1968). This work, long out of print, will soon be published in a second edition by the Trinity Foundation, Jefferson, Maryland.
3. Gordon H. Clark, *A Christian View of Men and Things* (Grand Rapids: Eerdmans, 1952). This work is now available from the Trinity Foundation.
4. Edward J. Carnell, *An Introduction to Christian Apologetics* (Grand Rapids: Eerdmans, 1948).
5. Of course, other influences were also at work in Carnell's early work, such as Cornelius Van Til and Edgar Sheffield Brightman.

were devoted to an analysis of worldviews in general and to the Christian worldview in particular.[6]

It should be easy to understand therefore why I am so delighted to see this new book on the biblical worldview by William Brown and Gary Phillips. It is my hope that this outstanding work will serve to introduce new generations of Christians—young and old—to this important way of thinking.

RONALD NASH

---

6. See Ronald Nash, *Faith and Reason: Searching for a Rational Faith* (Grand Rapids: Zondervan, 1988).

1996 PREFACE

Not long ago in Kiev, a dozen public school teachers surrounded William E. (Bill) Brown near the back of the auditorium where he had completed a week of lectures on the biblical worldview. They presented Bill with a gift, a beautiful commemorative coin honoring the independence of Ukraine from communist and Russian control.

"We want you to have this so you will always remember us," they said. "This week we have changed our worldview."

Bill was moved by their gift and the choice of their words. The desire of these people to become Christians was more than "trusting Christ." They recognized that they were making a deliberate change in their basic assumptions about life and the world.

Since *Making Sense of Your World* was first published, we have been overwhelmed with the response. Not only is it being used in colleges and schools across the country, it is being translated into Russian to be distributed to teachers and administrators throughout the former Soviet Union.

We have found that a worldview approach to education is essential. Socrates knew that we enter this world in ignorance, and that in order to learn we must first become aware of our ignorance. God has created us to be reflective beings, and yet often we don't reflect. We focus deeply on our life vocation, but don't think deeply about our life. Students who begin worldview studies go through an awakening process. They begin to realize, "Wait a minute. This is what life is about!" When we are forced to deal with the big questions of life, we may come to realize that our answers are more slogans anchored in sand than principles anchored in Truth. A physicist outside of Moscow said, "I never thought about it before. Now I know that my worldview is naturalism. Maybe I need to change."

And that is, of course, the point; it is why we wrote this book. Our thanks go to those who have encouraged us in this continuing project, to Sheffield Publishing Company for reissuing it, and to our families for their ongoing support.

— William E. Brown and W. Gary Phillips
April 1996

PREFACE

"There is no longer a Christian mind."

With this proclamation, Harry Blamires begins his book *The Christian Mind: How Should A Christian Think?*[1] Blamires points out that there is a Christian ethic, a Christian practice, and a Christian spirituality, but that consistent thinking on the part of Christians does not exist. The fragmentation of American culture has found its way into the very heart of American Christianity. The resulting spiritual schizophrenia provides a sad model for the coming generation of Christians who must forge a biblical agenda into the 2000s.

For this reason, thinking and living "Christianly" have become a mandate for this generation. Under the banner "Christian worldview," prophetic voices call for a breadth and depth in understanding the biblical perspective of the world and life. A number of books on a Christian worldview have been written that provide a good survey of the issues involved. Among them are *Building a Christian World View,*[2] a two-volume series that approaches the subject historically, topically, and from a distinctly Reformed slant. The *Turning Point Christian Worldview Series* discusses the application of a Christian worldview from the perspective of contemporary issues.[3] The Christian College Coalition is publishing a

1. Harry Blamires, *The Christian Mind: How Should A Christian Think?* (Ann Arbor, Mich.: Servant, 1978), p. 3.
2. W. Andrew Hoffecker and Gary Scott Smith, eds., *Building a Christian World View*, 2 vols. (Phillipsburg, N.J.: Presby. & Ref., 1986, 1988).
3. This series is jointly sponsored by Crossway Books and the Fieldstead Institute. See Herbert Schlossberg and Marvin Olasky, *Turning Point: A Christian Worldview Declaration* (Westchester, Ill.: Crossway, 1987). Other titles in the series reflect the intention to speak to contemporary areas of concern from a biblical perspective. They include: *Prodigal Press: The Anti-Christian Bias of the American News Media; Freedom, Justice and Hope: Toward a Strategy for the Poor and Oppressed; Beyond Good Intentions: A Biblical View of Politics;* and *Prosperity and Poverty: The Compassionate Use of Resources in a World of Scarcity.*

number of supplemental texts ("Through Eyes of Faith" series) for the purpose of helping Christian college professors present the biblical implications of their disciplines.[4] The fine series *Contours of Christian Philosophy*, edited by C. Stephen Evans, is more specific in its application of a Christian worldview, but it targets the philosophical foundations of several areas of study.[5] Other books exploring a Christian worldview will be mentioned later.

Seeing the need to present college students and laypersons with the "why and wherefore" of a biblical worldview resulted in several years of study, discussion, and debate, which further led to a number of papers, articles, a book, and eventually a "biblical worldview" freshman class at Bryan College. Putting the research and development into this book is another step in the process of helping all Christians (including ourselves) hammer out their faith against the hard realities that competing and conflicting worldviews present.

In a book of this scope, many important issues must be left for other works to explore and explain. For this reason, each chapter includes a bibliography for further reading. Discussion questions and case studies provide direction for continued thinking in the subjects explored in each chapter.

Developing a biblical worldview is no easy task—but it is a necessary one. Christians are called to "mature thinking," which means we must lay aside an immature simplicity in our approach to life (1 Cor. 14:20). If we are to take captive every thought to the obedience of Christ (2 Cor. 10:5), we must allow the Lord through His Word to set the agenda for our views and values. The hope is that consistent godly thinking will lead to consistent godly living with the result that the Christian community will confidently confront the slings and arrows of a secular world with the truth of God's revealed Word.

We would like to express our deepest appreciation to the following special people.

To the students of Bryan College who, through the biblical worldview course, all serve as perpetual "guinea pigs" for our ideas and plans.

To the Upper East Tennessee Chapter of the Bryan College Alumni Association (Jim and Judy Barth, Ralph and Ruth Green, Maxie and Zoe Green, Joe and Lynne Runyon, Gene and Joey Broughton, David and

4. The series is published by Harper & Row and includes such works as *History Through the Eyes of Faith*, by Ronald A. Wells (San Francisco: Harper & Row, 1989) and *Biology Through the Eyes of Faith*, by Richard T. Wright (San Francisco: Harper & Row, 1989).

5. This series is published by InterVarsity Press and includes works by Arthur Holmes on ethics, Del Ratzsch on science, Michael Peterson on education, and Stephen Evans on religion.

Beth Sault, and Barbara Howard), a very strange and fun-loving group of people who provided the funds for computer equipment.

To Barbara Howard and Nick Decosimo who read portions of the manuscript and gave helpful suggestions.

To James Muecke, for his constant availability to "debug" our computer problems.

To Garry Knussman of Moody Press, for his encouragement along the way.

To Dana Gould, formerly of Moody Press, who was instrumental in getting the first stages of this project off the ground.

To Ronald Nash for his "world-viewish" perspective that has motivated us over the past years.

To Carl F. H. Henry who refined our thinking with his gentle but pointed questions.

And, most important, to our families: Betsy Phillips, David, Beth, and Rebecca Ann; and Lynne Brown, April, and Alex. Their love and support was always there to make all the work worthwhile. We love you.

INTRODUCTION

It is time to recover the Christian mind. But even while some lament the nonexistence of the Christian mind, American Christianity charges full-speed ahead in its course of incessant activity, indomitable individualism, and irrepressible pragmatism. "Doing the work" and "getting results" make up the all-consuming objectives of the Christian church and leave little room (and time) for tough-minded contemplation of the role of a Christian worldview. Quantifying the work of the ministry has resulted in sanctified versions of the Fortune 500 (the largest churches and ministries), the top forty (Christian pop music), and the Nielsen ratings (Christian television). The "feel-good" religion that Christianity has become casts a jaundiced eye toward anything that smacks of "intellectual pursuit." Historian Mark Noll quips, "Comprehensive and coherent Christian thinking has never been a major part of religious life in America."[1]

Society in general gives little evidence of thinking about ultimate questions and important issues. The resulting self-indulgent values permeate every strata of social interaction. Many in higher education lament the shift away from altruistic ideals to an obsession with "having it all." The well-known study by the American Council on Education and the Higher Education Research Institute at UCLA revealed that over three-fourths of college freshmen feel that being financially well off is an "essential" or "very important" goal. A key reason for their decision to attend college was "to make more money," while at the same time only thirty-nine per cent of freshmen put any emphasis on developing a meaningful philosophy of life.[2] Miles Hardy, professor of psychology at the

1. Mark Noll, "Christian World Views and Some Lessons from History," in *The Making of a Christian Mind,* ed. Arthur Holmes (Downers Grove, Ill.: InterVarsity, 1985), p. 29.
2. Reported in "Freshmen Found Stressing Wealth," *New York Times*, 14 January 1988, p. A-14.

University of South Florida, grieves the lost values of the current college community. Students of the 1960s, he notes, at least had a concern for other people. He goes on, "Today's students are more interested in money, in what they can turn into bucks. They have little interest in the fine arts and social sciences but want a short cut to quick rewards."[3]

Christian higher education is not immune from this mercenary approach to education and life. As formal institutions of education, the Christian college, even more than the local church, must set the agenda for Christian thought. For this reason, setting forth a biblical worldview is no longer optional for institutions that desire to be distinctly Christian in their educational philosophy. The presentation and defense of a biblical worldview must be aggressive in its engagement with alternate worldviews; it must be well-rounded in its integration with the full scope of truth. Carl F. H. Henry delivers this charge: "Just as the Enlightenment in its revolt against Biblical theism sought to explain law, religion, science, ethics, and all aspects of culture without reference to miraculous revelation and redemption, so Christian supernaturalism must bring into its purview every sphere of reality and activity. It will involve all the disciplines of a liberal arts education."[4]

Developing a biblical worldview involves both a *mindset* and a *willset*.[5] The former includes the essentials of a biblical view *of* the world. How does the Bible explain and interpret my life and the world around me? Once this question is answered and accepted as a matter of principle, the latter aspect of a biblical worldview presents the challenge to put this view into practice. This is a biblical view *for* the world; an application of this view to life. My values, plans, and decisions are informed by—even prescribed by—the worldview perspective given by the Scriptures.

This twofold description of a worldview forms the framework for this book. Part one examines the first of these worldview functions: a view *of* the world. We will begin this exploration by describing the nature of worldviews in general, then we will focus on the essential elements of a worldview that is decidedly biblical. Following this we will confront the challenges to a biblical worldview and attempt to give adequate answers to those who find the biblical perspective inadequate or in error. The purpose of part one is to present a coherent and compelling explanation and

---

3. Quoted by Marie Deibler, "Activism, Apathy, Apartheid: Times They Are A Changin' (again)" *USF Magazine* (March 1986), p. 17.
4. Carl F. H. Henry, *Twilight of a Great Civilization: The Drift Toward Neo-Paganism* (Westchester, Ill.: Crossway, 1988), p. 121.
5. Ibid., p. 19.

defense of a biblical worldview. Part two explores applications of the biblical worldview to life: a view *for* the world.

The primary goal of any worldview exploration must be the attainment of truth. Let us begin our quest by exploring the world of worldviews.

PART 1:

A VIEW OF THE WORLD

What the meaning of life may be I don't know; I incline to suspect that it has none.

H. L. MENCKEN

The man who regards his own life and that of his fellow creatures as meaningless is not merely unhappy but hardly fit for life.

ALBERT EINSTEIN

Is life worth living, or is it a meaningless absurdity?

How one answers this question sets the stage for how (and even why) one chooses to live. The disagreement between Einstein and Mencken evident in the opening quotes cuts deeply into the fundamental differences among religions and philosophies.

Mencken's way is by far the easier path to travel. A meaningless existence requires nothing from anyone. There is no need to check for bearings along the way, no need to justify one's choices, values, or goals. Life is a lark at best, a tedium at worst. Such a philosophy agrees with Brendan Gill, who once quipped, "Not a shred of evidence exists in favor of the idea that life is serious."

On the other hand, there exists a "quiet desperation" that drives humanity to think about the question, "Does life have meaning?" Deciding that life *does* have meaning is not the end but the beginning of a quest. Life becomes a continual pilgrimage to find, affirm, and reaffirm a philosophy of life. One may join a church (or leave a church), change religions, switch jobs, get married, get divorced, or make any number of changes in an attempt to find meaning and purpose.

This is the stuff of worldviews.

The tragedy in American culture is that thinking has given way to feeling, pragmatism has replaced principles, and "how to" takes the place of "how come." Robert Bellah describes a woman whose worldview epitomizes many: "I just sort of accept the way the world is and then don't think about it a whole lot."[1] The results of this approach are the autonomy and individualism that are so much a part of current American public thought.

Raising the basic questions addressed by the worldview inquiry is an imperative for evangelical Christians. In the face of New Age irrationality, Islamic fanaticism, and existential sensuality, Christianity must present an alternative that sweeps away stereotypes and answers the central longings of man's existence.

The vital step is for Christians to think in terms of worldviews. Some argue that God merely requires a childlike faith and that a breadth of understanding of worldviews is unnecessary, but this confuses "childlikeness" with "childishness." As a child is unusually focused on his own needs and desires, so many Christians brandish a commitment to a biblical worldview that goes little beyond their personal well-being. Harry Blamires warns, "We cannot make sense of adult life with the mental equipment of a child. We cannot afford to carry into adult life a Christian consciousness so undernourished and anaemic that we slide into accepting faddish convenience recipes for worldly well-being as our daily diet."[2]

If a superficial knowledge of a biblical worldview continues to dominate the evangelical community, we cannot expect that community to stand unblemished against the onslaught of other worldview choices. David Wolfe cautions, "Our ungrounded belief is easily swayed and abandoned, even though it may be correct."[3]

It is time for Christians to put away childish thinking (1 Cor. 13:11; 14:20) and boldly confront the world with the message of Christ. We may best accomplish this by exploring worldviews to discover where the biblical view agrees and conflicts with other views. This involves knowing both the essentials of a biblical worldview and the basic tenets of the alternate views. A person often finds it helpful to understand what he believes by knowing what he does not believe, and why. Then, he must confront the challenges to a biblical worldview raised by those from other

1. Robert Bellah et al, *Habits of the Heart: Individualism and Commitment in American Life* (New York: Harper & Row, 1985), p. 14.
2. Harry Blamires, *Recovering the Christian Mind* (Downers Grove, Ill.: InterVarsity, 1988), p. 9.
3. David Wolfe, *Epistemology: The Justification of Belief* (Downers Grove, Ill.: InterVarsity, 1982), p. 15.

perspectives. Are there good answers to the crucial questions asked by critics? Can a biblical worldview withstand the scrutiny of its detractors?

To this end we shall undertake the subjects of developing a biblical view *of* the world in part one.

1

WHEN WORLDVIEWS COLLIDE

WORLDVIEWS: MAKING SENSE OF LIFE

Early in the afternoon of July 19, 1989, United Airlines flight 232 lifted off from Denver's Stapleton International Airport and headed east for Chicago. The 296 passengers and crew aboard the airliner anticipated an uneventful two-hour trip, but soon after lunch was served, tragedy struck. The number two engine near the tail of the aircraft exploded. The plane never reached O'Hare International Airport in Chicago. The graphic pictures of the DC-10 spinning and cartwheeling across the cornfields near Sioux City, Iowa, caused even the most hardened news reporters to gasp in horror. Miraculously, 185 people survived the fiery crash.

In the aftermath, the survivors of this tragic event were asked to philosophize on the reason for the crash. Why did it happen? Why were some saved? Why did 111 people die?

Many believed there was no particular reason for the crash. "Things happen," some said. The people on board just happened to be there coincidentally; it could have been anyone. Survivor Peter Wernick stated: "I am a humanist. I don't believe there is a kindly Supreme Being who responds to people one-on-one. People ask me if I am still a non-believer after my life was saved. If everybody had had his life saved except the bad people on the plane, maybe I'd believe a little more. But that's not what happened."

Others believed that a personal God was directly involved. Helen Young Hayes, a securities analyst from Denver, believed God took her through the crash for her own personal benefit. She claimed: "I think I went through this for a purpose—to show that God can still be seen and felt and glorified in the face of this tragedy."[1]

Still others postulated that the crash was planned, unwittingly it seems, by the "negative psychic energy" of some of the passengers. "Everything that happens to us is a creation of our minds and spirits," explained one psychic in a televised interview.

A coincidence . . . a personal God . . . cosmic forces? This single event spawned different interpretations that represent more than just isolated opinions. Identifying which view is the "correct" view is not the point. What is important is that each of the three explanations is the reflection of a differing worldview; a different understanding of how the world works.

A worldview has been compared to a pair of glasses through which we see the world. Without these glasses, the world would appear as an unfocused, meaningless blob. The glasses not only allow us to see, but to make sense out of what we see.

Everyone has a worldview. It is not only a human prerogative, but a human necessity. Some people have well-defined worldviews, which they can articulate clearly as their "philosophy of life." Others possess a worldview that is not so systematically arranged—at least not consciously—yet it still serves to give direction and meaning to their lives.

Our existence in the world screams for meaning. We cannot merely live like the animals in passive submission to the forces around us. Our minds question our existence and crave to know the meaning of life. The individual knows this is not *his* world and that he did not create himself, yet he has the frightening task of trying to make sense of it all. The universe would go on if he never lived; yet he is here. Why?[2]

---

1. Quotes taken from *Life*, September 1989, pp. 29-35.
2. These feelings of insecurity and dependence are what Reinhold Niebuhr calls man's "natural contingency." See Reinhold Niebuhr, *The Nature and Destiny of Man* (New York: Scribners, 1941), vol. 1, *Human Nature*, p. 178.

Even the nonreligious recognize that man has a "crying need" to make sense out of his life. Humanist Deane Starr writes, "Humans find their most complete fulfillment, whether real or imaginary, in some sort of intimacy with the ultimate."[3] The inability of many to find some reason for living results in an array of emotional and behavioral aberrations. Anthropologist Paul Hiebert concludes "to lose the faith that there is meaning in life and in the universe is to lose part of what it means to be human."[4] Bruno Bettelheim adds, "Our greatest and most difficult achievement is to find meaning in life. It is well known that many people lose their will to live because such meaning evades them."[5]

All around us, people desperately try to make sense of their lives and put their worlds together. Unconsciously, many accept popular views of life because they are glitzy, fashionable, or just downright fun. Worldview evangelists are everywhere: the New Age actress, the television scientist, the libidinous teenagers in the latest Hollywood youth movie, and even the characters on Saturday morning TV cartoons.

Amid the din of varied views clamoring for attention, the real issue is often overlooked: Which worldview is the "correct" one? Which view represents reality? Which one adequately explains the events in the universe and the experiences of a person's mind and emotions? We must always keep in mind that it does not matter whether or not a particular worldview suits *us;* the question is, Does it suit *the world*?

Christians believe God has spoken and revealed the essentials of a worldview that is genuine, that is, objectively true. Through His creation (the universe) and His Word (the Bible), God has shown man how to make sense of his world and his life. God explains why He made the world and where He is leading it. In Scripture He unveils the cause of suffering, the remedy for evil, and the ultimate end of all things.

The purpose of this book is twofold. The first is to describe and defend a distinctly biblical worldview. Biblical Christianity is more than a religious facet of life; it is even more than a view of God and religion. Ronald Nash notes, "Christianity is not simply a religion that tells human beings how they may be forgiven. It is a total world- and life-view."[6]

---

3. Deane Starr, "The Crying Need for a Believable Theology," *The Humanist*, July/August 1984, p. 13.

4. Paul Hiebert, *Cultural Anthropology* (Philadelphia: Lippincott, 1976), pp. 355-56.

5. Bruno Bettelheim, "Reflections: The Use of Enchantment," *The New Yorker,* 8 December 1975, p. 50. Bettelheim also notes that some people *do* attempt to live "from moment to moment" without giving any thought to their existence. For such people, finding a "meaning in life" is not important.

6. Ronald Nash, *Faith and Reason* (Grand Rapids: Zondervan, 1988), p. 39.

Whether a person is Christian or not, he must acknowledge that the Bible describes a comprehensive perspective of life and the world. But what is this perspective? To gain insight into the nature of the biblical worldview we will examine how it compares with competing worldviews.

A second purpose of this book is to take the biblical worldview and apply it to the life of the individual. If a biblical worldview is true, then what difference does it make in the way we live? How should one view himself, his family, church, job, society, government, and world?

First, we shall lay the groundwork for our discussion by exploring the smorgasbord of worldviews available. We shall begin by defining a worldview, and then probing the essentials of various ones.

WORLDVIEWS: HOW DO THEY WORK?

"The goal in life is to survive; you gotta keep out of trouble. You know, party and have a good time, but don't overdo it and hurt somebody."

Most prison inmates I talk with have no problem articulating their worldview—whatever it might be. Harry was no exception. He told me his story of how the world works and what is important in life.

"So you survive," I asked. "What happens then?"

"You die," he replied matter-of-factly.

"And after that?"

"Nothing." He looked insistent. "When you die, you die."

"You mean there's no God or life after death?"

"Nope." He responded. Then he looked away and sighed. "If there is, I'm in big trouble."

THE DEFINITION OF A WORLDVIEW

Harry recognized that the choices he made in his lifestyle reflected his views of God and immortality. His rejection of God and life after death were a part of his worldview. Before I left, he had narrated his own story about the existence of the world and man's purpose in life.

We all have a "story," a description of why we are here and where we are going. This helps us see where we fit into the world and how to get the most out of life. In one sense, our story is our worldview.

The concept of worldview has been defined in various ways. A popular definition is given by Charles Kraft in his thought-provoking work *Christianity in Culture*. He describes a worldview as "the central systematization of conceptions of reality to which the members of the culture assent (largely unconsciously) and from which stems their value system."[7] Kraft's definition highlights the two elements of a worldview: (1) a perspective of reality; and (2) the resulting value system that forms the basis for lifestyle choices.

Philosopher Nicholas Wolterstorff echoes this twofold emphasis of a worldview: "A people's world view is [1] their way of thinking about life and the world, [2] coupled with the values they set for themselves in the context of that way of thinking."[8] Biologist Richard Wright agrees. He describes a worldview as "[1] a comprehensive framework of beliefs that helps us to interpret what we see and experience and [2] also gives us direction in the choices that we make as we live out our days."[9]

It is this twofold perspective that will serve as the framework for our working description of a worldview. A worldview is, first of all, *an explanation and interpretation of the world* and second, *an application of this view to life.* In simpler terms, our worldview is a view *of* the world and a view *for* the world.[10] It is my blueprint for reality describing my understanding of the world and prescribing how I will live in it.

THE ELEMENTS OF A WORLDVIEW

When we unpack the components of a worldview we can arrange them in a number of ways. We can describe the elements philosophically, theologically, or culturally. Because worldviews are essentially *personal,* it seems best for our purposes to examine them from the perspective of our personal encounter with the world.

Worldviews are never passive; they are by their very nature confrontational. My worldview is a confrontation of my presence in the world. I must orient myself to my world and make sense of it or I lose the desire to exist as a human being. As I grapple with my place in the world, I must confront three major features of my existence: (1) *God,* the concept of ultimate reality; (2) *humanity,* the reality of human existence and my own self-consciousness (as well as that of other persons); and (3) *nature,* the existence and purpose of the world around me, both physical and

---

7. Charles H. Kraft, *Christianity in Culture* (Maryknoll, N.Y.: Orbis, 1979), p. 53.
8. Cited in Brian J. Walsh and J. Richard Middleton, *The Transforming Vision* (Downers Grove, Ill.: InterVarsity, 1984), p. 9. (Numerals added.)
9. Richard T. Wright, *Biology Through the Eyes of Faith* (San Francisco: Harper & Row, 1989), p. 247. (Numerals added.)
10. For this "dual focus" of a worldview see Clifford Geertz, "Religion as a Cultural System," in *Reader in Comparative Religion,* ed. W. A. Lessner and E. Z. Vogt. 3d ed. (New York: Harper & Row, 1972), p. 169. A fuller treatment is given in Geertz's *The Interpretation of Cultures* (New York: Basic Books, 1973), p. 93.

spiritual. How I respond to this upward, inward, and outward confrontation forms the framework for my worldview.[11]

Confronting God

One's view of God is the starting point for all worldviews. Mortimer Adler, in the Great Books series, comments, "More consequences for thought and action follow the affirmation or denial of God than from answering any other basic question."[12] When *confronting God,* I come face to face with that which is of ultimate concern. Even those who reject the existence of God have confronted the "God-question." It is not optional. An atheist may merely shrug off the existence of God, or he may face it with more sincerity than many Christians. However he arrives at his atheism, he must confront "God."

If I deny the existence of God, I still must explain certain qualities of man and the world that have been traditionally answered by appealing to God. Why does humanity even have the idea of God if no such being exists? How did the universe come into existence? How do we account for the apparent design and purpose within nature? Why is there a sense of right and wrong within the heart of man?

Denying the existence of God usually results in a worldview that focuses on the more immediate concerns of humanity rather than on "ultimate" questions. A "God-less" philosophy of life generally emphasizes the "here and now" because there is no "out there and later." We shall explore the implications of a worldview without God in chapter two.

If I take the step to acknowledge the existence of God, I am forced to answer several questions about Him. Is He a personal being or an impersonal force? Is He actively involved in human events? Is He a moral God who will judge His creation? Can He communicate with man? Does He desire to communicate with man?

If I believe that God is the Creator of all things, I move myself from the center of my universe and see God as the most important being. I ask Him the crucial questions, "Why did you make me?" and, "What do you expect from me?" If He is the final judge, then I desperately need to know by what criteria He will judge me and what I must do to pass acceptably. What I say about God embraces everything else I believe.

11. These three aspects of man's existence became the focal point of many nineteenth- and twentieth-century theological inquiries. Schleiermacher's theological system utilized man, nature, and God as a framework; see Friedrich Schleiermacher, *The Christian Faith*, ed. H. R. Mackintosh and J. S. Stewart (Edinburgh: T. & T. Clark, 1928). See also William Temple's *Nature, Man and God* (London: Macmillan, 1934).
12. Mortimer J. Adler, *Great Books of the Western World*, ed. Robert M. Hutchins (Chicago: Encyclopedia Britannica, 1952), 2:561.

Confronting Humanity

"Man," wrote Reinhold Niebuhr, "has always been his own most vexing problem. How shall he think of himself?"[13] In confronting humanity I am laying the foundation for my worldview. Why? Because whatever I decide about humanity's place in the world affects me; it is my worldview. I am setting the agenda for my life.

The question of the nature of humanity is where my worldview connects with my philosophy of life. Before he became a Christian, Russian novelist Leo Tolstoy listed six questions he had to answer:

Why am I living?
What is the cause of my existence and that of everyone else?
Why do I exist?
Why is there a division of good and evil within me?
How must I live?
What is death — how can I save myself?[14]

Tolstoy's quest to understand the ultimate questions of life is the heart and soul of a worldview. Consciously or unconsciously we all face ultimate questions such as these. How we answer them personally gives us meaning and purpose in our lives and provides the framework for how we live.

Beyond the question of my presence in the world, I ponder the kind of being I am. I must come to grips with my intellectual, social, moral, and religious natures. How can I know anything? Why can I think? Why can I feel? Why can I even ask why?

I am me. How did I get to be "me"? Why am I the way I am? Further, I see other people who all have this same concept of personal identity. They are like me, but they are not "me." What is my responsibility to them? What is their responsibility to me? Confronting ourselves is a difficult and unnerving task. We are both the subject and the object of the investigation.

Whatever I decide about my purpose and future will set the values I place on my family, job, and others. If I conclude that my life has no purpose, then I will live accordingly. If I reason that my existence has some meaning, then I will generally conform my life to that purpose (or at least I should).

---

13. Niebuhr, *Human Nature*, p. 1.
14. Stephen Zweig, *The Living Thoughts of Tolstoy* (Philadelphia: David McKay, 1939), p. 4.

Confronting Nature

A final aspect in the development of one's worldview is the *confrontation with nature;* or, as Redfield puts it, "man" confronting "not-man."[15] To possess a *world*view, I must have an explanation that includes all the elements of the universe—one that first describes the origin of the world and explains its apparent design.

How am I related to the physical universe? At times I am the master of nature; at other times I am its slave. Is the natural world friendly, hostile, or indifferent to man?

In times past, the confrontation with nature was often the major influence in man's comprehending his place in the world. His understanding and response to nature set the agenda for the life and practice of his culture. Some of the earliest worldviews saw man and nature as partners in the universe. There was a personal relationship with the world that emphasized a need on the part of man to be in harmony with his environment. For example, to the early Egyptians, two central events in nature helped to shape their worldview: the triumphant daily rebirth of the sun and the triumphant annual rebirth of the Nile River.[16] Their confrontation with nature led them to assume a regularity in the universe. Nature was a friendly and benevolent partner in the cycles of life. For this reason, the people of Egypt considered themselves to be the special object of care by the gods of nature. The word *human*, in fact, was used by the Egyptians only to refer to themselves.

The ancient Mesopotamians, on the other hand, did not have the benefit of the Nile River or the somewhat predictable seasonal changes of Egypt; rather, they were overwhelmed by the power within natural events. The cosmos seemed capricious, often antagonistic. To the Mesopotamians, nature was a hostile, degrading feature of life. This may have led to their strong emphasis on submission and authority within society as a whole.[17]

The confrontation with nature by these ancient societies resulted in a different understanding of man's place in the world. It is no wonder then that the Egyptians built to themselves impressive monuments that still stand today. The monuments of the Mesopotamian civilizations, in the words of the prophets, "have become heaps."

15. Robert Redfield, *The Primitive World and Its Transformations* (Ithaca, N.Y.: Cornell U., 1953), p. 92. It is important to note that Redfield included beliefs about God and spirit beings in his category of "not-man." However, this confrontation with "not-man" is first of all a confrontation of that which makes up the physical universe. It is in this sense that we refer to his term.
16. John A. Wilson, "Egypt," in *The Intellectual Adventure of Ancient Man*, ed. H. and H. A. Frankfort et al (Chicago: U. of Chicago, 1946), p. 36.
17. Thorkild Jacobsen, "Mesopotamia," ibid., p. 202.

Unlike ancient cultures (and many non-Western cultures today), Western societies do not generally confront nature with the same sense of respect. For us, the physical realm of "not-man" is indifferent to man. Nature is lifeless and spiritless, operating according to predetermined forces. It exists for man to harness for his own purposes. There are no gods to appease, no magic formulae to recite. Science and technology probe the cosmic machine for clues to increasing the well-being of humanity. We do not conform to the universe, rather we seek to conform the universe to us or our needs.

In spite of this indifference, there is another dimension in the confrontation with the created world. Is there a realm of reality that cannot be seen with physical eyes? Are there nonhuman personal beings who populate the universe? The belief in spirit beings permeates the worldviews of ancient civilizations. In their view of the universe, Persian, Greek, Jewish, Egyptian, Asian, and Roman cultures included demigods, angels, demons, and other beings.

Various mythologies ascribed certain powers to unseen personalities. Some were godlike beings and traveled between earth and the heavens, manipulating humans and circumstances for their own purposes. Other mythologies considered the unseen world populated with less-powerful beings of questionable character, or the spirits of the dead that remained to "haunt" the living.

The modern mind, which drinks heavily at the well of naturalism, has no room for the existence of spirits. Metaphysical "objects" cannot exist in a materialistic scheme. Belief in angels, demons, and other spirit beings is considered a remnant of archaic and superstitious thinking.

But the possible existence of a spirit world cannot be so easily dismissed. In spite of the great and numerous strides made by science and technology over the past two centuries, the scientific enterprise has not eradicated belief in another realm beyond the physical. In fact, interest in "the spiritual world" is on the rise. To admit to the existence of realities that cannot be empirically observed opens a flood of possibilities in the worldview arena.

My response to the confrontation of God, humanity, and nature gives much of the basic information about my worldview. Now a practical question arises: How many of us consciously confront these three features of our lives to arrive at our worldview? Often, at times of great change or loss, we become acutely aware of what our beliefs are; but this is usually a retrospective encounter with a worldview we have already developed. Yet, how did we get this worldview? There is no time in a young child's life in which he is given an opportunity to choose from the many worldview options, yet each of us clearly has chosen one of these.

WORLDVIEWS: THE CULTURAL MOLD

Worldviews are rarely isolated perspectives. Looking back at Kraft's definition of a worldview, he described it as "the central systematization of conceptions of reality *to which the members of the culture assent (largely unconsciously)* and from which stems their value system."[18] One of his points is that worldviews are shared perspectives of life that become part of the culture. A particular worldview thus pervades a culture and is passed on to succeeding generations as a "social inheritance."[19] In other words, I have my particular worldview because it was the prevailing one of the environment in which I was reared.

WHAT IS CULTURE?

When we say a person has "culture," we usually have in mind a refined individual who enjoys the "finer things in life." But in the broadest sense of the term, everyone has culture—at least *a* culture, because it is the social environment in which one is reared.

A group of people within a particular locality will generally adopt certain behavior patterns that become normative for the group. These accepted forms of conduct are passed on by teaching and modeling. For this reason, culture is often described as our "social and intellectual heritage."[20] One's culture is "the integrated system of learned behavior patterns which are characteristic of the members of a society and which are not the result of biological inheritance."[21]

Suppose a friend walked up to you, smiled broadly, and then spit on your chest. As an American, you might not be pleased with such a greeting. But if you lived among the Siriano of South America, you would smile and spit back, the normal manner of greeting.

In America, men generally shake hands when they meet. In Mexico, they embrace; whereas in parts of Europe, they kiss one another on the cheek. None of these behaviors is "right" or "wrong." They are

---

18. Kraft, *Christianity in Culture*, p. 53 (italics added).
19. Linton refers to culture as man's "social heredity." (See Ralph Linton, *The Study of Man: An Introduction* [New York: Appleton-Century, 1936], p. 76.)
20. James F. Downs and Herman K. Bleibtreu, "The Evolution of Our Capacity for Culture," in *Cultural and Social Anthropology*, ed. Peter B. Hammond, 2d ed. (New York: Macmillan, 1975), p. 4.
21. E. Adamson Hoebel, *Anthropology: The Study of Man*, 4th ed. (New York: McGraw-Hill, 1972), p. 6.

merely the culturally accepted (and expected) modes of conduct within a particular group.

Our culture takes a visible form in everything from the institutions of society (government, schools, churches, etc.) to eating and sleeping patterns (midnight meals, siestas, etc.). Economic, social, and religious institutions reflect what the group considers important. This is also seen in what the group chooses to commemorate through rituals: weddings, funerals, graduations, and other rites of passage. When and how these rituals are carried out (including religious worship) become a matter of cultural agreement.

CULTURE AND WORLDVIEW

How is a worldview related to culture? The visible aspects of a culture are to some extent a reflection of an underlying ideology or worldview, which gives the reasons for the customs. Kraft notes, "Thus, in its explanatory, evaluational, reinforcing and integrating functions, world view lies at the heart of a culture."[22] *Culture* suggests the way a group of people may appear to an anthropologist; *worldview* suggests how the universe looks to the group.

A worldview, as the heart of the culture, is passed from generation to generation. For example, we see a pantheistic view of God dominant in the Eastern world, whereas a theistic view prevails in the West. These views are certainly not genetic; an Asian child can be reared in Western society (or an American child in the East) and will adopt the cultural views of his social environment. In other words, the earliest worldview I accepted was the prevailing view of the culture in which I was reared—it was an "accident of birth." In the same way that culture gives us the impression that our way of doing things is the "right way to behave," the worldview of our society instills within us an overwhelming sense that our outlook is the "right way to believe."[23]

From the beginning of human history man has speculated, studied, and dreamed about the purpose of his existence. He has confronted the issues of God, humanity, and nature and constructed worldviews that attempt to interpret life. Worldviews have been adapted, modified, and enshrined in the various cultures. Now a smorgasbord of worldviews

22. Kraft, *Christianity in Culture*, p. 56.
23. This of course does not mean that a person's worldview cannot change. Through the process of growth and adaptation, one's worldview does modify slightly. Drastic changes often occur when one is confronted with a worldview that is radically different from his own. At such a time, a decisive choice may be presented either to affirm one's own worldview or to embrace the new. This is what happens in evangelism, for example, especially in cross-cultural missions.

confronts us as we explore our global village. How are we to sift through all these views and determine which (if any) reflects true reality?

WORLDVIEWS: THE BIBLICAL PERSPECTIVE

Father Brown, the clergy-sleuth of G. K. Chesterton novels, often solved crimes by putting together the evidence in a creative manner that baffled the experts. Sometimes, investigators would view the scene of a crime and make elaborate guesses as to how the crime was committed. Father Brown would usually sigh and remark, "There are many explanations that may fit the evidence. What we want to know is, which one is right?"

In the same way, many different worldviews seem to fit the evidence found in our world. Atheistic naturalism seems to fit the view of the world as we investigate it by the scientific method. On the other hand, a pantheistic view of the world seems to explain the spiritual realities that are common to our experience. More and more new worldviews clamor for attention. With all these competing claims, what we, like Father Brown, want to know is, Which one is right?

Man's attempts to explain his existence are just that: *man's attempts*. Within the world, man's experience and perceptions of the infinite universe are limited and inadequate. We need help from the "outside." This is what a biblical worldview claims to be: help from the outside. It acknowledges that God, the Creator and controller of all things, has given light in the confused darkness. He has not given us all the answers, but He has supplied us with enough information sufficient for our need.

As we mentioned earlier, a worldview can function as a pair of glasses through which we observe and understand our world. Everything we perceive must come through these glasses. If such glasses have "Christian" lenses, then everything we observe will be "tinted" Christian. We will explain the universe and life's events from a Christian perspective. We will not understand why others do not see the world as we do—it is so obvious to us.

The same is true for those who wear atheist glasses or Buddhist glasses. They will "see" the same world, but it will be understood differently. Their "glasses" (worldview) do not shape reality nor do they ensure a correct perception, but they do determine a person's *explanation and interpretation* of life and the world.

A biblical worldview is thus a perspective that sees everything through the "glasses" of Scripture. Rather than allowing culture or experience to determine a worldview, it allows the Bible to make that determination.

Claiming that the Bible gives a perspective of reality that is uniquely true sounds narrow-minded and obscurantist. Immediately challenges to such a position arise.

Is not the Bible just one of many cultural attempts at piecing together a worldview? After all, the biblical writers were merely reflecting their own cultural worldview, were they not?

What allows the Bible to dictate the answers to my life? Do I not have a say? It presents such a mental straight-jacket; I am not free to sort things out for myself.

How can an ancient book speak to our situation today? The Bible does not address our modern technological society. Times are changing; the Bible does not.

We will not sidestep these (and many other) difficult challenges to a biblical worldview. Essentially, these challenges concern the nature of the Bible. Does it have the authority to dictate the correct worldview? Are we being foolish in allowing it to do so? We will take up these challenges in chapter four.

However, before a person dismisses a biblical worldview, he should be honest enough to consider the Bible's claims and its comprehensive view of reality. The question is: Does a biblical worldview fit the actual world? If it does not, then it may be discarded onto the heap of misguided philosophies. If it does, then a careful search into its implications and consequences is the reasonable response.

Where does a biblical worldview start? Two basic truths are at its heart: (1) God exists; (2) God has uniquely revealed His character and will in the Bible.

Both of these statements are more complex than they first appear. We hope to demonstrate that they can be accepted with genuine intellectual integrity. If both statements *are* true (in the sense that we will define them), then we are driven to the conclusion that the Bible holds the answers to man's basic questions and longings about life. We will allow the Bible to give us a view *of* the world by detailing the answers to the ultimate questions of life. Then we will discuss how we should allow the Bible to determine both our view *for* the world and how we ought to live *in* the world.

Obviously, not everyone agrees that the Bible should be man's guide to truth. Many worldviews claim the right to be called "the way."

What are these worldviews? How does a biblical worldview compare with them? In the next chapter, we will explore the world of worldviews.

CASE STUDY: *A Worldview Smorgasbord*

The array of worldview options present in the United States is vast and confusing. Nowhere is this more clearly seen than in the world of entertainment, especially Hollywood films. The big box office draws offer a kaleidoscope of worldviews that no doubt contributes to the desultory quality of intellectual life in America.

For example, from a naturalistic perspective, the "blood and guts" adventure movies bludgeon audiences with an approach to life that borders on nihilism. The focus is on victory at any cost, even wholesale slaughter. From the same perspective, but somewhat tamer in action, teenage movies poke fun at authority and locate ultimate concerns in immediate experiences and relationships.

The shallowness of these movies is overshadowed by the deeply "spiritual" nature of a number of other popular movies that give a worldview glowing with glimpses of the "other side." A preoccupation with death and life beyond rallies New Age troops in what we shall describe later as a transcendental worldview. The popularity of movies such as *Always*, *Field of Dreams*, *Ghost*, and *Flatliners* demonstrates that the "scientific" perspective does not dominate current popular thinking.

A theistic view of life and the world is rarely treated as credible. The favorable handling of Christianity in movies such as *Chariots of Fire*, *Tender Mercies*, *The Trip to Bountiful*, and *A Cry in the Dark* is overwhelmed by the openly antagonistic portrayal of religion in *Monsignor*, *Crimes of Passion*, *The Blob*, *Poltergeist II*, *The Last Temptation of Christ*, and others.

Even if the average person avoids the movie theater, the staggering speed at which first-run movies are converted into video format and sold or rented for home use, not to mention showings on cable and network television, makes them an "in-home" influence. The pervasive impact of movies stresses the importance of Christians' thinking "worldviewishly." They need to know their worldview and have the ability to evaluate alternate views.

CASE STUDY: Jimmy Swaggart and the Islamic Evangelist

Several years ago a public debate was held at Louisiana State University between evangelist Jimmy Swaggart and Islamic writer Ahmed Deedat. The format of the debate was an exchange of questions between Swaggart and Deedat concerning the validity of their respective religions. The most notable feature of the exchange was Deedat's consistent quotations from the Old Testament, the New Testament, and the Koran. Deedat displayed an understanding of the Christian message, knew the teachings of Jesus, and was well-versed in the difficult passages found in the Bible.

Swaggart, on the other hand, relied heavily on his evangelist background and dramatics. He knew the gospel message well but admitted he knew little about the Islamic faith. At times, he had problems articulating the basics of the Christian faith. For example, Deedat asked Swaggart to "prove" that the Bible is the Word of God. The challenge is, of course, somewhat ambiguous, but Swaggart's response was even more so. He quoted John 3:16 and claimed that his own "changed" life is evidence that the Bible is the Word of God. This answer took an ironic twist when, months later, revelation was made of Swaggart's exploits with a prostitute.

Both Swaggart and Deedat were viewed as national spokesmen for their religions. However, Swaggart's inability to articulate a biblical worldview and his lack of understanding of an Islamic worldview made Deedat's convictions appear thoughtful and well-rounded. No doubt the Islamic community agrees: a videotape of the debate is available as a Muslim evangelistic tool from the Islamic Teaching Center.

DISCUSSION QUESTIONS

1. Why do people search for meaning in their lives? In what ways is this universal search evident?
2. Discuss Mortimer Adler's statement: "More consequences for thought and action follow the affirmation or denial of God than from answering any other basic question."
3. Turn to Tolstoy's ultimate questions on page 31. Give as many plausible answers as you can for each question.
4. Why do you think Western society has taken an "indifferent" perspective of nature? Validate your response by giving examples in the media, industry, technology, education, and so forth.

5. Describe your worldview. Discuss the origin of that view and how it has changed since you were a child.

6. Note the following statements introduced on page 37: "God exists"; "God has uniquely revealed His character and will in the Bible." Why are both statements crucial if a biblical worldview is true?

FURTHER READING

Clark, Gordon H. *A Christian View of Men and Things*. Grand Rapids: Eerdmans, 1952.

Geisler, Norman L., and William D. Watkins. *Worlds Apart: A Handbook on World Views*. 2d ed. Grand Rapids: Baker, 1989.

Halverson, William H. *A Concise Introduction to Philosophy*. 4th ed. New York: Random House, 1981. See especially Part XIII, "World Views," pp. 411-42.

Kraft, Charles H. *Christianity in Culture*. Maryknoll, N.Y.: Orbis, 1979.

Lockerbie, D. Bruce. *Thinking and Acting Like a Christian*. Portland, Oreg.: Multnomah, 1989.

Nash, Ronald H. *Faith and Reason: Searching For a Rational Faith*. Grand Rapids: Zondervan, 1988. See Part 1, "The Christian World View," pp. 21-66.

Orr, James. *The Christian View of God and the World*. 7th ed. New York: Scribner's, 1904.

Redfield, Robert. *The Primitive World and Its Transformations*. Ithaca, N.Y.: Cornell U., 1953.

Sire, James W. *The Universe Next Door*. 2d ed. Downers Grove, Ill.: InterVarsity, 1988.

Walsh, Brian J., and J. Richard Middleton. *The Transforming Vision*. Downers Grove, Ill.: InterVarsity, 1984.

2

THE WORLD OF WORLDVIEWS

ORGANIZING THE WORLDVIEWS

A group of experts sat in a university lounge discussing the meaning of life. The scholars-in-residence represented philosophies and religions from all over the world. The conversation was engaging and stimulating, especially to those who had never before openly debated these questions. Eventually, their discussion centered on a single question, "What is ultimate reality?"

The Hindu teacher spoke up, "All is one. The universe is but a part of the organic fabric of all reality. All that exists sways to the movement of the goddess Shiva; it dances with Kali, the Divine Mother of Hindu mythology."

The American physicist grimaced. "But the universe is governed by the irrevocable laws of nature. The forces within the universe are the cause for all motion and life. Even the subatomic world can be described by the laws of quantum physics and superluminal influences.''

The Hindu teacher half-closed his eyes and smiled. ''That's what I said.''

There is a crisis in worldview thinking. On the one hand, many try to dissolve all worldviews into one scheme that suits everyone. This approach takes two forms: the pantheistic and the scientific. For the first, books such as *The Tao of Physics, The Dancing Wu Li Masters,* and *Taking the Quantum Leap* have taken the implications of modern scientific theory and merged them with ancient Eastern pantheism. For the second, Carl Sagan, Stephen Hawking, and others of the ''scientific'' community view any religious thinking as outdated superstition that must be replaced by the certainty of scientific discovery. The goal in both cases is to rid the world of culturally based worldviews and produce a view that can be embraced by everyone.

The worldview crisis at the personal level arises from neglect. The average person forges ahead in life giving little thought to worldviews, philosophies of life, or any other such ''intellectual'' endeavors. The compartmentalization of life and thought have resulted in the fragmentation of everything from education to entertainment.

The invitation is thus to call all people, especially Christians, to think and live consistently by the tenets of their worldview. The important issues will become clearer and the challenges better defined. In chapter 1 we described a worldview as *an explanation and interpretation of the world* and *an application of this view to life.* Because every individual perceives the world differently, there are as many worldviews as there are people. With so many worldviews around, the best we can do is organize them into groups. Worldviews can be sorted into geographical families, such as a Western worldview, an Eastern worldview, an African worldview, and so on. Worldviews may also be arranged by ethnic group, as is usually the case with anthropological studies. Such a grouping would yield a Cherokee or a Hopi worldview, a Hispanic or a Slavic worldview, and so on.

Books discussing current worldviews catalog a number of diverse views and explain their beliefs. For example, in James Sire's *The Universe Next Door: A Basic World View Catalog* he lists and discusses seven major worldviews.[1] Geisler and Watkins in their *Worlds Apart: A*

---

1. James W. Sire, *The Universe Next Door: A Basic World View Catalog*, 2d ed. (Downers Grove, Ill.: InterVarsity, 1988). Sire discusses Christian theism, deism, naturalism, nihilism, existentialism, Eastern pantheistic monism, and the New Age.

Handbook on World Views, also discuss seven worldviews but group them into three categories, according to the view of God.[2]

Although it is true that one's view of God determines the direction of his worldview, for our purposes a more comprehensive arrangement of worldviews is necessary. The crucial feature of any worldview is what it says about ultimate reality, that is, what is "at the bottom" of everything that exists?

From this perspective of ultimate reality we may divide all worldviews into three major groups: naturalism, transcendentalism, and theism. Briefly stated, *naturalism* is the view that ultimate reality is the physical matter of the universe; *transcendentalism* is the view that ultimate reality is spiritual or psychic (mental energy); and *theism* is the view that ultimate reality is a personal God who created the material and spiritual universe.[3]

These are not the *only* three worldviews, but most of the major ones can be placed into one of these categories. Similar threefold perspectives of worldviews have been given by C. S. Lewis,[4] William Halverson,[5] and Arthur Holmes.[6] On the next page is a chart showing the major worldviews grouped into these three categories.

A biblical worldview falls under the accompanying chart's category of Traditional Theism. In chapter three we shall explore the essentials of a biblical worldview as they relate to theism in general. Before we do, we must set the stage by exploring and evaluating the cases for the two major alternative views: naturalism and transcendentalism.

EXPLORING THE WORLDVIEWS

NATURALISM: THE WORLD AS WE SEE IT

"When I became convinced that the universe is natural—that all the ghosts and gods are myths, there entered into my brain, into my soul, into

2. Norman L. Geisler and William D. Watkins, *Worlds Apart: A Handbook on World Views*, 2d ed. (Grand Rapids: Baker, 1989). Geisler and Watkins organize their seven worldviews as each view relates to a perception of God: (1) *no God*—atheism; (2) *one God*—panentheism, finite godism, pantheism, theism, and deism; (3) *many Gods*—polytheism.
3. These are working definitions to explain how we are using the terms.
4. C. S. Lewis, *Mere Christianity*, reprint ed. (Westwood, N.J.: Barbour and Co., 1952), pp. 18-23. Lewis called the three worldviews the *materialist* view, the *life-force* view, and the *religious* view.
5. William Halverson, *A Concise Introduction to Philosophy*, 4th ed. (New York: Random House, 1981), pp. 411-41. Halverson's views are: *ethical theism, naturalism,* and *transcendentalism*. He also includes *humanism*, which he claims is not a worldview but "a group of insights that must be incorporated into any world view if that world view is to be regarded as adequate" (p. 436).
6. Arthur Holmes, ed., *The Making of a Christian Mind* (Downers Grove, Ill.: InterVarsity, 1985), p. 12.

CLASSIFYING MAJOR WORLDVIEWS

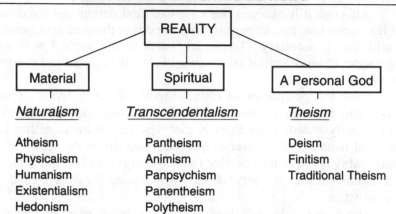

REALITY		
Material	Spiritual	A Personal God
Naturalism	*Transcendentalism*	*Theism*
Atheism	Pantheism	Deism
Physicalism	Animism	Finitism
Humanism	Panpsychism	Traditional Theism
Existentialism	Panentheism	
Hedonism	Polytheism	

every drop of my blood, the sense, the feeling, the joy of freedom
. . . There was for me no master in all the world—not even in infinite
space. I was free . . . free from all ignorant and cruel creeds, all the 'inspired' books that savages have produced, and all the barbarous legends
of the past. . . . I stood erect and fearlessly, joyously, faced all worlds.''[7]
Such was the manifesto of Robert Green Ingersoll (1833-1899), one of
the leading statesmen and orators of the nineteenth century. His bold
proclamation of freedom arises from his worldview, which we define as a
populist expression of naturalism.

Naturalism[8] projects the view that ultimate reality is material. The
physical universe is all there is. There is nothing beyond or separate from
that which we can see, touch, and measure. Matter and energy are the
basic "stuff" from which all existence is derived. Such a view of reality
implies that all obtainable answers for the questions relating to the universe and mankind can be found by the investigation of physical phenomena. Naturalists do not deny the real existence of such things as thoughts,
plans, language, and so on, but they claim that these things are explain-
able as a form or function of some material entity.

In order more fully to understand the implications of naturalism as a
total philosophy of the world and life, we shall now examine the major

---

7. Quoted by Philip Mass, "Robert Green Ingersoll," in *The Humanist* (November/December 1988): 29.
8. We are using *naturalism* to denote the philosophy that denies real existence beyond the physical world. This definition also includes the views commonly called *materialism* and *physicalism*.

tenets from the perspective of its confrontation with God, the self, and nature.

Confronting God

The God Who Is Not There. A university biology professor traditionally began his semester with the quip, "Christians say, 'In the beginning, God'; I say, 'In the beginning, hydrogen.'" His remark was more than a joke, it revealed the starting point of his worldview: the cosmos. In naturalism, the supernatural God is replaced by natural elements.

Ernest Nagel, in his essay "Naturalism Reconsidered," defends a materialistic view of reality. In naturalism, he states, "there is no place for the operation of disembodied forces, no place for an immaterial spirit directing the course of events, no place for the survival of personality after the corruption of the body which exhibits it."[9] If there are no spiritual realities, then it is impossible for God to exist.

However, one may challenge the naturalistic assertion that the existence of God is impossible. If God does not exist, then from where does the idea of God originate? Why is it that belief in God is almost a universal characteristic of man?

Most naturalists respond by asserting that man created God in his own image to satisfy his dreams and hopes for purpose in life and immortality. Humanist Paul Kurtz claims "the theist's world is only a dream world; it is a feeble escape into a future that will never come."[10] Sigmund Freud described belief in God as "the fulfillment of the oldest, strongest, and most urgent wishes of mankind."[11] Bertrand Russell disparaged Christians as "timid seekers after the childish comforts of a less adult age."[12]

For the naturalist, reality is understood only by the careful use of the scientific method, not wishful thinking. This perspective borders on scientism, which is "the belief that all truth is scientific truth and that the sciences give us our best shot at knowing 'how things really are.'"[13] Such a scientific view of the world seems strange when we remember that so many of the earliest scientists were strong Christians. But we can gain an insight into this scientism by analyzing the development of naturalism.

9. Ernest Nagel, "Naturalism Reconsidered," in *Essays in Philosophy*, ed. Houston Peterson (New York: Washington Square, 1959), p. 487.

10. Paul Kurtz, *Forbidden Fruit: The Ethics of Humanism* (Buffalo, N.Y.: Prometheus, 1988), p. 243.

11. Sigmund Freud, *The Future of an Illusion* (London: Hogarth, 1961), p. 30.

12. Bertrand Russell, *The Scientific Outlook* (London: Unwin, 1931), p. 30.

13. C. Stephen Evans, *Preserving the Person: A Look at the Human Sciences* (Downers Grove, Ill.: InterVarsity, 1977), p. 18.

The Growth of Naturalism. Naturalism, as a full-blown atheistic worldview, is a relatively new perspective. The modern roots of naturalism are found in the scientific revolution of the eighteenth century. James Turner points out that atheists were practically unheard of before 1800. Even the skeptic David Hume once noted that he never laid eyes on an atheist.[14] The scientific enterprise continued to view God as part of the universal scheme of things for two reasons.

The first was the "God-habit," that is, the fact that humanity had persistently held to a belief in God. Such an ingrained tradition was hard to extract from any area of thinking, in public or private life. Atheist Max Otto admitted, "For those who have reasoned themselves into a naturalistic position, there still remains a substratum of allegiance to the supernatural."[15]

The second reason science held so tenaciously to a belief in God was the conclusion that the orderly Newtonian universe served as a constant proof for an orderly God. All truth was God's truth, and the starry heavens above blinked down God's favor. As late as the nineteenth century, most scientists gave the purpose of scientific investigation, in the words of John Herschel, "to shore up religious belief."[16]

However, such a perspective began to change. The Marquis de Laplace spent the better part of thirty years investigating the effect of gravitational force in the world. The result of his labors was a five-volume work entitled *Celestial Mechanics*, published in 1827. When he presented an early volume to Napoleon, he was surprised the monarch studied it so carefully. Calling for Laplace, Napoleon remarked, "You have written a large work on the universe without once mentioning its author." Laplace replied, "I have no need for that hypothesis."[17] A practical atheism slowly began to be a part of a scientific worldview that no longer found the "God-hypothesis" necessary.

One question lingered: atheistic scientists in the nineteenth century had no genuine explanation for the design of the universe. In 1859, Charles Darwin gave skeptical thinkers the mechanism they had been looking for. The design of the universe was not the handiwork of an intelligent and purposeful God, but the result of natural selection, the "blind, unconscious, automatic process which Darwin discovered, and which we

14. James Turner, *Without God, Without Creed: The Origins of Unbelief in America* (Baltimore: Johns Hopkins, 1985), p. 44.
15. Max Otto, "A Humanist Questioned by Youth," *The Humanist* (Spring 1941; reprinted May/ June 1988): 27.
16. John F. W. Herschel, *A Preliminary Discourse on the Study of Natural Philosophy* (London, 1830; reprint edition, Chicago: U. of Chicago, 1987), p. 7.
17. Eric Temple Bell, *Men of Mathematics* (New York: Simon and Schuster, 1937), p. 181.

now know is the explanation for the existence and apparently purposeful form of all life.''[18] Now the order of the universe could be described as the result of mechanical laws. Darwin did not prove God's nonexistence, he merely left God out of the picture.

A new sense of urgency and excitement about the natural world developed. Science was taking a turn and began to uncover the "secrets" of the universe. Metaphysical questions paled in the brilliant light of scientific discovery. However, for several years after the 1859 publication of Darwin's *The Origin of Species* the term *atheist* was still negative and unpopular. It took Thomas Huxley in 1869 to articulate a new viewpoint that freed naturalistic thinking from the impediments of the "God-question." Huxley coined the term *agnosticism* to describe a tentative, uncertain attitude toward any question about God and the meaning of life.

Huxley stated, "Agnosticism is not properly described as a 'negative' creed, not indeed as a creed of any kind, except in so far as it expresses absolute faith in the validity of a principle, . . . This principle may be stated in various ways, but they all amount to this: that it is wrong for a man to say that he is certain of the objective truth of any proposition unless he can produce evidence which logically justifies that certainty.''[19] Agnosticism revitalized science and philosophy with a spirit of adventure and freedom. "Truth" became synonymous with "scientific fact," and the great sin became holding to certainty in metaphysical questions.

Whether atheistic or agnostic, naturalism sets forth a worldview in which God is unnecessary. Although most naturalists consider themselves agnostic about questions of ultimate concern, such questions actually do not matter in their worldview. The naturalist's approach to God is no approach to God. The implications of this attitude are seen in the naturalist's confrontation with the self.

Confronting Humanity

Life from the dust. For the naturalist, man originated from the dust of the earth . . . without the breath of God. Humanity is solely a part of the mechanistic universe. Even the most abstract facets of man's behavior are reduced to component natural processes. For example, Herbert Spencer concluded that the human mind was the end product of the evolution of the nervous system.[20] Thoughts and personality were described as

18. Richard Dawkins, *The Blind Watchmaker: Why the Evidence of Evolution Reveals a Universe Without Design* (New York: W. W. Norton, 1986), p. 5.
19. Thomas H. Huxley, *Science and Christian Tradition* (London: Macmillan, 1894), p. 310.
20. Herbert Spencer, *Principles of Psychology*, 3d ed. (New York: D. Appleton, 1898), 3 vols., 1:145ff. Spencer described mental processes as a series of "nervous shocks."

electrical impulses in the brain. Birth is the absolute beginning and death is the absolute end. Man is merely a machine that works for a while and then eventually runs down and quits.

Christians believe that man's ethical nature is the result of God's moral standards impressed into his soul. The naturalist responds by claiming that morality is the result of social convention. The sense of right and wrong within each person does not indicate the existence of moral absolutes but rather reflects conditioning of acceptable behavior by authority figures. Like a dog whose behavior is shaped by his master, human behavior is shaped to society's norms by reward and punishment.

The ethical system of naturalism is usually utilitarian and individualistic. For example, in his book *Ethics Without God,* Kai Nelson concludes, "happiness, self-consciousness and self-identity are essential to give significance to human living."[21] Whatever promotes happiness, self-consciousness and self-identity in my life and in the lives of others is "good"; whatever hinders them is "bad."

Life without meaning. Naturalists, because of their view of ultimate reality, see no overarching meaning for the universe or humanity. Human destiny, according to Nagel, is "an episode between two oblivions."[22] Natural history and human history are the same thing. By a series of random and chance events, humanity has evolved and possesses the capability to reflect on the past and project his thoughts to the future. These abilities give man the illusion of uniqueness and superiority.

At the personal level, the consequences of existence without God are disturbing. Naturalists do not consider their view one of despair, yet they admit there is no consolation for the injustice in life or hope beyond the grave. Some naturalists believe their worldview ultimately makes life absurd. Such an approach is called nihilism, from the Latin word *nihil,* which means "nothing." Because life is meaningless, man's existence and quest for purpose amounts to nothing. Novelist Albert Camus summed up a nihilist point of view when he wrote, "There is but one truly serious philosophical problem, and that is suicide."[23]

By its very nature, naturalism excludes the quest for meaning in life. For example, Sigmund Freud admitted that his naturalistic worldview would not allow him to accept any purpose for his existence. Such

21. Kai Nelson, *Ethics Without God* (London: Pemberton Books, 1973), p. 65.
22. Nagel, "Naturalism," in *Essays in Philosophy*, p. 496.
23. Quoted in Louis P. Pojman, *Philosophy: The Quest for Truth* (Belmont, Calif.: Wadsworth, 1989), p. 453. (This statement was originally in Albert Camus, *The Myth of Sisyphus and Other Essays*, trans. Justin O'Brien [New York: Alfred A. Knopf, 1955].)

ultimate concerns, he claimed, could be raised only by religion.[24] But this does not stop naturalists from asserting that life can be lived with some purpose. Atheist John Mackie bravely concludes that man gets all the purpose he needs from within himself.[25]

The despair of nihilism is a logical consequence of naturalism, yet man cannot live with such emptiness. This gives rise to several approaches to life that attempt to surmount this despair. One of these is *existentialism*, an approach to life that ventures to overcome the hopelessness of naturalism by creating one's own meaning for life. In a world of emptiness, each person must fill life with experiences, love and joy, making the most of the time he has. Each person must find his own meaning. There are no rules except those which he chooses to follow, there are no truths except those which he chooses to believe. He is justified in pursuing anything that will give meaning to his life.[26] Thus existentialism attempts to overcome the terrifying consequences of a naturalistic world view by locating man's purpose within himself.[27]

Another approach is *hedonism*, which views the goal of life as pleasure. Hedonism makes a great deal of sense if naturalism is true. Because this life is all there is, we should make the most of it and enjoy it to the fullest. Therefore, whatever brings pleasure in life is good, whatever brings pain is bad.

Certain naturalists choose to focus their energies on making the world a better place to live. Overcoming poverty, disease, handicaps and other natural limitations of this life is their agenda. Peace and love for all people is their goal. This approach, known as *humanism*, discards any ultimate meaning for life and places the needs of humanity as a whole at the center of all universal concerns. This focus is seen clearly in the two Humanist Manifestos (presented in 1933 and 1973) that proclaim "the quest for the good life is still the central task for mankind."[28]

24. Freud states, "So again, only religion is able to answer the question of purpose in life. One can hardly go wrong in concluding that the idea of a purpose in life stands and falls with the religious system" (*Civilization and Its Discontents*, The Great Books [Chicago: U. of Chicago, 1952], 54:772).

25. John Leslie Mackie, *The Miracle of Theism* (Oxford: Oxford U., 1982), pp. 250-51. Mackie states, "Still less do we need anything like a god to counter the supposed threat of aimlessness. Men are themselves purposive beings. In their own nature they unavoidably pursue aims and goals, they do not need these to be given from the outside."

26. Jean-Paul Sartre, *Existentialism and Human Emotions*, trans. Hazel E. Barnes (Secaucus, N.J.: Castle, n.d.), p. 51.

27. Here we have described what is commonly known as pessimistic or atheistic existentialism. There are many streams of Christian thought that embrace a more positive form of existentialism, especially in the thought of Soren Kierkegaard and Karl Barth.

28. "Humanist Manifesto I," in *Humanist Manifesto I and II*, ed. Paul Kurtz (Buffalo, N.Y.: Prometheus Books, 1973), p. 10.

The naturalist's desire to find purpose in life in a purposeless universe is noble, but it is small comfort in light of a meaningless existence. Sartre honestly evaluated the plight of man from a naturalistic perspective when he stated, "Man is a useless passion, condemned to freedom."[29] How can the average person live with such a perspective on life? Cab driver Jose Martinez summarizes it best. When asked about the meaning of life, he replied bluntly, "We're here to die, just live and die. I drive a cab, I do some fishing, take my girl out, pay taxes, do a little reading, then get ready to drop dead. Life is a big fake."[30]

Confronting Nature

As its name implies, naturalism defines every existence and every event by natural causes. Nothing is "super"-natural. Therefore it is up to mankind to understand how nature works so that he will be able to harness its power for the improvement of human life.

This view of nature, however, does not absolve the naturalist from grappling with the two basic questions concerning the physical universe: From where did the universe come? (the question of origins); and, Why is the universe organized as it is? (the question of design).

The naturalist will answer the question of design, as discussed above, by appealing to natural selection. The laws of nature have caused the resulting appearance of design and purpose within the universe. Whatever design is present is the result of completely natural processes, many of which we do not presently understand.

But the nagging question, "From where does the universe originate?" causes the naturalist to search for credible answers. Something cannot come from nothing, and the evidence seems to indicate that the universe had a definite beginning. Christians appeal to this evidence as proof that the universe was set in motion by God, a claim the naturalist must reject. How, then, does he respond to the question of origins?

One response by recent writers is to attempt to prove that something *can* come from nothing. For example, Paul Davies applies the theories of subatomic physics to the universe (an application known as quantum cosmology) to conclude that creation can be explained as a completely natural, impersonal process. He concludes, "It is no longer entirely absurd to imagine that the universe came into existence spontaneously from nothing

---

29. Jean-Paul Sartre, *Being and Nothingness*, trans. Hazel Barnes (Secaucus, N.J.: Citadel Press, 1957), pp. 755ff.
30. Quoted in "The Meaning of Life," *Life*, December 1988, p. 80.

as a result of a quantum process."[31] Davies sees the universe as self-creative and self-organizing.

From another perspective, elaborate theories have been generated to explain the existence of the universe without the need of a creator. Cambridge University physicist Stephen Hawking believes the universe is not infinite and eternal but rather finite and temporal with no boundary and no beginning. He concludes, "If the universe is really completely self-contained, having no boundary or edge, it would have neither beginning nor end; it would simply be. What place then, for a creator?"[32]

Thus, in naturalism, the cosmos is the beginning and end of all questions; matter is all that matters. Hopes and beliefs that go beyond the physical realm are illusory. The best man can do is live his life to the fullest and not concern himself with questions for which there are no answers.

Naturalism: A Limited Perspective

To the Western mind, naturalism is an appealing worldview because it seems so closely tied to the scientific enterprise. Science has the aura of objectivity and progress, which generates confidence. Further, naturalism teaches that each individual chooses his or her own goals and morality. The ethical relativism and freedom from ultimate judgment are inviting.

Positively, naturalism affirms the importance of the physical world. Naturalism demonstrates to us the design and uniformity of the universe, which are truths necessary for science to be possible. Science has taken away the superstitions associated with earlier views of nature. Demons do not cause lightning, and spirits do not make crops grow. Science also illustrates that truth can be derived by our senses as we investigate the world.

Practically, some streams of naturalism remind us of our responsibility to care for the world's human needs. Often, Christians are put to shame by the indefatigable efforts of some humanist organizations to care for the needy.

Science and Reality. In spite of its contributions to understanding the world around us, there are two major hesitations about naturalism as a full-blown worldview. The first hesitation is the *limitation of science*. Naturalism is often "proved" to be true by an appeal to the scientific nature of knowledge. Even though it claims great objectivity and certainty, science begins with presuppositions about knowledge, the objective exis-

---

31. Paul Davies, *The Cosmic Blueprint* (New York: Simon and Schuster, 1988), p. 5.
32. Stephen W. Hawking, *A Brief History of Time* (New York: Bantam, 1988), p. 141.

tence of the universe, the orderliness of natural law, and so forth. Carl Henry points out, "No historian and no scientist approaches historical or physical events without presuppositions. He may not wear his view of total reality on his lapel, but he nonetheless interprets the particularities of his life by it."[33]

By its very nature, science is limited to observable and repeatable events in the physical realm. But to reduce all knowledge to this realm excludes the possibility of real things existing beyond the physical. Therefore, even though science does give us true knowledge it does not give us full knowledge. Robert Jastrow, professor of astronomy and geology at Columbia University, acknowledges that science "is one avenue of truth. But it is clear to me that it is not the only one."[34]

Paul de Vries notes that the scientific method "cannot pretend to provide answers to the ultimate questions. At some point in every explanation of phenomena, the question 'Why?' can no longer be answerable within science."[35] Science cannot even give final truth about matters of science, let alone about matters of morals or religion.[36]

Such an admission of science's limitations is also acknowledged by nontheistic scientists. For example, as we pointed out above, Stephen Hawking attempts to prove that if there is no "edge" of the universe there is no God. But Hawking's theory, while it appears to explain away the need for a creator, still fails to answer the fundamental question, "Why is there something rather than nothing?" Simply saying, "The universe just *is*," does not advance our understanding beyond that of the ancient Greeks who believed the universe was eternal. Even Hawking himself admits limitations. He notes, "When I was eleven, I wanted to know how and why the universe works. Now I know how, but I still do not know why."[37] Scientists may one day discover all the "how's" of the universe and be able to explain every event in the universe, but such a knowledge of the mechanics of the physical world will not answer the question "why" the world is as it is.

Further, the speculations of the so-called quantum cosmology are questionable. Davies's claim that quantum physics "routinely produces

33. Carl F. H. Henry, *God Who Speaks and Shows*, vol. 1 of *God, Revelation and Authority* (Waco, Tex.: Word, 1976), p. 261.
34. Quoted in an interview with Bill Durbin in "A Scientist Caught Between Two Faiths," *Christianity Today*, 6 August 1982, p. 15.
35. Paul de Vries, "Naturalism in the Natural Sciences: A Christian Perspective," *Christian Scholar's Review* 15:4 (1984):394.
36. See Carl F. H. Henry, *God Who Speaks and Shows*, pp. 165-80.
37. Stephen Hawking, quoted in "The Creation of the Universe," special edition of "Nova," Public Broadcasting Service, 1985.

something from nothing''[38] is unfounded and misleading. Quantum physics has never discovered "something being created from nothing," because even it adheres to basic laws. As William Craig points out, the experiments to which Davies refers require pre-existing energy in a system for there to be any conversion of energy into matter.[39]

To believe that science is valid does not mean that one must adopt a naturalistic worldview. Naturalism does not have a corner on the scientific enterprise. Christianity affirms that science is a valid means of uncovering truth about the physical world, but Christianity goes further and affirms the existence of real things beyond the reach of scientific investigation.[40] Science gives a view that embraces the material realm but is not a comprehensive view of all reality.

The choice is not between science and faith. Princeton physicist Freeman Dyson acknowledges, "Scientific materialism and [religion] are neither incompatible nor mutually exclusive. We have learned that matter is weird stuff. It is weird enough, so that it does not limit God's freedom to make and do what he pleases.''[41] Science and religion are better seen as partners in the quest for truth. Philosopher Richard Westfall notes, "If Christianity is true, the valid conclusions of science can never be in conflict with it.''[42]

Humanity and Emptiness. The second hesitation in accepting naturalism as an adequate worldview is the *problem of human thought and meaning*. Seeing the universe as a closed system of physical events appears fine when we consider rocks, mountains, planets, and stars; but when humanity is brought into the picture, everything comes unglued. How is it that man has the ability to reason abstractly and transcend his own existence? The very fact that the human mind can apprehend objects outside itself goes beyond physical explanation. How did unconscious forces give rise to minds and sound reasoning? Pascal noted, "Thought constitutes the greatness of man. Man is a reed, the most feeble thing in nature, but he is a thinking reed.''[43]

38. P. C. W. Davies, *God and the New Physics* (London: J. M. Dent, 1983), p. 216. Davies more fully develops this statement in his later book *The Cosmic Blueprint*, referred to earlier in this chapter.
39. William Lane Craig, "God, Creation and Mr. Davies," *British Journal for the Philosophy of Science* (1986):165-69.
40. For example, the Bible affirms the existence of God and angels, the existence of a human soul and life after death, the existence of "things not seen" (2 Cor. 4:18; Heb. 11:1), and so forth.
41. Freeman Dyson, *Infinite in All Directions* (New York: Harper & Row, 1988), p. 8.
42. Richard S. Westfall, "The Trial of Galileo: Bellarmino, Galileo, and the Clash of the Two Worlds," 1988 Gross Memorial Lecture (Valparaiso, Ind.: Valparaiso U., 1988), p. 17.
43. Blaise Pascal, *Pascal's Pensees* (New York: Dutton, 1958), p. 97 (fragment numbers 346 and 347).

Naturalists have consistently struggled with the implications of their worldview as it applied to certain facets of man's nature. Darwin was mystified by the human eye, and Freud was baffled by human creativity. That human beings possess such powers of reasoning, art, and morality calls into question the premise of purely materialistic explanations.

Naturalism assumes that reality is completely physical and there is no purpose or meaning to be found. But if the universe is meaningless, then so is the statement "The universe is meaningless." How can such an evaluative statement be made if indeed there is no meaning in the universe? By what criterion is meaning being judged? If the universe is meaningless, how would we know?

As a means of understanding the world around us, naturalism provides the tools necessary to explore and discover truth. As a full-blown worldview, however, naturalism fails to explain far too many aspects of the world and life as we see them. For this reason, many have turned away from a naturalistic perspective and embraced a view that sees ultimate reality as metaphysical. This view we are calling *transcendentalism*.

TRANSCENDENTALISM: THE WORLD AS WE WANT IT

"The currents of the Universal Being circulate through me; I am part or parcel of God."[44]

These words may sound familiar to one who is acquainted with Eastern religions or the contemporary New Age thinking; but Ralph Waldo Emerson made this statement more than 150 years ago. He represents a line of thinking that came to be known as New England Transcendentalism.

Unhappy with what they considered the stale and rational theology of Christianity and the spiritual bankruptcy of deism, the transcendentalists sought to return God to the experience of everyday life. They perceived a godlike character for man and proclaimed that nature was not a vast machine but a living organism. God was not "out there," He was "right here," all around us, in everything we see and do. God could not be known by finely figured syllogisms but was experienced as a part of everything we feel. God was active in me, around me, and through me. Imagination triumphed over reason; creativity over theory.

New England Transcendentalism of the nineteenth century reflects a mood present in Western society today. Reacting against the authoritarian nature of some religions and the distressing implications of naturalism,

44. Ralph Waldo Emerson, "Nature," in *Collected Works of Ralph Waldo Emerson*, ed. Robert E. Spiller and Alfred R. Ferguson (Cambridge: Cambridge U., 1971), 1:10.

many have tried to find a middle ground. Such an approach is what C. S. Lewis called the "Life-Force" philosophy, a view that imparts a spiritual nature to all of reality.[45]

This perspective of ultimate reality is a second worldview that we are labeling transcendentalism. A number of religions and movements reflect this worldview. Among them are Hinduism, Buddhism, Taoism, Confucianism, Hare Krishna, Baha'ism, Christian Science, Unity School of Christianity, and the many New Age organizations and groups. We are viewing transcendentalism as a melting-pot of mystical and psychic movements.

A great deal of variation can be found among those who take a transcendental approach to reality. For example, most Buddhist thought concludes that ultimate reality is impersonal, whereas Hare Krishna believe that it is personal. Some believe that the physical world is unreal whereas others believe it is merely an illusion. A transcendental worldview can take so many avenues that it will be impossible to explore all the current expressions. In fact, squeezing a transcendental worldview into a Western mindset is tenuous. Our discussion here shall focus on some of the general areas of agreement that such a worldview demands.[46]

Confronting God

Much transcendental thought is based on the fundamental idea that all things are a unified whole, a concept known as *monism*. Everything that exists comes from the same stuff; there is no essential difference between a rock, a tree, a cow, and a man.[47] All "objects" are separate manifestations in different forms of the one reality. This ultimate reality is spiritual or psychic in nature. In this way transcendentalism denies naturalism's basic tenet that all reality is material.

---

45. C. S. Lewis, *Mere Christianity*, pp. 18-23.

46. Among the many religious expressions of transcendentalism, the most important are: *animism*, the primitive belief that nature is filled with spirits; *panpsychism*, a "modernized" view of animism, which claims that all objects in the universe are animated and possess a soul; *panentheism*, the "progressive" view that the universe is God's "body"; and most if not all of the mystical and occultic movements and religions. *Polytheism*, the belief that the universe is populated with many gods, is difficult to categorize. However, it shares more affinities with animism and pantheism than with theism. (See Alasdair MacIntyre, who concludes that pantheism grew out of primitive polytheism; *The Encyclopedia of Philosophy*, 8 vols. [New York: Macmillan, 1967], 6:32.)

47. There is no easy way accurately to depict the variations of monistic thought. What we are describing here is generally referred to as classical pantheism or a form of absolute monism. Modified views of pantheism and monism view God as the energizing force or "soul" of the material universe. However, even in these views God is still not a personal being nor is He separate from the material universe.

Two major characteristics of the transcendental "God" differ from the God of Christian theism.

First, the transcendental God and the universe are inseparable. This does not necessarily mean that God and the universe are equal (although pantheistic monism believes this is true) but that the two are inextricably intertwined in one fabric of reality.

This leads to the second difference: the transcendental God is not a personal being. The concept of personality is a construct of human thought and therefore not an essential feature of reality. God is thus beyond personality and possesses none of the qualities necessary for personal interaction. For the transcendentalist, God is the impersonal force, principle, or spirit behind the created world.

Confronting Humanity

According to transcendental thought, man's nature is an extension of the divine oneness. Therefore, it is readily claimed that each person is divine. Why is it, then, that each of us is not conscious of his divinity? Transcendentalism answers that awareness of this divine nature is muddled behind the encumbrances of the physical life and individual distinctiveness. According to early Buddhism, a person could be separated into five elements or parts. What we call an individual ego is no more than a temporary combination of form, feeling, perceptions, impulses, and consciousness.[48]

If such a view of the self is true, how is the internal struggle with right and wrong explained? In transcendental thought, man's moral nature is a product of his physical limitations and not an indication of a moral Lawgiver. The Hindu *Upanishads* state, "The immortal man overcomes both the thoughts, 'I did evil' and 'I did good.' Good and evil, done or not done, cause him no pain."[49] Much of transcendentalism has little to do with ethics, at least as far as the Western mind perceives moral systems.[50] However, this does not mean that an ethical lifestyle is ignored by transcendental religions and movements. Moral behavior, although not based upon absolute norms given from heaven, still allows a person to attain oneness. A life of wanton behavior, because it is usually a quest for individual sensual fulfillment, is a hindrance to the recognition of the individual's divine unity with all things.

48. See Edward Conze, *Buddhism: Its Essence and Development* (Oxford: Bruno Cassirer, 1951; reprint, New York: Harper & Row, 1975), p. 107.

49. *The Upanishads*, trans. F. Max Muller. *Sacred Books of the East* (Oxford: Clarendon, 1900), Brhadaranyake 3.4.

50. Albert Schweitzer, *The Quest for the Historical Jesus* (New York: Macmillan, 1964), p. 43. Schweitzer refers to Hinduism as "supra-ethical."

Man's problem is manifested by the rampant suffering and injustice in the world. Two characteristics of man's nature are the cause for these deficiencies. First, mankind possesses a fragmented vision of the oneness of all things. Because of man's incarnation his perspective is impaired by the limitations of human thought and reasoning. He sees life in fragments. For instance, I can choose to focus attention on my unique self and ignore my connection with the universe. I can crave things that are impermanent (such as sex, power, or possessions) and make them symbols and goals of my individual pleasures or accomplishments.

Such a perspective is what Alan Watts called our "ego illusion."[51] As long as a person sees himself as a separate reality he will never escape the prison of incarnation. He is doomed to the cycle of birth and death until he breaks free from the bondage of selfish living. Thus, reincarnation is a fundamental feature of transcendental philosophy. Successive rebirths form the links in the chain of the individual soul's journey back to the One.[52]

The second cause of suffering and injustice is man's ignorance of his own divine nature. He has a fundamental ignorance of truth, which results in selfish pursuits. Man looks too often for answers to his problems outside himself, in the world of shadows and illusions. As a result, the spark of the divine nature within is ignored and overwhelmed by the false perceptions of the world.

Man's solution to his problems is not to be found outside himself. Truth, salvation, peace, and enlightenment are all found within. The transcendentalist view of salvation is one of overcoming the fragmented vision of his incarnation. A person's ideal goal should be some form of enlightenment by which he moves beyond his individualness and "becomes one" with ultimate reality. Many different paths are proposed to overcome man's ego illusion. Some find it in meditation, others through good works and a denial of desires, still others through intellectual achievement. All approaches have two common elements: (1) the need to see the unity of all things; (2) the need to actualize the divinity within each person.

At the emotional level transcendentalism becomes an appealing alternative to naturalism. The drive toward intellectualism and scientific discovery seems cold and lifeless to many who desire a view of reality that surges with warmth and love. For the transcendentalist, even nature

---

51. Alan Watts, *Spirit of Zen* (New York: Dutton, 1936), p. 23.
52. For an explanation of the purpose and nature of reincarnation from a transcendental perspective, see *Coming Back: The Science of Reincarnation, based on the teachings of A. C. Bhaktivedanta Swami Prabhupada* (Sydney, Australia: The Bhaktivedanta Book Trust, 1982).

possesses the emotional characteristics of life and joins with man in the quest for universal peace and unity.

Confronting Nature

The world, at least the material aspect of creation, is viewed differently among transcendentalists. Even among the Eastern religions there is much disagreement as to the exact nature of the physical world. Hindu thought, for example, holds to the doctrine of *maya,* that is, that the physical world as perceived by human senses is not true reality. Certain Buddhist groups view the material world as unreal, an illusion. Jainism, on the other hand, considers the material world to be real. In general, the physical realm is at best a part of reality and at worst a bad dream. The focus of transcendentalism is upon the fabric of reality that underlies the physical world. "What we take to be real self-subsisting entities in the phenomenal world are in reality interdependent structures existing only momentarily."[53]

Transcendentalism commonly sees the physical realm as a profound manifestation of the divine nature; however, the divine is not dependent upon the physical realm. Still, there is the sense that the universe emanates from God necessarily. Radhakrishnan states, "Creation is a necessary part of God's being. God needs it for the fullness of His being."[54] The distinctions between ultimate reality and the physical world are clear.

SOME TRANSCENDENTAL DISTINCTIONS

Ultimate Reality	Physical World
Impersonal (Beyond Personality)	Personal (Many Personalities)
Oneness	Multiplicity
Unity	Diversity
Truth	Deception
Unchanging	Changing

Transcendentalism accuses both naturalism and theism of focusing too much attention on the physical realm. The diversity and change of the physical realm is deceptive, according to transcendentalism. As a result, the alternate worldviews have applied human reason and personality to

53. Mark R. Mullins, "The Worldview of Zen," *Update* 7:4 (December 1983):48.
54. S. Radhakrishnan, *Eastern Religions and Western Thought,* 2d ed. (New York: Oxford U., 1940), p. 92.

ultimate reality and/or the material world. In seeking reasonable answers for the meaning of life, they ask temporal questions of a nontemporal order.

The transcendental perspective rejects the subject/object dichotomy that is a major part of naturalism and theism. To the transcendentalist, all is subject. The world is not indifferent or hostile to man, it is a part of the organic fabric of all reality. We are one. We are the world.

The Popularization of Transcendental Thought

The transcendental view of nature has practical outworkings in several areas. For éxample, there has been little emphasis on scientific inquiry in cultures where a transcendental worldview is dominant. This makes a great deal of sense if the physical world is viewed as deceptive and illusory. For this reason a lack of interest in science and technology and their advancements is pervasive in many Eastern countries.

On the positive side, if the world is seen as an organic whole, then care for all aspects of the environment and life is important. Only a crass form of selfishness causes a person to view humanity as more important than other aspects of the world. The ecological gospel of saving the whales, rescuing seals, preserving redwoods, and so forth, promises our own salvation from mutual destruction and the achievement of universal harmony.

"All animals have the same rights as humans" is the rationale of many behind the animal-rights movement. Organizations such as the Animal Liberation Front and the Guardian Apes have taken a vigilante approach to protecting animals from human exploitation. Demonstrations and marches by the new "Transcendental Right" seek protection for animals from fur-traders and medical researchers. Although many animal rights activists do not resort to extreme tactics, the transcendental foundation of their rhetoric is clear.

From a broader perspective there are two elements of transcendentalism that make it a popular worldview. The first is that transcendentalism promises a progression toward unity. Modern society is enamored with the concept of progression. The belief that the world is ultimately moving toward global unity is a promising alternative to predictions of Armageddon.

Albert Einstein saw man's religious feelings developing over history in three progressions. First, man held to a religion of fear in which his superstitious beliefs resulted in rituals and prayers. Second, mankind developed the religion of morality in which social feelings were dominant. The final stage is what Einstein called the "cosmic religious feeling."

Here the individual is overwhelmed by his own nothingness compared to the marvelous order in nature and human thought. At this stage man will "look upon individual existence as a sort of prison and want to experience the universe as a single significant whole."[55]

Einstein's view is part of an interesting phenomenon whereby scientists and the scientific fields are being used to promote a transcendental worldview. Some are using the tentative results of quantum physics to prove a universal pantheism.[56] Still others, by claiming that the universe has a "free will" to create new things,[57] view the cosmos as not only self-creative but also self-organizing and possessing a "personality." This coming together of science and religion is viewed as a positive step toward the unity of human thought and experience. The most positive aspect of transcendentalism is the promise of a "New Age" of global harmony and peace. As mankind progresses toward this unity, the shackles of theistic religions and atheistic naturalism must be removed.

A second element resulting in its popularity is that transcendentalism presents a positive view of the human situation. It replaces the theistic view of man's depravity with a positive acclamation of man's divinity. Such a view fits in well with an American culture that prides itself on individual determination and accomplishment. Actualizing one's divine nature results in breakthrough experiences for individuals in their jobs and relationships. Capitalizing on certain forms of transcendentalism can be profitable. If we really possess the "divine Oneness" within ourselves, why not use this connection to our advantages? Many people are trying. The *Wall Street Journal* describes individuals who project "positive energy" by chanting in order to obtain expensive cars and better jobs.[58] Most of this thinking is promoted by the many New Age organizations currently in vogue. Although New Age thinking is really old age pantheism, to the Western mind it appears fresh and full of potential.

Using teachings based on Eastern mysticism, pantheism, and "self-actualization" philosophies, New Age-related firms provide employee training for various businesses. These sessions often include hypnosis, chanting, meditation, channeling, and even tarot cards and fire walking.

55. Albert Einstein, *The World As I See It*, trans. Alen Harris (New York: Citadel Press, n.d.), p. 26.
56. For example, see Gary Zukav, *The Dancing Wu Li Masters* (New York: Morrow, 1979); Fred A. Wolf, *Taking the Quantum Leap* (San Francisco: Harper & Row, 1981); and Fritjof Capra, *The Tao of Physics* (Boulder, Colo.: Shambala Publications, 1975).
57. See for example, Eric Jantsch, *The Self-Organizing Universe* (Oxford: Pergamon, 1980), pp. 96ff.
58. Kathleen Hughes, "Enlightenment Is Fine, But Now a New Car Will Do," *Wall Street Journal*, 9 May 1986, pp. 1, 16.

Firms offering these programs to businesses include Transformational Technologies, Inc. (which franchises training seminars), FORUM (founded by Werner Erhard), Sterling Management (operated by the Church of Scientology), and Krone Training (developed by Charles Krone).

These "training seminars" are not limited to the voluntary participation by adventurous self-seekers but are sometimes mandated by major employers, such as Pacific Bell, California's largest utility company.[59] Other corporate giants, such as Proctor & Gamble, TRW, Ford Motor, and Polaroid, have officially enlisted the aid of New Age consultants. It is estimated that four billion dollars a year of corporate spending directly finances New Age programs.[60]

New Age thinking influences every area of life in America. A survey of the abundance of New Age-related writings makes this clear. There is a *New Age Bible*, a *New Age Politics*, a *New Age Medicine*, a *New Age Handbook on Death and Dying*, a *New Age Yellow Pages*, and a *New Age Community Guide Book*. There is even a book on *New Age Tennis*, a *New Age Brown Rice Cookbook*, and the *New Age Baby Name Book*. If there is a New Age coming soon, the book publishers will certainly have prophesied (and profited from) the event.

Transcendentalism: An Unreal Reality

Transcendentalism has a tremendous appeal at the emotional level. It promises everything a person could desire: divinity, self-reliance, moral freedom, and a second chance. C. S. Lewis concluded that such a worldview was "the permanent natural bent of the human mind."[61]

From a Christian perspective, transcendentalism makes several positive *contributions*.

First, transcendentalism recognizes that ultimate reality is beyond the human categories of thought and language. Whereas naturalism teaches that all truth potentially can be uncovered by the scientific method, transcendentalism holds that a complete understanding of the physical universe does not begin to exhaust the knowledge of truth.

Second, transcendentalism recognizes that ultimate reality is not only beyond human understanding but is also spiritual in nature. There is

---

59. See Steve Rabey, "Karma for Cash: A 'New Age' for Workers?" *Christianity Today*, 17 June 1988, pp. 69, 71, 74.
60. Annetta Miller and Pamela Abramson, "Corporate Mind Control," *Newsweek*, 4 May 1987, pp. 38-39.
61. C. S. Lewis, *Miracles* (London: Geoffrey Bles, 1959), p. 100.

a bond between our own spiritual make-up and that which is the final reality of the universe.

Third, transcendentalism sees the unity of all creation. All things are one in spite of the diversity present in the world.

However, there are several major *hesitations* one should have regarding a transcendental worldview.

The first and most glaring difficulty is the inability to evaluate transcendentalism. It appeals more to the emotions than the mind. Since, in the view of transcendentalism, ultimate reality goes beyond human thinking, then there no doubt will be logical inconsistencies and contradictions. For this reason, transcendentalism is not only beyond proof, it is also beyond disproof. This aspect of transcendentalism is often no problem for its proponents, many of whom enjoy the logical absurdities of their view. But does such a perspective of reality actually fit the world in which we live?

The second difficulty is the problem of origins. How did a perfect "oneness" produce the diverse universe of the physical realm? How did an impersonal force produce individual personalities? If all things are one, why is there such a problem with so many persons not being aware of this oneness?

A third and related issue concerns the problem of evil. If all is one, how can evil be such a real and powerful part of the physical universe? Is ultimate reality also evil? The only recourse is to claim that the physical realm is totally an illusion, thus evil is not real. However, this is small consolation for those who suffer. Denying the reality of evil does not make it go away. "Illusory" pain ends up hurting just as much as real pain.

A fourth problem, from a biblical perspective, is the promise of reincarnation. The Bible clearly excludes any possibility for "other lives" when the writer of Hebrews states, "And inasmuch as it is appointed for men to *die once* and after this comes judgment" (Heb. 9:27, italics added). It is popular among New Agers to discuss the influences of "past lives" (and even future lives![62]) on their personalities. This romantic sense of history makes the whole idea of reincarnation an exciting future hope. However, this is a distortion of the common pantheistic view of reincarnation. To the Eastern mind, reincarnation is a *curse* not a romantic cycle of interesting, exciting lives.[63]

62. See Bruce Goldberg, *Past Lives, Future Lives: Accounts of Regression and Progression Thru Hypnosis* (New York: Ballantine, 1988).

63. Some New Age teachers refer to biblical passages to support reincarnation. For examples and a brief analysis of this usage of Scripture, see Norman Geisler and J. Yutaka Amano, *The Reincarnation Sensation* (Wheaton, Ill.: Tyndale, 1984), pp. 133-54. See also Doug Groothuis, *Confronting the New Age* (Downers Grove, Ill.: InterVarsity, 1988), pp. 94-103.

A fifth problem is that transcendentalism is a religious step backward. Rather than giving humanity the hope of a maturing "new age," transcendentalism actually forges a retreat to an earlier period of human development when man attempted to appease "the spirits" for his own benefit. Rabbi Harold Kushner concurs: "For me, New Age religion infantalizes our relationship with God. It would take us back to the premoral stage of religion, asking for something, trying to manipulate God to get what we want, without our having to meet any standards at our end of the relationship."[64]

WHERE DO WE GO FROM HERE?

Naturalism and transcendentalism prevail in Western culture. Naturalism dominates the outlook of the university and the government. Charles Malik, former president of the General Assembly of the United Nations, concludes, "Because scientific naturalism is deeply entrenched in the university, the university has become a principal disseminator of atheism."[65]

In government, employing the separation of church and state doctrine has resulted in the attempt to be "God-neutral." The secularization of legislation and public school education has rendered God a *persona non grata* in the public square. (See the first case study at the end of this chapter.)

Whereas naturalism is predominant in the intellectual and institutional spheres, transcendentalism dominates the emotive spheres. All forms of media and art are influenced by transcendental thinking, especially under the guise of New Age thought. (See the second case study at the end of this chapter.) The open-minded character of transcendentalism, accompanied by the shining promises of a "new age" of hope, is an offer too good to pass up.

What is interesting is that both naturalism and transcendentalism fit in nicely with the thrust of American thinking and living. The "national religion" of America is "the belief that we are each in full command of our own destinies."[66] Naturalism and transcendentalism reject the possibility of help from beyond ourselves. Both worldviews allow the focus and control of life to reside within the individual. For the naturalist, life may have no meaning, but this should not lead to despair. In fact, the na-

64. Harold Kushner, *Who Needs God?* (New York: Summit Books, 1989), p. 80.
65. Charles H. Malik, *A Christian Critique of the University* (Downers Grove, Ill.: InterVarsity, 1982), p. 44.
66. Stephen Budiansky, "What Remains Beyond Our Power to Control," *U.S. News and World Report,* 7 August 1989, p. 6.

turalist will claim that this meaninglessness leads to freedom: freedom from guilt and accountability for my past; freedom from future judgment; and freedom from the forces and values of the people around me.[67] I am free to live each moment as it happens.

For the transcendentalist, the mastering of forces within nature (especially those within me) is the prime objective. Whether through meditation or occultic practices, I *alone* am responsible for my lot in this life and in the life (lives?) to come. I am free to choose my own course in life and make my own decisions.

From the perspective of naturalism and transcendentalism, theism endangers man's freedom. Believing in God implies that I am totally subject to Him and must bow my will to His. Is this a compelling alternative to either naturalism or transcendentalism? We shall explore theism and the essentials of a biblical worldview in the next chapter.

CASE STUDY: *Secularization of Government—"Scopes II"*

The domination of naturalism in society is no clearer seen than in the government's attempts to secularize all phases of public life. The overall attitude is to appear "God-neutral" and "nonsectarian" in public education, government-sponsored programs, and judicial decisions. Sex education, religious symbols on public property, prayers before high school football games or any other "public" event, and many other issues have become subjects for debate.

A case in point is the well-known "Scopes II" trial in Little Rock, Arkansas, during the winter of 1981. The late Judge William Overton ruled against the teaching of creation-science in public schools because such an approach to origins was not "scientific." To come to such a conclusion the judge had to define science. He wrote: "More precisely, the essential characteristics of science are: 1) It is guided by natural law; 2) It has to be explanatory by reference to natural law; 3) It is testable against the empirical world; 4) Its conclusions are tentative, i.e., are not necessarily the final word; and 5) It is falsifiable."[68]

His description of science leaves the impression its process is an objective and certain endeavor that makes no metaphysical assumptions and has no room for God. Judge Overton's points have all been challenged by

67. This perspective of "freedom" is vividly portrayed in the works of Albert Camus, particularly, *The Stranger,* trans. Matthew Ward (New York: Knopf, 1988).
68. This part of Judge Overton's decision is cited in Norman L. Geisler, *The Creator in the Courtroom* (Milford, Mich.: Mott Media, 1982), p. 176.

scientists,[69] especially the implication that science and religion have no common ground. Yet the impact of the judge's ruling is effectively to rule out any supernatural assumptions or references to God in public education. This approach is not "God-neutral" but "God-less," making a strong statement that any consideration of God is not necessary to become an educated person.

CASE STUDY: Cosmic Comedy—Children's Cartoons

The move to a transcendental view of reality in popular culture is portrayed especially well in the development of children's TV programs and cartoons over the past two decades. In the past, "superheroes" (Superman, Batman, Spiderman, the Incredible Hulk, etc.) performed superhuman feats in order to overcome evil. In each case, there was a "rational" explanation for the hero's power (e.g., an alien, a laboratory experiment, superior intellect, etc.). The cartoon viewing fare for smaller children, dominated by such familiar characters as Mickey Mouse, Donald Duck, Bugs Bunny, Porky Pig, Yogi Bear, Tom and Jerry, and many others, generally involved human and animal characters in wacky, but normal, situations. The Saturday morning TV cartoon line-up from 1947 to 1980 included only a few programs that could be construed as containing transcendental tendencies.[70]

This is not to imply that mystical elements were absent from these earlier programs and films. Big-screen productions such as *The Wizard of Oz, Fantasia, Alice in Wonderland*, and many other children's stories were built around themes dominated by fantasy. But the fantasy was undisguised, and the story often resolved itself as being unreal (as in *The Wizard of Oz*, in which Dorothy's adventures were a dream).

More recently, the popular children's programs have taken a decidedly mystical slant. Now, many cartoon characters take advantage of a power or force present in the world in order to achieve the strength they need to overcome evil. Superhuman powers are accessible through crystals, mystical spells, and magic swords. The animated feature film *Land Before Time* is an eighty-minute commercial for New Age philosophy.

The religious implications of such programming are usually not obvious; however, at times religious themes are decidedly the focal point of

69. See Ernan McMullin, "Introduction: Evolution and Creation," in *Evolution and Creation*, ed. Ernan Mcmullin (Notre Dame, Ind.: U. of Notre Dame, 1985), pp. 46ff.
70. The most notable were "Shazami," "The Secrets of Iris," and "Birdman." See Gary H. Grossman, *Saturday Morning TV* (New York: Crown, 1987).

the story. In one Saturday morning cartoon, for example, a unicorn had lost his power until his magical horseshoe was found in a manger, surrounded by an adoring group of gentle animals—a scene reminiscent of Christ's nativity.

How young minds integrate the underlying worldview of these stories is uncertain. It is clear, however, that both theism and naturalism are edged out by the unbridled appeal to transcendentalism.

DISCUSSION QUESTIONS

1. The average person forges ahead in life giving little thought to worldviews, philosophies of life, or any other such "intellectual" endeavors. Why is this true? If every person has a worldview, then why are so many fragmented in their thinking and living?
2. Describe the starting point of each of the three major worldviews. How are they similar? How do they differ?
3. How was reference to God excised from science? In what ways did Darwin's theory help to change the philosophical base of science and set the stage for modern agnosticism?
4. Describe how existentialism, hedonism, and humanism are practical responses to a naturalistic worldview.
5. What elements of a transcendental worldview contribute to its popularity? What are manifestations of this worldview with which you are familiar?
6. Why is reincarnation such an important aspect of transcendental thought? In what ways is reincarnation contrary to biblical teachings?
7. In what ways are transcendentalism and naturalism similar? How do these similarities make both worldviews particularly appealing to the American way of thinking and living?

FURTHER READING

Naturalism, Science, and the Christian Faith:

Barbour, Ian G. *Issues in Science and Religion*. New York: Harper & Row, 1966.

Bube, Richard. *The Human Quest: A New Look at Science and the Christian Faith*. Waco, Tex.: Word, 1971.

Clark, Gordon. *The Philosophy of Science and Belief in God*. Nutley, N.J.: Craig, 1964.

Dooyeweerd, Herman. *The Secularization of Science*. Memphis: Christian Studies Center, 1954.

Greene, John C. *Science, Ideology and World View: Essays in the History of Evolutionary Ideas*. Berkeley, Calif.: U. of California, 1981.

Jaki, Stanley. *The Road to Science and the Ways to God*. Chicago: U. of Chicago, 1978.

Kekes, John. *The Nature of Philosophy*. Totowa, N.J.: Rowman and Littlefield, 1980.

Ratzsch, Del. *Philosophy of Science*. Downers Grove, Ill.: InterVarsity, 1986.

Rolston, Holmes. *Science and Religion: A Critical Survey*. New York: Random House, 1987.

Transcendentalism and the Christian Faith:

Albrecht, Mark. *Reincarnation: A Christian Appraisal*. Downers Grove, Ill.: InterVarsity, 1982.

Chandler, Russell. *Understanding the New Age*. Waco, Tex.: Word, 1989.

Clark, David, and Norman L. Geisler. *Apologetics in the New Age: A Christian Critique of Pantheism*. Grand Rapids: Baker, 1990.

Cox, Harvey. *Turning East*. New York: Simon and Schuster, 1977.

Groothuis, Douglas R. *Confronting the New Age*. Downers Grove, Ill.: InterVarsity, 1988.

————. *Unmasking the New Age*. Downers Grove, Ill.: InterVarsity, 1986.

Sire, James W. *The Universe Next Door*. 2d ed. Downers Grove, Ill.: InterVarsity, 1988.

Tucker, Ruth A. *Another Gospel: Alternative Religions and the New Age Movement*. Grand Rapids: Zondervan, 1989.

3

THE ESSENTIALS OF
A BIBLICAL WORLDVIEW

The Beginning of a Biblical Worldview: God
    A Description of Theism
    An Explanation of Theism
    Some Variations of Theism
The Substance of a Biblical Worldview: Scripture
    A Description of Biblical Revelation
    An Explanation of Biblical Revelation
The Development of a Biblical Worldview: Steps
    Comprehension
    Application

Every man who occupies himself with the construction of a god, or merely
even agrees to it, prostitutes himself in the worst way.

                                        VLADIMIR LENIN

Nothing will be changed if God does not exist.

                                        JEAN-PAUL SARTRE

When Zarathustra was alone, however, he said to his heart: "Could it be
possible! This old saint in the forest hath not yet heard of it, that God is
dead!"

                                        FRIEDRICH NIETZCHE

There is no end to classic statements denying the existence of God.
Yet the statistics reveal that more than ninety percent of Americans believe in God, whereas only one in twenty-five is a professing atheist.

Three-fifths of the world's population hold to a belief in some form of personal deity.[1]

However, truth cannot be determined by opinion polls. Either God exists or He does not. Theism must wrestle with the same questions and cover the same territory as any other worldview.

THE BEGINNING OF A BIBLICAL WORLDVIEW: GOD

A DESCRIPTION OF THEISM

Naturalism builds its system on the assumption that the material universe is all that exists. Transcendentalism assumes that all reality is one great mind or spirit. Theism begins with the assumption that God exists.

Acknowledging the existence of God is not merely a sentimental belief in a kindly "Father in the sky"; it is a bold and powerful declaration concerning the origin and meaning of the universe. Unlike naturalism, theism holds that real things do exist beyond the physical realm: God, angels, the human soul, immortality, and the like. Christians can speak of eternal things not seen (Gen. 1:1; 2 Cor. 4:17; Heb. 11:1)—there is more than meets the eye. Unlike transcendentalism, theism sees the created world as a work of art from the hand of the Creator. Theism also delivers an indictment against man because of his personal rebellion against God.

AN EXPLANATION OF THEISM

A theistic worldview and a biblical worldview are not synonymous. Theism is usually understood to be any view that holds to belief in a Supreme Being. Although this is also the starting point for a biblical worldview, many variations of theism depart drastically from the essentials of biblical teachings. We shall discuss these variations briefly later in this chapter. Theism, however, does contain certain elements that we must understand before a biblical worldview can be placed into proper perspective. We shall narrow our description of a biblical worldview by first outlining the essential truths of a theistic worldview as it confronts God, humanity, and nature. Then we shall fill in the specific teachings of a biblical worldview as it also faces this threefold division.

Confronting God

Whereas transcendentalism views the term *God* as a reference to the impersonal life-force of all reality, theism sees God as a personal being

---

1. Information taken from David Barrett, ed., *World Christian Encyclopedia* (New York: Oxford, 1982), pp. 1-21.

who is separate from the natural world. Therefore, God exists in a different way than does the creation He brought into existence. Douglas Groothuis explains, "God differs from His creation not in degree (of being) but in kind. He is uncreated, unchanging and self-sufficient; creation is created, subject to decay, and dependent on its Creator."[2]

Theism agrees that God's nature is beyond the world He has created, but does not agree that He is removed from it. Most theists hold that God is also active within the physical realm. Such an understanding of God opens up the possibility of His interceding in the affairs of His creation. This involves both revelation (God communicating with man) and miracles (God "interfering" with nature or the course of events).

But before we move on in our discussion of the theistic view of God, a challenge must be explored. Because theism is built squarely upon belief in God's existence, can this belief be proved?

The Proofs of God. *Proof* may not be an appropriate term to describe the evidence for the existence of God. The idea of "proving" that something exists usually refers to the realm of science that is limited to the physical world. For example, I can prove that I know how to make banana nut pancakes by cooking a stack for you, or I can prove that my car is brown by showing it to you. But the essential nature of God is not physical. As the final reality, God is beyond the material world—the physical universe was created by Him. However, this does not mean the physical universe provides no clues to God's existence. The Christian may point to evidence within the physical realm as "proof" for God's existence: the order of creation, human conscience, miracles, or religious experiences. Thus, to search scientifically for the presence of God in the physical universe is like searching for the artist in the canvas of a painting. All that can be found is evidence of the artist's handiwork. In the same way, by searching the physical realm we would expect to find evidence of God's handiwork in creation.

This evidence is seen in several ways in what have traditionally been called the arguments for God's existence. Because other works explore these arguments at length, we shall simply summarize three of them here: the cosmological argument, the teleological argument, and the moral argument.

1. The cause of the universe. The *cosmological argument* points to the existence of the cosmos as evidence of God's existence. The cosmological argument has been a part of Greek, Arabic, Jewish, and Christian

2. Douglas Groothuis, "The Christian Mind," *CSSH Quarterly* VII:2 (Winter 1984):13.

thought. It is found in the works of Plato, Aristotle, Maimonides, Spinoza, and Leibniz.[3] The classic exposition of the cosmological argument was given in the thirteenth century by Thomas Aquinas in his "Five Ways."[4]

The argument generally takes two forms.

The first is to claim that something outside the universe is required to explain its existence. The universe itself consists of a series of cause/effect relationships: for everything that exists there is something that existed prior and caused its existence. Such relationships could not move infinitely into the past; there had to be a first cause. However, some have argued that an infinite regression of cause/effect is not absurd. Although this may be true philosophically, the actual evidence within the present form of the material universe points to a definite starting point.

George G. Simpson, Harvard paleontologist and evolutionist, acknowledges the limitations of science in this area. He states, "The origin of the cosmos and the causal principles of its history remain unexplained and inaccessible to science. Here is hidden the First Cause sought by theology and philosophy."[5] A theistic worldview identifies this first cause as God.

A second form of the cosmological argument focuses on the *necessary* existence of God. It is argued that God is the only existence that *must* exist, all other "things" are not necessary. For example, you can imagine many of the things around you not existing: your car, the pine tree in your front yard, your neighbor's house, even your neighbor. In fact, there is nothing in the universe that absolutely must exist. Things that do not have to exist are said to be contingent, that is, dependent on something else for their existence. Because the universe is made up of contingent things, it seems reasonable to assume the universe itself does not have to exist—it is contingent on something else for its existence.[6] This "something else" is God.

2. The design of the universe. A second argument for the existence of God is the *teleological* argument, which looks beyond the mere existence of the cosmos and extends the scope of inquiry to the apparent design within the creation. If not the strongest, the argument for design is

3. For a good explanation of the history and development of the cosmological argument, see William L. Craig, *The Cosmological Argument from Plato to Leibniz* (New York: Macmillan, 1980).

4. Thomas Aquinas, *Summa Theologica*, Part 1, Question 2, Article 3, in *Basic Writings of Saint Thomas Aquinas,* ed. Anton C. Pegis (New York: Random House, 1948).

5. George G. Simpson, *The Meaning of Evolution* (New Haven, Conn.: Yale U., 1967), p. 279.

6. Because the universe consists of contingent things, it does not *necessarily* follow that the universe itself is contingent. However, for the naturalist to claim otherwise is a bold statement of faith. How can a universe of contingent things be necessary?

certainly the most popular approach to demonstrate the existence of God.[7] The argument is based on the analogy of human design and purpose. When we see evidence of intelligent design within the world (i.e., an automobile, a watch, a building, etc.) we naturally assume that an intelligent designer was responsible for constructing the object.

The teleological argument claims that the universe also shows evidence of an intelligent scheme. Of course, it is not the same kind as that of human design, but at least three aspects of the created world show evidence of conscious design. The first is in the natural realm. The laws of nature discovered by science are regular and irrevocable. Without these laws the created "order" would be chaos and science would be impossible.

The second area of evident design is within the organic realm. The intricate and purposeful functions of plant and animal life sustain the biological cycles. Processes such as photosynthesis, digestion, reproduction, and thinking are more complex than anything mankind has produced.

The third area of evident design is the beneficial arrangement of the natural and organic realms. The "balance of nature" both within and between these two realms allows for their nourishment and growth. The existence of such design in the universe at a magnitude far beyond human capability is seen as evidence for the existence of an intelligent designer, or God.

Not everyone is convinced by the argument for design. Philosophically, some believe that the analogy between human design and the apparent design within the universe is not so evident. Further, they argue, there is a great deal of disorder within the universe. If God is a God of order, they ask, why did He seem to fall short of a universe that is completely ordered?[8]

Scientifically, as we mentioned in chapter 2, the natural selection theory of Charles Darwin, which has been expanded to include a host of other natural processes, supposedly takes away the mystery of design within the biological world. Darwin claimed, "The old argument of design in nature . . . which formerly seemed to me so conclusive, fails, now that the law of natural selection has been discovered."[9]

Neither of these arguments is sufficient to reject completely the teleological approach to God's existence. The concept of "disorder" implies

7. See J. L. Mackie, *The Miracle of Theism* (Oxford: Clarendon, 1982), p. 133.
8. See David Hume, *Dialogues Concerning Natural Religion*, ed. Nelson Pike (Indianapolis: Bobbs-Merrill, 1970) and Anthony Flew, *God and Philosophy* (New York: Dell, 1966).
9. Quoted in John C. Greene, *Darwin and the Modern World View* (Baton Rouge, La.: Louisiana State U., 1961), p. 43.

an understanding of "order." From where does this idea arise except from a divine orderer? The theory of natural selection, even if it is true, certainly does not rule out God.

The classic explanation of the teleological argument was given by William Paley, who used the analogy of a watch discovered in a field. Because a watch is an instrument of intricate design, the natural conclusion, claimed Paley, is that the watch is the product of a watchmaker. The intricate design of the universe, therefore, leads us to conclude that it is the product of a "universe-maker," or God.[10] Richard Swinburne has updated this argument by taking into account the philosophical and scientific objections.[11]

The teleological argument has great appeal because it fulfills the aesthetic longings *within* us as we view the beauty of the world *around* us. The argument may be summed up in a statement by Martin Luther, "All creation is the most beautiful book of the Bible; in it God has described and portrayed Himself."[12]

3. The morality in the universe. A third argument for God's existence is the *moral argument*, which sees the reality of man's moral nature as evidence for a "moral Lawgiver." This argument focuses on the pervasive sense of right and wrong that is present in humanity. Morality may have different expressions in different cultures, but the fact of moral standards is a most striking feature. Among all people there is an approval of benevolent behavior and the tendency to act benevolently toward others. This of course does not mean that people always behave kindly toward others, but actions are consistently judged as being "right" or "wrong"; "good" or "bad"; "fair" or "unfair."

By what standard are such judgments made? Why do we believe we are answerable to some moral standard for our behavior? Who imposed this standard on us? Theists believe God has given mankind an obligation to meet up to certain behavioral standards that are a reflection of His character. Morality is an intensely personal matter and thus only a personality could have imposed such standards.

Not everyone agrees that human morality is a proof for the existence of God. Atheists argue that morality is the natural product of biological and social evolution. Further, many atheists consider the idea of a moral law to be an unlikely "miracle." For example, J. L. Mackie believed it was impossible for God to impose His will on mankind. He claimed,

10. William Paley, *Natural Theology*, 2d ed. (Oxford: J. Vincent, 1828).
11. See his *The Existence of God* (Oxford: Oxford U., 1979), pp. 135.
12. Quoted by Martin E. Marty, *Health and Medicine in the Lutheran Tradition* (New York: Crossroad, 1983), p. 27.

"Moral values, their objectivity and their supervenience, would be a continuing miracle . . . , a constant intrusion into the natural world. But then our post-Humean scepticism about miracles will tell against this whole view."[13] Mackie concluded that because David Hume "proved" that miracles are impossible, anything resembling a miracle (i.e., God imposing His will on mankind) is dismissed as impossible.

The moral argument is best suited to complement the other arguments for the existence of God. Although it makes strong statements about the source of man's moral nature, the moral argument nevertheless interprets human behavior and cultural norms from a metaphysical perspective.

The moral argument, however, has been a formidable proof over the past few centuries. The German philosopher Immanuel Kant considered the moral argument to be the only compelling one for God's existence.[14] Later apologists, such as J. H. Newman[15] and C. S. Lewis,[16] used the moral argument as a powerful statement for the existence of God.

Other arguments are often set forth to demonstrate God's existence. Among them are the arguments from religious experience (If there is no God, how is it that millions of people have religious experiences?); the arguments from consciousness (How can a material object give rise to conscious thought?); and the ontological arguments (Is not the very idea of God proof of His existence?). Many theists would say that even though the individual arguments may be answered, the overwhelming impact of the arguments as a whole is compelling and not easily dismissed—they give reasonable evidence to believe that God does exist.

However, it is crucial to recognize that the theistic arguments alone are not solid proof for God's existence. Metaphysical arguments usually end up where they begin. An atheist will take the evidence of the world order and conclude that God, in fact, does not exist. Using the same evidence, theists conclude that God does exist. One's assumptions determine the outcome of his arguments.

The arguments, however, are not useless. They do point out that belief in the existence of God is not a foolhardy "leap of faith." Further, they show that a monotheistic interpretation of the world can be a "thinking man's" view. Belief in God's existence does not violate a logical and

13. Mackie, *Miracle*, p. 118.
14. Immanuel Kant, *Grounding for the Metaphysics of Morals*, trans. James W. Ellington (Indianapolis: Hackett Publishing, 1981).
15. J. H. Newman, *A Grammar of Assent* (London: Longmans, 1870).
16. C. S. Lewis, *Mere Christianity*, reprint ed. (Westwood, N.J.: Barbour and Co., 1952).

rational approach to the particular evidences and experiences in the world.

The Nature of God. The sum of the arguments for the existence of God, however, gives us only scant insight into the nature of a Supreme Being, a view that barely resembles the God revealed in the Bible. God's general revelation of Himself through nature gives us scant specific or reliable information about Him. For example, "Nature can teach one about divine wrath, for the universe can be a terrible and savage place, but nature will teach nothing of mercy. Nature suggests both the omnipotent and the omniscient, for the universe is vast, intricate, and well-ordered; yet it knows of no God who would be a friend of man."[17]

Much like reading the résumé of a person we do not know, we are left wondering about the personality of the individual, as well as his plans and goals. We can derive from the evidence around us that God is a powerful, orderly, moral being, but little about His character traits and His plan for the world and humanity.

For this reason, the theistic religions do not rely solely upon God's revelation in nature for the foundation for their beliefs. Much is derived from their own scriptures and teachings of "holy men." A good description of the theistic understanding of the nature of God is given by Richard Swinburne: God is "a person without a body (i.e., a spirit), present everywhere, the creator and sustainer of the universe, a free agent, able to do everything (i.e., omnipotent), knowing all things, perfectly good, a source of moral obligation, immutable, eternal, a necessary being, holy, and worthy of worship."[18] While one may quibble about the exact meaning of some of these terms, this represents a basic description of God, which most theists would accept.

Confronting Humanity

In light of God's existence, when I try to understand my place in the world I am able to look beyond myself for answers. I am not the product of transcendental emanation or of naturalistic evolution. I have been brought into existence by an intelligent being—God. My existence is not by chance, but the result of a purposeful choice. My existence as a human can be summarized by three major themes: dependence, dignity, and dominion.

17. Alan J. Birkey, Fred Van Dyke, and Ted D. Nickel, "Integration and the Christian College: Reflection on the Nineteenth Psalm," *Faculty Dialogue* (Fall 1987), p. 92.
18. Richard Swinburne, *The Coherence of Theism* (Oxford: Oxford U., 1977), p. 2.

To claim that man is *dependent* means that he is not autonomous. Even his life is not merely a biological event, but an intelligent choice by God to bring that individual into existence. Practically, I recognize that I am dependent on God for my existence and continuance. I am not the captain of my own fate. Further, if God is a moral being, then I must admit that I am dependent on Him as the moral judge of my life. Theism teaches that each person will be evaluated for how he lives and either be rewarded or punished by the supreme authority, God.

To claim that man has *dignity* is to make a strong assertion about the nature of man's being. Unlike naturalism, which centers the essence of the individual in physical matter, theism sees each individual as a special creation by God. In some way, man shares in the nature of God. However, unlike transcendentalism, man is not "part or parcel" of God. He is separate from God and shares in the divine nature only as a direct act of God's will.

Such a share in God's nature causes man to ask the ultimate questions of life. Thus all human life has dignity — not because of the inherent worth of the person, but because God ascribes worth to humanity created in His image. Our abilities to seek that which is true, good, and beautiful are profound indicators of God's imprint in the soul of each person.[19]

Man's dignity is further highlighted by his immortality. Our birth is the beginning of our personal history, but through God's will and power all people continue eternally. There is no cycle of continued incarnation as in transcendentalism. In theism there is one life, one death, one judgment.

Each person is unique. The individual ego is not evil or an illusion as in transcendentalism, but another mark of God's special creation. Biologically, psychologically, and spiritually, each person bears a unique imprint from the Creator.

The fact of man's dignity leads to the paradox of humanity. Humanity is capable of the greatest acts of kindness and selflessness, the greatest discoveries of the universe, the greatest thoughts of creativity, and the greatest acts of courage; yet he is also capable of the grossest acts of violence against himself and others. This paradox is often understood by the theistic religions as the result of the conflict between God's image in man and man's rebellion by sin, which has resulted in an alienation from God.

19. The three categories of human reason, human volition, and aesthetic sensitivity are celebrated faculties that are distinctly human. The classical philosophers expounded man's exploration of these capabilities. Immanuel Kant devoted his major works to them in *Critique of Pure Reason, Critique of Practical Reason,* and *Critique of Judgment.*

The only remedy is deliverance from this sinful state. How this is accomplished constitutes the various salvation schemes of the theistic religions.

The concept of *dominion* is difficult to articulate, yet there is a compelling notion that mankind is, in a small way, ruler over his environment. In one sense we are a part of nature. We are born through natural processes and our activities are governed by natural laws. But our essential qualities go beyond the natural world. By our free will we may act contrary to nature, and with our imaginations we are able to transcend our own existence. Man's dominion over nature is, of course, not a blank check to exploit the earth to benefit his own desires. Rather, theism calls for man to nurture his world as a steward.

While reflecting some of the most positive features of naturalism and transcendentalism, theism solves the mysteries concerning man's purpose and meaning, his individual personality and destiny. From a personal point of view, the naturalist would claim, "There is no God"; the transcendentalist would affirm, "I am god"; but the theist would insist, "I am God's."

Confronting Nature

Theists believe that God created the universe *ex nihilo* ("out of nothing"). He did not form the universe out of eternal pre-existing material, as was thought by the early Greek cosmologies, but instead He brought matter and energy into existence. The world exists as the result of God's free decision to create. This is a crucial point in the understanding of theism. God alone is the ultimate reality and everything else is derived from Him.

The first verse of the Bible declares, "In the beginning God created the heavens and the earth" (Gen. 1:1). This is a bold proclamation of God's existence, His transcendence over the universe, His creative power, and His authority. Unlike naturalism, nature is not autonomous and purposeless, but is dependent and purposeful. Unlike transcendentalism, nature is not divine but designed.

The natural world is not only created by God but is also sustained by Him. The natural laws that describe physical events are God's design to maintain an orderly universe. The created world is not eternal; even physicists point out that the universe is "running down." Whatever future the natural world has is held in the hands of the One who brought it into existence.

Most of the major theistic religions would generally agree with the description above. It is clear that merely acknowledging the existence of

God does not set a single agenda for a worldview. The differences among the various theisms involve disagreements concerning the nature of God and His plan for the world. Is He the God of Abraham and/or Jesus and/or Muhammad? Is He active in the world today? Is He limited in His ability to control world events or the influence of evil? From a biblical perspective, God has spoken and given the answers. Let us look at the essential elements of a biblical worldview as it responds to the confrontation of God, the self, and nature.

SOME VARIATIONS OF THEISM

Within the realm of a theistic worldview, there are several worldviews that run counter to traditional theism. We will look briefly at four of them here. The first two are derived from Christianity: deism and finitism. Both of these views alter the traditional view of God as an all-powerful, all-good Being who is active within His creation.

Deism

Deism claims that God is beyond the world, not within it. The deistic God created the physical universe and instilled within it natural laws to ensure its orderly operation. Now the world runs according to God's precise initial design without any need for His intrusion. A watchmaker or engine designer is no longer needed after the instrument is constructed.

Because deism rejects divine intervention in the affairs of the created world, the only means available for man to know God is through what has been made—creation itself. Verbal revelation in the Bible, the deity of Christ, and miracles are all discarded as possibilities. Deism flourished in Europe and later in America in the latter days of the Renaissance until the early part of the nineteenth century. Well-known American deists of that era were Thomas Jefferson, Benjamin Franklin, and Thomas Paine.

Finitism

Another alternate form of theism is known as *finitism*, the belief that God is limited in certain aspects of His nature and power. Finitism attempts to solve the dilemma of evil that plagues traditional theism. This is more fully explored in chapter 5; however, we can summarize at this point. How can an all-good, all-powerful God allow evil to persist in a universe He created? Finitism attempts to solve the problem by claiming that God is limited and incapable of destroying evil.

Such a perspective of God has been popularized by Rabbi Harold Kushner in his best-selling *When Bad Things Happen to Good People* and

When All You've Ever Wanted Isn't Enough.[20] Kushner notes, "God has a hard time keeping chaos in check and limiting the damage that evil can do."[21]

However, both deism and finitism unnecessarily limit God. Deism implies that God supernaturally created the world but does not supernaturally work within it. Finitism renders the future uncertain: if God cannot control evil, then there can be no assurance that He will ever overcome it. In both cases God must be redefined and the biblical evidence rejected.

Two other variations of theism arise from the two world religions —Judaism and Islam—that compete with Christianity. All three religions believe in a personal God who has revealed Himself through holy writings. However, many differences exist among the three concerning their views of God.

Judaism

The various sects of *Judaism,* for example, view God as the single, supreme ruler of the universe. Judaism locates the authoritative source of its theism in the Torah (Old Testament) and the Talmud.[22] The God of Judaism is the God who specially chose Israel as His people and who is working out His covenant with them through history.

Islam

Islam (the Arabic term for "surrender") was founded by Muhammad (A.D. 570-632) and is generally touted as Christianity's greatest challenge for the future.[23] The strict legalistic lifestyle of the *Muslim* ("one who surrenders") is a result of the Islamic view of God as one who exacts justice according to a stern ethical and ritual code.[24] The Islamic view of God is a mixture of Jewish, Christian, and Arabic religious concepts derived from four sacred books: the Torah (delivered through Moses), the Psalms (through David), the Gospel (through Jesus) and, most important, the Koran (through Muhammad).

20. Harold Kushner, *When Bad Things Happen to Good People* (New York: Avon, 1981); *When All You've Ever Wanted Isn't Enough* (New York: Summit, 1986).

21. Kushner, *When Bad Things Happen,* p. 43.

22. Although Judaism relies upon the Torah as the authoritative Word of God, the Talmud serves as the official interpretation and application of the Torah to life. The Talmud is made up of the *Mishnah* (early teachings and discussions of the Rabbis dating until A.D. 210) and the *Gemara* (a rabbinical commentary on the Mishnah).

23. See George Fry, "Christianity's Greatest Challenge," *Christianity Today,* 7 November 1969, pp. 9-12.

24. The Islamic system of works is described by the "Five Pillars": (1) recitation of the Islamic creed ("There is no god but Allah and Muhammad is his prophet"); (2) prayer (five times daily facing Mecca); (3) pilgrimage to Mecca once during a lifetime; (4) observance of the Fast of Ramadan (abstaining from food, drink, and sexual relations from sunrise to sunset during one month of the year); and (5) charity (giving alms to the poor).

In spite of their differences, Judaism and Islam share a common understanding of God as a single, personal Being. Christianity, on the other hand, views God as "tri-personal," a view that is expressed by the doctrine of the Trinity. We shall refer to this later in our discussion of the biblical worldview.

The most important point of theism is that God exists. He is the final reality. Everything that exists is ultimately dependent upon Him. To acknowledge God is to cast all of human history and all personal destiny upon the will and character of the Creator and Judge.

THEISTIC RELIGIONS

	Judaism	*Christianity*	*Islam*
Inception	ca. 2,000 BC	ca. AD 30	ca. AD 600
Founder	Abraham, Moses	Jesus	Mahammad
Scripture	Old Testament	Old Testament New Testament	Torah, Psalms Gospels, Quran

---

Similarities and Agreements

- Belief in one personal God
- God's will revealed through "Scripture"
- Rewards or punishment in afterlife determined by this life

THE SUBSTANCE OF A BIBLICAL WORLDVIEW: SCRIPTURE

A DESCRIPTION OF BIBLICAL REVELATION

Much has been written about a "Christian" worldview. Unfortunately the concept of "Christian" varies to such an extent that it often designates little more than "theistic." It is for this reason that we are focusing our attention on the idea of a "biblical" worldview. Although the term *biblical* may be just as ambiguous as *Christian*, the center at least is more focused. Our usage of *biblical* follows the conservative, evangelical understanding of the Bible as the divinely inspired writings constituting the canonical Old and New Testaments.

A biblical worldview assumes one basic presupposition: "the living and personal God intelligibly known in his revelation."[25] A biblical

25. This proposition is the focal point of Carl Henry's six-volume series, *God, Revelation and Authority* (Waco, Tex.: Word, 1976-83). This particular reference is found in volume one, page 212.

worldview presents itself not as a metaphysical theory hammered out by the speculations of human thought, but as revelation. God has spoken and revealed to humanity the truth. Is this so irrational? Hardly. A biblical worldview does no violence to reason, science, or any of the intellectual endeavors of man.

A biblical worldview assumes that God can speak and that man can understand. John Stott states, "God has revealed himself in words to *minds.*"[26] God has formed man with his rational and moral capabilities to understand and respond to God's revelation.

AN EXPLANATION OF BIBLICAL REVELATION

What is necessary for a biblical worldview to be true? Ronald Nash gives the "touchstone proposition" that defines a biblical worldview: "Human beings and the universe in which they reside are the creation of God who has revealed himself in Scripture."[27] If this proposition is not true, then a biblical worldview is false. Carl Henry delineates a sample of "disproofs" for a biblical worldview:

> Evangelical theism would be falsified if one could disprove the existence of God or of the universe, since the self-revealed God is disclosed as the sovereign creator of all; or if one could disprove the bodily resurrection of Jesus of Nazareth from the dead (declared in Acts 17 to be a sign of judgment to come); or if one could prove the unqualified "success" of evil. By demonstrating that devotion to immorality and injustice is man's wisest, happiest, and most rewarding course, by exhibiting the remains of the crucified body of Jesus, or by logically demonstrating the self-existence or nonexistence of the universe, one could theoretically demolish biblical theism by attaching to it an insuperable weight of logical inconsistency.[28]

Can the "touchstone proposition" stated above be proved true? No, it becomes an assumption upon which the worldview is worked out. Many opponents will claim that to assume God's existence and revelation is an error that dooms Christianity to the status of personal opinion and experience rather than the status of comprehensive truth statement. However, *all* worldviews begin with certain assumptions and metaphysical claims that cannot be proved. Naturalism, for example, assumes that the universe is orderly, operated by fixed physical laws that can be under-

26. John R. W. Stott, *Your Mind Matters* (Downers Grove, Ill.: InterVarsity, 1973), p. 17.
27. Ronald Nash, *Faith and Reason: Searching for a Rational Faith* (Grand Rapids: Zondervan, 1988), p. 47. Nash calls this the touchstone proposition of a "Christian" worldview and notes that by the term *Scriptures* he is referring to the canonical Old and New Testaments.
28. Henry, *God, Revelation and Authority*, 1:270-71.

stood in terms of rational thought. Can these assumptions by *proved*? No, but they can be demonstrated to work when they are applied to practical experience.

The assumption of a biblical worldview also may be demonstrated to work when it is applied to practical experience. In fact, Christians accept the scientific assumptions of naturalism and go a step further: the source of the orderliness of the universe and man's rational abilities is God. At this point, naturalism counters with the claim: God and all other "non-material" entities do not exist. But how can such a claim be proved? Certainly not in the observable realm of science. It is an assumption naturalists make in order to work out their system. To deny the existence of God is an announcement of the naturalist's disbelief, not a pronouncement of his belief.

The biblical worldview rests solely on the revelation of God to His creation. This revelation is made alive by the Holy Spirit to those who embrace it. Let others attack a biblical worldview, but they must not feel they have destroyed it simply because it fails to match their own assumptions.

Now we come to the central task of the Christian: to explore, explain, and obey the revelation of God. Is it rational? Is it credible? What are its demands? Christians must proclaim to the world that "this earth has been indeed invaded — from outside its own being, outside its own resources, outside its own possibilities; it has been and, moreover, continues to be invaded by the transcendent Logos made known in divine revelation."[29]

Confronting God

The Bible gives us great insight into *who* God is and *what* God does. Whereas theistic arguments may point to the existence of an "Unmoved Mover" or "Moral First Cause," a biblical worldview fills in many of the gaps that tell us of God's nature and plans. In addition to the general evidence describing God from a theistic worldview, the Bible adds the following crucial truths about God.

The Self-revelation of God to His Creation. The transcendental view of God negates any possibility of God as a *personality*. God is rather the sum of all reality; human personality is an embarrassing fragmentation of that unity. Many Western thinkers, especially Georg Hegel, viewed God as a great thinking mind that permeates the physical realm and causes the

29. Ibid., 1:30.

progression of nature, history, and humanity.[30] However, such an impersonal view of God seems unnecessarily reductionistic. The presence of individual personalities in the world who are created in "His image and likeness" is a strong indication that God is also personal, while not denying that He is all-powerful and everywhere-present.

From the biblical perspective, God is seen as an individual Being with all the attributes of personality. As a person, God expresses emotions such as anger (Ps. 30:5), love (1 John 4:8-10), and sorrow (Gen. 9:6; Isa. 63:10). The most profound implication of God's personality is that He can personally relate to man. The relationship between God and man is a two-way street. The social aspect of personality allows for mutual communication and shared emotions. God also "speaks" to man. Verbal communication from God to man is possible. We shall explore the nature of this communication as it relates to the Bible in chapter 4. Essentially we will see that the Bible can serve as an authoritative source for truth, if indeed it is the record of God's speaking to man.

The Sovereignty of God in All History. Human history is not a series of random, unplanned events, neither is it a repetitive cycle of incarnations. History is ordained by God — there is a purpose and a goal for the course of human and natural events. God has made man's days (Ps. 139:13-16) and He knows the future. He "carries everything" (Heb. 1:3, Beck) for the fulfillment of His plans. Nothing escapes God's concern or His purpose, because He works "all things after the counsel of His will" (Eph. 1:11). History is not an inward private matter nor is it a personal interpretation of historical events; rather a biblical worldview is an all-embracing scheme of universal history.

The Triunity of God in His Personhood. Traditional theism holds that there is only one God. As we mentioned earlier in this chapter, the major theistic religions — Judaism, Christianity, and Islam — have always put forth the contention that a single, personal God exists. However, a biblical worldview adds the dimension of triunity to God's nature. He is three in personality yet one in essence; the Father, Son, and Holy Spirit are each God. Both Judaism and Islam argue strongly against the historic Christian view of the Trinity. Such a view of God has led to the charge of tritheism by Judaism, and particularly by Islam.

The Bible is clear that there is only one God (Deut. 6:4; 1 Cor. 8:4), yet this unity does not preclude statements that allow three persons — the

30. See George Hegel, *Lectures on the Philosophy of Religion* (New York: Humanities, 1962), 1:90-105.

Father, the Son, and the Holy Spirit — to be called "God" or "Lord" (Matt. 11:25; Rom. 9:5; 2 Cor. 3:17). Jesus told His disciples to baptize new converts in the "name" (singular) of "the Father and the Son and the Holy Spirit" (Matt. 28:19). The equality among the members of the Trinity is seen in many passages (i.e., Acts 2:32-33; 1 Cor. 6:11; 12:4-6; 2 Cor. 13:14; 2 Thess. 2:13-14; etc.).

Natural analogies will not suffice to portray the Trinity adequately. Because of man's limited understanding and language, the doctrine of the Trinity is impossible to comprehend.[31] This does not mean the doctrine is impossible to describe, only that the nature of God is beyond human understanding. C. S. Lewis illustrates the differences between the human and divine perspective: "On the human level one person is one being, and any two persons are two separate beings—just as, in two dimensions (say a flat sheet of paper) one square is one figure, and any two squares are two separate figures. On the Divine level you still find personalities; but up there you find them combined in new ways which we, who do not live on that level, cannot understand."[32] He continues the analogy by pointing out that in three dimensions, several squares can be combined to form one figure (as a cube). In a similar way, in the divine dimension several personalities can be combined to exist as one Person.

Many books discuss the tri-personal nature of God,[33] and the student of theology would do well to explore the biblical evidence and philosophical issues involved with the doctrine. The most practical implication of the biblical view of the Trinity is the insight we achieve into the nature of God. The respective roles and relationships within the Trinity present God as a dynamic fellowship rather than a static unity. God has exercised an eternal relationship of love and communication within His own nature. This relationship is the source of all actions directed toward His creation.

The incarnation of God in the Savior. Here we come to the most important focus of a biblical worldview: the Person of Jesus Christ. A bibli-

---

31. This does not mean that belief in the Trinity is absurd or that Christians have not attempted to understand the nature of the Trinity. The historic quest to comprehend the Trinity and its implications is a monument to man's desire and ability to think at levels beyond his own limited perspective. The quest continues. For example, Linda Zagzebski argues that the Persons of the Trinity do not differ in essential, external relations but do differ in accidental, external relations. Thus, the Persons of the Trinity can be numerically identical yet differ in some sense of identity. Linda Zagzebski, "Christian Monotheism," *Faith and Philosophy* 6:1 (January 1989): 3-16.

32. C. S. Lewis, *Mere Christianity*, pp. 138-39.

33. See for example, Arthur Wainwright, *The Trinity in the New Testament* (London: S. P. C. K., 1962); G. A. F. Knight, *A Biblical Approach to the Doctrine of the Trinity* (Edinburgh: Oliver and Boyd, 1953); and the more recent Alistair E. McGrath, *Understanding the Trinity* (Grand Rapids: Zondervan, 1988). Also see the standard systematic theologies that usually give extended treatment to the doctrine of the Trinity.

cal worldview is essentially *Christus Nexus,* Christ at the center. His life and teachings are the central core of truth. For example, Christians consider the Bible to be the authoritative Word of God because Jesus did. We shall discuss this at length in chapter 4, but it is necessary at this point to emphasize that a biblical worldview is "Bible-centered" because it is also "Christ-centered."

Transcendentalism views Jesus Christ as one of many "enlightened masters" (in the tradition of Buddha, Muhammad, Confucius) who has revealed mystical truth to the world. Naturalism feels that Jesus was at best a Jewish social reformer and at worst a deranged cult leader.[34] Neither approach is close to the biblical teaching of Jesus as the focal point of all creation and history. In fact, "all things have been created by Him and for Him" and "in Him all things hold together" (Col. 1:16-17). Paul states that history is moving toward "the summing up of all things in Christ, things in the heavens and things upon the earth" (Eph. 1:10). These are not references to some principle or ideal, but to the historic Person of Jesus Christ.

The earliest confession of the Christian church, "Jesus [is] Lord" (Rom. 10:9), will one day be the acclamation of all creation, "that at the name of Jesus every knee should bow, . . . and that every tongue should confess that Jesus Christ is Lord, to the glory of God the Father" (Phil. 2:10-11).

Who is Jesus? The Bible describes Him as a "real man." He passed through normal human processes: He was born (Matt. 1:18–2:11), He grew up (Luke 2:40,52), and He died (Luke 23:46). The Bible also points to the normal human functions and emotions displayed by Jesus: hunger (Matt. 4:2), thirst (John 19:28), weariness (John 4:6), sorrow (Matt. 26:37), joy (Luke 10:21), anger (Mark 3:5), and love (John 11:35-36).

But Jesus was not a man who became a god, He was God who became a man. His deity is affirmed by the direct references to Jesus as God (Rom. 9:5; Titus 2:13; John 1:1; etc.). Jesus claimed to exist with God, the Father, before the world was created (John 17:5; cf. 8:58). His actions while on earth (working miracles, forgiving sins, etc.) and expressed future intentions (coming in power, judging the earth, etc.) are clear indications that He claimed to be God.

The biblical writers are no less hesitant to ascribe deity to Jesus. Because God alone is the creator of all things (Isa. 44:24), the New Testament authors unequivocally designate Jesus Christ as God when they call

---

34. For a brief description of some contemporary views of Jesus compared to the biblical view, see "Why Believe in Jesus?" in William E. Brown, *Making Sense of Your Faith* (Wheaton, Ill.: Victor, 1989), pp. 86-89.

Him the creator of all things (John 1:3; Col. 1:16; Heb. 1:2). Although the disciples may not have fully *understood* the implications of the eternal God living in human flesh, they were clear that such an event had taken place and that Jesus was God-incarnate (Phil. 2:5-11; Col. 2:9).

Jesus is the *unique* incarnation of deity; He is not one among many as the New Agers claim. He is the only mediator between God and man (1 Tim. 2:5) and the only name by which men can be saved (Acts 4:12). Thus, a biblical worldview gives a very narrow explanation of the means of redemption.

In Christ the sum of God's plan for all creation is worked out: by His life, God is revealed; by His sacrifice, man is redeemed; by His return, the universe is restored to its original holiness.

The indwelling of God through the Spirit. God is active in the person of the Holy Spirit. The role of the third Person of the Trinity can be summed up in the phrase "relating God to man."[35] Imagine traveling in a country in which you did not understand the language. Conversations would be impossible; road signs would be unreadable; restaurant menus would be cryptic. How valuable a translator would be — a constant companion to make sense out of what you could not understand otherwise. You could then relate to the people and events around you.

The Bible presents the work of the Holy Spirit in a similar capacity: to translate to man the spiritual dimension of reality. The apostle Paul states, "Now we have received, not the spirit of the world, but the Spirit who is from God, that we might know the things freely given to us by God" (1 Cor. 2:12). Everything man can know about God is accomplished through the work of the Holy Spirit. He takes the raw evidence of creation and conscience and frames it in the understanding of general revelation (Rom. 1:19-21; 2:14-15; Ps. 19). His oversight in the recording of Scripture resulted in the product of special revelation (2 Pet. 1:19-21).

The Holy Spirit draws mankind to God by convincing him of his need for repentance (John 16:7-11) and spiritually "recreates" him when he responds to God's offer of salvation through grace (Titus 3:5; 2 Cor. 5:17). The Holy Spirit enters the life of every believer, an event that marks the beginning of a new relationship with God as Father (Rom. 8:15; Gal. 4:6; John 1:12-13). In a mysterious way, the Holy Spirit re-

35. The nature of the Holy Spirit has been the subject of debate for centuries. Is the Holy Spirit merely the "spiritual presence" of the omnipresent God or an impersonal "divine force"? Biblically, it seems clear that the Holy Spirit is a separate *person* from the Father and the Son and is, by nature, full deity. For a discussion of the various views concerning the nature and work of the Holy Spirit, see Millard Erickson, *Christian Theology*, one-vol. ed. (Grand Rapids: Baker, 1983-85), pp. 865-886; and Michael Green, *I Believe in the Holy Spirit* (Grand Rapids: Eerdmans, 1975).

mains present within the life of the believer to guide, empower, and convict (Rom. 8:14-17). The Holy Spirit provides the dynamic present witness of God in the world today. God is not just "out there," He is also "right here."

A biblical worldview presents a picture of God as the transcendent, sovereign, omnipotent Creator; the immanent, suffering, and redeeming God-man; and as the speaking, indwelling, empowering presence.

Confronting Humanity

Once we understand the nature and extent of God's working in the world, the place of the self in creation comes into sharper focus. We shall devote chapter seven to a discussion of a biblical view *for* the self. So let us summarize here briefly a biblical view *of* the self.

Mankind is the special creation of God. Man is "creaturely" in that he shares in the creation of the physical world. But each person is more than a physical being, because the Bible claims that the human race in total is created in the image of God. Even though the *imago Dei* of man is difficult to specify,[36] it is important to note that man was created in God's image (Gen. 1:26-27, 31; 5:1; 9:6). Thus, God's image involves man's essence, not his function; that is, it is part of what man is, not what he does. God's image in man seems to be his capacity to relate to God, which involves man's higher intellectual abilities, morality, spiritual sensitivity.

Every person shares in God's image by virtue of his creation by God. God has specially designed man to reflect His glory. For this reason, the Bible commands respect for the individual, specifically in the prohibitions against murder (Gen. 9:6) and cursing (James 3:9-10). Even the most physically fragile or mentally impaired person deserves respect because God has "crowned him with glory and majesty" (Ps. 8:3-6).

Mankind is separated from God by sin. Every person, without regard to his spiritual status (1 Cor. 11:7; James 3:9), bears the image of God. However, this image has been damaged by sin. The *imago Dei* has not been eradicated but skewed and distorted. When mankind fell into sin, he began seeking to love created things rather than the Creator (Rom. 1:25). He became self-serving rather than God-serving, and his ability to know God and His will was altered.

---

36. For different perspectives on the many views concerning the *imago Dei*, see Philip Edgcumbe Hughes, *The True Image: The Origin and Destiny of Man in Christ* (Grand Rapids: Eerdmans, 1989), pp. 1-69; Reinhold Niebuhr, *The Nature and Destiny of Man: A Christian Interpretation* (New York: Scribner's, 1943); G. C. Berkouwer, *Man: The Image of God* (Grand Rapids: Eerdmans, 1962); and Ray S. Anderson, *On Being Human: Essays in Theological Anthropology* (Grand Rapids: Eerdmans, 1982).

Man's rebellion against God is seen initially as his desire to be autonomous, self-reliant, and independent (Gen. 3:5-6), which resulted in an alienation from God (Rom. 3:23). But the Fall is more than a "spiritual" problem. As a result of man's rebellion, he finds he is alienated from himself. Francis Schaeffer noted, "The most striking part of this [self-alienation] is our coming physical death when the body will be separated from our spiritual portion. But also in the present we are each separated from ourselves psychologically. Each of us is to some extent 'schizophrenic.' There are degrees, but this present psychological separation is true of each of us."[37]

The Fall has affected man morally, physically, and intellectually. Morally, he is born in sin and by nature seeks the fulfillment of selfish desires apart from God (Eph. 2:1-3; Rom. 3:8ff.). Physically, man is dying (Rom. 5:12-21; 1 Cor. 15:21-22) and doomed to death. Intellectually, man's thoughts are darkened and hostile toward God (Col. 1:21; Eph. 4:17-24; Rom. 1:18-32), and the center of his being is couched in self-deceit (Jer. 17:9). However, certain aspects of man's reason are still intact. The Fall seems to have more impact on his will than on his reasoning powers.

The overall effect of man's situation is a terrifying sense of anxiety, alienation, and apprehension. Such feelings are not merely psychological phenomena, but the outgrowth of a real separation of man from his Creator, a condition that can be remedied only by the Creator Himself.

Mankind is redeemable through the initiation of God. Salvation is the restoration of the fullness of the divine image in man and the divine relationship with man. Many of the English terms related to salvation highlight that the act is a restitution of the relationship God intended: *rec*onciliation, *re*demption, *re*turn, *re*pentance. This restoration, of course, does not happen all at once, because the initial stages of salvation are effected within mortal bodies in a corruptible world. The terrible effects of sin upon man physically are taken away through the impartation of eternal life (Luke 18:30; John 3:16ff.; Rom. 6:23). The redeemed will not suffer eternal death but will live with the Lord forever (1 Thess. 4:17).

Morally, each of the redeemed receives the righteousness of Christ. Each is considered positionally holy through the removal of the penalty for sin and the imputation of Christ's righteousness (Rom. 3:21; 4:5). Intellectually, the redeemed has a mind that is made holy. Even though the full effects of this sanctified mind are still future (Rom. 7:18-24; 1 Cor.

37. Francis Schaeffer, "The Dust of Life," *Eternity*, March 1981, p. 37.

13:12), each redeemed person has the potential for a "renewed mind" through the power of Christ (Rom. 12:1-2; Eph. 4:22-24).

Salvation is initiated solely by God's grace on behalf of a sinful humanity that is incapable of restoring its own relationship with God (Eph. 2:1-8; Rom. 3:9-24; Titus 3:3-7). But bringing about the possibility of salvation was not just a discretionary decision by God. God could not deny His own holiness and justice and therefore had to remove the penalty of sin by an act of earned judgment. This was accomplished through the atoning death and glorious resurrection of Jesus Christ (Rom. 3:21-26; 4:25). That single event in history makes it possible for mankind to be free from the penalty of sin, since God, "having canceled out the certificate of debt consisting of decrees against us and which was hostile to us; and He has taken it out of the way, having nailed it to the cross" (Col. 2:14).

The *provision* of salvation is God's grace through the atonement of Christ, but the *personal possession* of salvation is accomplished by an act of trust: "But as many as received Him, to them He gave the right to become children of God, even to those who believe in His name" (John 1:12). The acquisition of salvation is a response to God's offer of forgiveness and restoration, not a result of human effort or achievement (Rom. 3:21-24; Eph. 2:8-10; Titus 3:3-5).

Mankind is destined for an eternal future existence. Man was created to live forever. However, this everlasting life is more than a long life, it is a specific destiny. Carl Henry notes, "Man's destiny is therefore not simply an endless existence, but is moral — either a life redeemed and fit for eternity, or a life under perpetual divine judgment."[38]

For the child of God, the promises of Scripture are very clear. C. S. Lewis summarizes the future for the Christian in five areas: "It is promised, firstly, that we shall be with Christ; secondly, that we shall be like Him; thirdly, with an enormous wealth of imagery, that we shall have 'glory;' fourthly, that we shall, in some sense, be fed or feasted or entertained; and, finally, that we shall have some sort of official position in the universe — ruling cities, judging angels, being pillars of God's temple."[39]

Naturalism promises only the grave; transcendentalism promises another incarnation; but a biblical worldview promises resurrection, "the transformation of a person's one mortal body to an immortal one."[40]

38. Carl F. H. Henry, "Man," in *Baker's Dictionary of Theology,* ed. Everett F. Harrison (Grand Rapids: Baker, 1960), p. 341.
39. C. S. Lewis, *The Weight of Glory and Other Addresses* (Grand Rapids: Eerdmans, 1949), p. 7.
40. James Sire, *Scripture Twisting* (Downers Grove, Ill.: InterVarsity, 1980), p. 92.

Confronting Nature

Throughout the Scriptures there is a consistent reference to nature as the product of God's creative will and power. The act of creation is thus the basis for the biblical view of nature. All things are not engaged in some impersonal, cosmic ebb and flow, but rather are controlled by the personal hand of the Creator.

The created world is distinct from the Creator. A biblical worldview presents the physical realm as created at the initiation of God. There was a time when the universe was not. Before the universe was, only God existed. The creation account in Genesis 1-2 is recorded to show Israel the transcendence of God. Unlike the Canaanite religions, which saw their gods within nature (and dependent upon it), the Bible affirms clearly that God is prior to, above, and beyond the material universe.

The created world reflects the person and character of God. The universe God created was initially "good" (Gen. 1:31), no doubt a reflection of the character of God, as Paul notes, "Everything created by God is good" (1 Tim. 4:4). This is unlike transcendentalism and ancient Greek cosmologies, which saw the physical world as evil. The seasons and regular harvests of the earth are also a testimony to God's goodness to man (Acts 14:17).

The created order testifies of God's invisible attributes, eternal power, and divine nature (Rom. 1:20). The general statement by the psalmist, "The heavens are telling of the glory of God" (Ps. 19:1), sums up the biblical view of nature's revelation of God.

The created world is ordered and purposeful. The prophet Jeremiah records the words of God:

> Thus says the Lord,
> Who gives the sun for light by day,
> And the fixed order of the moon and the stars for
>   light by night.
> Who stirs up the sea so that its waves roar;
> The Lord of hosts is His name:
> "If this fixed order departs from before Me,"
>   declares the Lord,
> "Then the offspring of Israel also shall cease
> From being a nation before Me forever." (Jer. 31:35)

The prophet points to God's control over nature as well as the "fixed order" of certain natural events. The natural "random" events (roaring waves) and the natural "regular" events (sun, moon, and stars) are the results of God's personal, creative control.

All things were created *for* God (Col. 1:16-17) and are the objects of His possession, thus there is a purpose in their existence and in the events that occur. The psalmist remarks, "O Lord, how many are Thy works! In wisdom Thou hast made them all; the earth is full of Thy possessions" (Ps. 104:24).

This biblical view of creation paves the way for the scientific enterprise. In fact, it was the Judeo-Christian perspective that led observers to see the diversity in creation as a unified whole. Such a view correlates with three basic aspects of science. Physicist Joseph Spradley enumerates these:

> First, the reality and goodness of creation provide a basis and motivation for experimental science. Second, the order and intelligibility of nature are essential for theoretical science. Third, the purpose and meaning of creation encourage the development of applied science. Each of these principles can be contrasted with Greek attitudes to show how a Christian view transcends the limitations of Greek science, as well as similar limitations in Oriental science.[41]

The created world is dependent upon God for its continuance. Not only did the Lord bring the universe into existence, but He continuously sustains it: "And He is before all things, and in Him all things hold together" (Col. 1:17). The writer of Hebrews claims, in a similar way, that the Lord "upholds all things by the word of His power" (Heb. 1:3). The repetition of the inclusive "all things" shows that the biblical writers were referring to *all* creation.

In spite of the power and expanse of creation, it is not eternal, at least not in its present form (Heb. 1:10-12). As a direct result of man's sin, the earth was cursed and subjected to decay (Gen. 3:17-18; Rom. 8:20). The Scriptures speak of a time in the future when the universe will be made new. The creation "will be set free from its slavery to corruption" (Rom. 8:21) and a "new heaven and new earth" will replace the old (Isa. 65:17; 2 Pet. 3:12-13; Rev. 21:1).

The created world is to be cared for by man. The declaration that the natural world was "good" (Gen. 1:31) expressed both God's pleasure in what He had made and its intrinsic value. God tends His "garden" and

41. Joseph Spradley, "A Christian View of the Physical World," in *The Making of a Christian Mind*, ed. Arthur Holmes (Downers Grove, Ill.: InterVarsity, 1985), p. 60.

cares for His creatures (Ps. 104:15-18). Man must also care for that which God created. Clearly man was granted dominion over nature (Gen. 1:28; 9:1-7; Ps. 8:3-8), but if "the earth is the Lord's and everything in it" (Ps. 24:1, NIV) man's rulership over nature is delegated and must reflect God's attitude.[42] The key concept is "stewardship"—we are managers but not owners.[43]

The biblical view concerning the natural world is all-encompassing: it describes the past origin and development of the universe; it prescribes man's involvement with the created world in which he lives; and it predicts the ultimate end of all things and the reconstitution of the present world into a new world where "righteousness dwells" (2 Pet. 3:13).

THE DEVELOPMENT OF A BIBLICAL WORLDVIEW: STEPS

The preceding discussion is only a brief sketch of the basic tenets of a biblical worldview. The implications and applications of such a view are inexhaustible. So now we ask the question, What does it mean to develop a biblical worldview?

The idea of "developing" involves more than merely "accepting," "believing," or even "knowing" the teachings of a biblical worldview. It is a dynamic two-step process that is constantly being refined. It involves both a "mindset" and a "willset."

COMPREHENSION

The first step is to *comprehend the biblical worldview.* Although there are unchangeable truths at the foundation (truth often has a way of being narrow), a biblical worldview is not a procrustean bed upon which every question or issue must be made to fit. When answers are inconclusive and options are many, a biblical worldview is better seen as a light to illuminate the darkness. Therefore, knowing the content and teachings of the Scriptures is imperative for every Christian. This involves not only a knowledge of the facts contained in the Bible, but also an understanding of the theological, philosophical, and practical implications of those

---

42. Many claim that the Christian worldview is at the root of the modern ecological crisis. The belief that man was "special" and detached from nature allegedly allowed him to exploit the natural realm for his own pleasure. See, for example, Lynn White, Jr., "The Historical Roots of Our Ecological Crisis," *Science* 155 (1967):1203-6. However, the case is not convincing. A misunderstanding of biblical teaching in this area certainly could have resulted in a misuse of natural resources, but because a Christian worldview has dominated Western culture for centuries, it could conceivably be seen as the "root" of *all* current social and ecological problems.
43. Richard T. Wright, *Biology Through the Eyes of Faith* (San Francisco: Harper & Row, 1988), p. 173.

COMPARISON OF WORLDVIEWS

	GOD
NATURALISM	God does not exist (atheism) Man cannot/does not know if God exists (agnosticism) The idea of God is a creation of man
TRANSCENDENTALISM	Essence: Impersonal force/spirit within all things Attributes: Beyond morality and human categories Actions: Moves all things toward unity
THEISM	Essence: Personal spirit, uncreated, eternal Attributes: Benevolent, holy, just Actions: Creator/sustainer of physical realm; Source/standard of truth and morality
BIBLICAL WORLDVIEW	Same as Theism, also: Essence: Triune nature Attributes: Involved in the affairs of His creation 1. Reveals His character/will through the Scriptures 2. Redeems humanity through the sacrifice of Christ 3. Judges all humanity

HUMANITY	NATURE
Essence: Totally material/physical Behavior: Self-directed; ethics self- determined Future: Life ends at death	Essence: Eternal, uncreated matter Behavior: All events governed by innate physical laws
Essence: Spiritual/psychic; uncreated part of divine oneness Behavior: Human ethics unnecessary; goal is for self-realization of divinity and unity with all things Future: Eternal existence; successive incarnations until "enlightenment"	Essence: Physical realm either an illusion or a manifesta- tion of divinity Behavior: Laws of nature lim- ited to physical realm; not a reflection of true reality
Essence: Composite of spiritual/material; created by God and for God Behavior: Ethics determined by God; individual's life judged by God Future: Eternal life with God or (some) eternal judgment	Essence: Physical realm created by God from nothing Behavior: Physical realm sustained and ordered by God; reflects certain aspects of God's character; mankind given mandate to care for created world.
Same as Theism, also: Essence: Created in God's image/likeness; corrupted by sin; separated from God Behavior: Ethics determined by God's will communicated through the Scriptures Future: Eternal life with God for the re- deemed; eternal judgment for all others	Same as Theism, also: Essence: Physical realm corrupted by man's sin Behavior: Physical realm to be restored to perfect state

facts. As imposing as this task may sound, thinking in terms of world-views helps put a tremendous amount of information in its proper place.

APPLICATION

The second step is to *apply a biblical worldview consistently.* If the biblical worldview is true, then we should seek to conform our lives to that truth. A biblical worldview cannot be developed in a vacuum but must be active in changing the individual and society. Both in our person-al lives and in public issues, the biblical worldview should determine the course of decision and action. This is a view *for* the world that we shall explore in the second half of this book.

However, before we turn our attention to the application of a bibli-cal worldview to life, we must address three major concerns or challenges to this worldview. The first is, Why a biblical worldview? What are the reasons for allowing the Bible to serve as the authority for determining a worldview? We shall discuss this challenge in chapter 4.

The second challenge concerns the problem of evil and suffering in the world. How can the all-powerful and all-good God of the Bible allow evil to persist in His creation? We shall confront this issue in chapter 5. The third challenge is the dilemma of pluralism. With so many conflict-ing worldviews, how can any one of them be the correct view? What about those who never hear "the truth"? Are they held accountable? This challenge shall be the subject of chapter 6.

CASE STUDY: Not Everyone Is Happy—The American Atheist

Theism, although the dominant profession of American society, is not without its detractors. Philosophical atheists and agnostics often raise anti-theistic banners in the context of civil and personal rights issues. Among the most radical of the anti-theistic organizations is the American Atheists, founded by Madalyn Murray O'Hair in Baltimore on July 1, 1963. O'Hair gained national prominence in the early 1960s for her bat-tles against Bible reading and prayer in public schools. When the Su-preme Court ruled in her favor (*Murray* v. *Curlett*), she capitalized on the publicity and organized Other Americans, Inc., with the intention of "ad-vancing and promoting the philosophy of materialism" and erasing reli-gion from public life.

The first years of the fledgling organization were marked by turmoil and public opposition. By her own account, O'Hair and her family were driven from Maryland by state officials and twenty-six police officers who beat her and her family (although, oddly, it was O'Hair who was charged with assault in the "attack"). The family fled to Hawaii where O'Hair claims they were again harassed by government agencies and forced to flee to Mexico.

After being returned to the United States "illegally at gunpoint," the family settled in Texas and organized the Society of Separatists on January 1, 1966. Based in Austin, the state capital, O'Hair's society struggled for ten years to gain a credible following. In 1976, believing the organization had gained enough strength to function openly, she began operating under the new name of American Atheists.

Since that time, while maintaining a small constituency, the American Atheists have attempted to secularize American public life by challenging church influence and governmental acknowledgment of religion. Consistent targets are the "In God We Trust" motto on coins, prayer before government and public school functions, and the tax-free status of church property.

The main organ of the society is the monthly magazine *American Atheist*. Other programs include a radio talk show, the "American Atheist Forum" television series, and a nation-wide "Dial-An-Atheist" phone service. The American Atheist Center in Austin is a clearinghouse for atheist literature and produces current and out-of-print atheist works. The Center houses the Charles E. Stevens American Atheist Library and Archives with more than twenty thousand books and one hundred thousand newsletters, pamphlets, and flyers.

O'Hair and her cohorts find themselves fighting not only Christians but reasoned agnostics as well, whom they refer to as "gutless atheists." Because of its emotional approach, caustic rhetoric, and simplistic approach to theistic arguments, the American Atheist organization will continue to appeal only to the fringe and radical elements of the "nonbelieving" public.

CASE STUDY: The Joys of Ignorance— The Society of Evangelical Agnostics

The American Atheist organization is one of the few that takes an extreme anti-theistic approach to life. These hardliners are critical of organizations that are more agnostic in their position against theism. Among the more interesting of these groups is the Society of Evangelical Agnostics (SEA) founded in 1975 in Auberry, California. With a membership of about one thousand, SEA promotes the "good news" that agnosticism saves people "from being seduced into unreasonable dogmatic conclusions and frees them from possible guilt for having rejected some of their past beliefs."[44] SEA literature claims that members can boldly affirm "Here I stand: committed to being open-minded, demanding evidence before coming to conclusions, and being willing to live without final answers."

The SEA philosophy falls within the mainstream of classical agnosticism. The approach is not a position for or against God, but an open admission that ultimate questions have no answers. This allows many from various schools of thought to embrace SEA's philosophy. The administrator of SEA, William H. Young, notes that SEA's membership includes "Christians of various persuasions." Further research revealed that the "Christians" were Universalist-Unitarian, not orthodox Christian.

SEA is not alone in its agnostic approach to life and the world. Members of SEA also serve in leadership positions for similar organizations. Among these are the American Humanist Association, the Committee for the Scientific Investigation of Claims of the Paranormal, Council for Democratic and Secular Humanism, and the Freedom from Religion Foundation. Publications by these groups include *The Humanist, The Skeptical Inquirer, Free Inquiry,* the *Religious Humanist,* and *Free Thought Today.* The common element in all of these groups is an agenda that promotes freedom from theistic assumptions and personal autonomy in matters of ethics and behavior.

DISCUSSION QUESTIONS

1. How does theism as a worldview differ from a biblical worldview?
2. What is the value of the "proofs" for God's existence?
3. Ronald Nash gives the "touchstone proposition" that defines a biblical worldview: "Human beings and the universe in which they reside are the creation of God who has revealed Himself in Scripture." What are the basic elements of this proposition? Do you agree that this proposition gives the essential elements of a biblical worldview? Why or why not?
4. "A biblical worldview is essentially *Christus Nexus*, Christ at the center." Why is this true?

---

44. All direct quotes are taken from promotional materials published by the Society of Evangelical Agnostics, Box 515, Auberry, CA 93602.

5. How do the major points of confrontation (God, humanity, and nature) of a biblical worldview differ from those of naturalism and
   transcendentalism?

FURTHER READING

Anderson, J. N. D. *The World's Religions*. Grand Rapids: Eerdmans,
1955.

Davis, John Jefferson. *Foundations of Evangelical Theology*. Grand Rapids: Baker, 1984.

Evans, C. Stephen. *The Quest for Faith*. Downers Grove, Ill.: InterVarsity, 1986.

Frame, John M. *The Doctrine of the Knowledge of God*. Phillipsburg,
N.J.: Presby. & Ref., 1987.

Henry, Carl F. H. *God, Revelation and Authority*. 6 vols. Waco, Tex.:
Word, 1976-83.

Lockerbie, D. Bruce. *Thinking and Acting Like a Christian*. Portland,
Oreg.: Multnomah, 1989.

Mavrodes, George. *Belief in God: A Study in the Epistemology of Religion*. Rev. ed. New York: University Press of America, 1983.

Neill, Stephen. *Christian Faith and Other Faiths*. Downers Grove, Ill.:
InterVarsity, 1984.

Noll, Mark, and David Wells, eds. *Christian Faith and Practice in the
Modern World*. Grand Rapids: Eerdmans, 1987.

Purtill, Richard. *Reason to Believe*. Downers Grove, Ill.: InterVarsity,
1974.

Sire, James W. *Discipleship of the Mind*. Downers Grove, Ill.: InterVarsity, 1990.

4

WHY A BIBLICAL WORLDVIEW?

"How do you know the Bible is God's Word, rather than the Koran? Isn't establishing the Bible's integrity by appeal to the Bible simply reasoning in a circle?

"And by the way," David continued, "why do we say these sixty-six books are inspired and other books are not? Didn't the early church disagree on some of them? Why don't people answer my questions? I want to believe the Bible is God's Word, but nobody at church takes my questions seriously."

David was a college senior about to enter law school and was experiencing the frustration that many feel when their most fundamental questions about the Bible go unanswered. He was a Christian and did not have a skeptic's nature. But suddenly he realized he was about to leave his Christian womb—a safe, comfortable, Bible-believing environment—and he knew he did not have answers to questions skeptics ask.

Many Christian young people have been reared in "the Christian ghetto" and have never been outside its walls. Their families have attended church faithfully; many have gone to Christian schools or have been schooled at home. For some, their faith is not their own, but is *faith in others' faith*, whether parents, pastors, or professors. They have been told what to believe, and this has been enough—until their faith is challenged.

When they are asked *what* they believe, whether they have answers or not, they know their answers should come from the Bible. But when they are asked *why* they believe in the Bible itself, where do they go for answers? How can they give a reasonable defense and at the same time avoid reasoning in a circle?

As we said in the last chapter, a biblical worldview appeals to the Bible as its authority. The Bible tells me that God exists, that the world is His creation, and that I am accountable to my Creator. God's Word tells me how to view my unsaved neighbor, how to treat my spouse, how to rear my children, how to use my money—in short, my view *of* and *for* the world. But why should Christians submit themselves to the authority of an ancient book for both mundane and momentous decisions?

IS REVELATION INTELLIGIBLE?: CREDIBILITY

FROM GOD TO US

Is it possible for a "book of God" to exist? Think carefully. If God is our Creator, we may assume we have been created for a purpose that He has determined. Because man forms relationships, God may have created us for some kind of relationship with Him. "Indeed, would a patently wise, intelligent creator leave his creatures to grope in the dark for some clue to his existence without making himself known? The thought is palpably absurd."[1] Our relationship with God would begin at the point of revelation, in which God communicates Himself to us.

If God's Person is such that He can function with human language (certainly being greater than man!), then God *can* communicate verbally

---

1. Bruce Milne, *Know the Truth* (Downers Grove, Ill.: InterVarsity, 1982), p. 20.

to man. If God's character is such that He is both a truthful and loving Creator who is concerned about His creatures, then God *will* communicate Himself to man. No loving God would play cosmic hide-and-seek with His beloved ones.

What would we expect of this communication from God? It might take different forms, according to the needs of His creatures. Some oral revelation might be through dreams, visions, or words spoken through prophets. But if God wanted His revelation to be used by His followers throughout the centuries He would have His truth permanently written down. Because human writings are often mixtures of truth and error, we would expect a divine book to be absolutely true (inspired), reflecting the character of its Author. Thus the idea of a book such as the Bible becomes not only possible, but probable.

The Bible claims to be God's absolutely true Word. Of course, simply making that claim does not mean it is true. But surely it would be folly for Christians to make such claims about the Bible if the book itself did not.

Building a case for Scripture's trustworthiness is an enjoyable task; the problem is deciding where to start. Consider the following valid deductive argument:

A. God is true (= without any mixture of falsehood).

B. Whatever God says is true.

C. Scripture is God's Word.

Therefore: Scripture is true (= without any mixture of falsehood).

"Aha!" some would say, "you have ignored the fact that the Bible did not drop from the sky, but is the product of human beings. The fact that fallible men wrote the Bible shows it is no more reliable or authoritative than the frailties of those men."

Therefore, when premise C (above) is changed to read "Scripture is God's Word *through human agents*," the whole argument is thrown off. But this objection ignores first the *process* of inspiration: the Holy Spirit guided human authors ("borne along" — 2 Pet. 1:21) to produce Scripture. Second, it ignores the *purpose* for inspiration: the Holy Spirit guaranteed that the (potential) limitations of human finiteness would be overcome to protect Scripture from untruth.

But did God *actually* overcome human limitations so that Scripture was written without error? Some argue strongly that the Bible is filled with mistakes and therefore is not a reliable source for a coherent and consistent worldview. In 1859 William Henry Burr published *Self-Contradictions of the Bible*. In the preface to the 1987 edition, Joseph Hoffman charges, ''The fact is that fundamentalism—the belief that the Bible is the inspired, inerrant, and literally true word of God—thrives on ignorance, *not* just of a general sort, but an ignorance of the Bible.''[2]

If true, Hoffman's challenge undercuts the *sole* foundation of a biblical worldview—the Bible. We say without apology that the Bible is the sole authority, but not without *apologetic*. The Bible speaks *for* itself (with intrinsic authority); but we must not ignore what it says *about* itself as our source of authority.

If we accept claims about the Bible that come from within the Bible, is this not circular reasoning? Actually, all worldviews operate with non-provable assumptions. The alternatives are not objective proof on the one hand and subjective circularity on the other, but rather competing sets of assumptions. The thinking person will make sure his assumptions are coherent (internal *logical fit*), consistent with reality (external *factual fit*), and satisfying (existential *psychological fit*). We believe a biblical worldview can be established that will ''fit'' all these criteria. C. S. Lewis said, ''I believe in Christianity as I believe the sun has risen, not only because I see it, but because by it I see everything else.''[3]

In our society science is worshiped. People say, ''Seeing is believing!'' or, ''I'm from Missouri—show me!'' In our empirically-oriented world we tend to trust *most* what we see, hear, touch, and experience personally. But the worldview of the Bible is broader.

First, as we discussed in chapter 2, the scientific method offers a limited view of reality and limited options for knowing. The Bible speaks of realities that cannot be reduced to empirical testing. The scientific method cannot adequately encompass subjective realms of human knowledge: ''I feel depressed,'' ''I love you,'' or ''Murder is wrong.''

Second, we may misinterpret what we perceive through the senses. The New Testament records sensory *mis*-interpretation even of direct communication from God (John 12:28-30; Acts 22:9). In contrast to sources of knowledge that may be limited—or distorted—Peter regarded the written ''prophetic word'' *more certain* than his empirical experience

2. R. Joseph Hoffman, Introduction to William Henry Burr, *Self-Contradictions of the Bible* (reprint; New York: Prometheus, 1987), p. 7.
3. C. S. Lewis, *The Weight of Glory and Other Addresses* (New York: Macmillan, 1980), p. 92. See also Greg L. Behnsen, ''Inductivism, Inerrancy, and Presuppositionalism,'' *Journal of the Evangelical Theological Society*, 20 (December 1977), pp. 289-305, and James M. Grier, ''The Apologetic Value of the Self-Witness of Scripture, *Grace Theological Journal*, 1:1 (Spring 1980), pp. 71-76.

of seeing and hearing the Transfiguration (2 Pet. 1:16-21). Thus a biblical worldview can reasonably ask the believer to trust the authority of God's Word in areas that cannot be objectively verified.

In this chapter, however, we do not intend to *prove* the inspiration of the Bible, but rather to show that belief in an inspired book from God is a serious option that any thinking person must consider. The purpose of this chapter is fourfold: first, to discuss the source of a biblical worldview (the question of *authority*); second, to discuss the extent of "Scripture" (the question of *canon*); third, to ask if it has come to us in reliable historical form (the question of *textual reliability*); and finally, to probe just how trustworthy Scripture is (the question of *inerrancy*).

JESUS' BIBLICAL WORLDVIEW

In chapter three we maintained that Jesus is who He claimed to be: the second Person of the Trinity, God incarnate. He also claimed to be truth incarnate (John 14:6). Jesus regularly confronted error with truth. He never hesitated to confront His disciples—and even the religious leaders—with their inconsistent behavior or with their bad theology. At one point He told His disciples, "if it were not so, I would have told you" (John 14:2). Jesus would not allow error to remain in the minds of His disciples for long.

The authority of Jesus is the final word that settles all issues for Christians, including questions raised about Scripture. His Bible should be our Bible and His view of Scripture—its authority, its extent, its authenticity, and its integrity—should be our view. As we shall see, Jesus' view of Scripture was embraced by the apostles and by the early Christians.

IS THE CANON GENUINE?: CERTIFIABILITY

THE CHRISTOLOGICAL TEST

Our discussion of biblical authority must include the question of *extent*, or the "Canon."[4] Why these sixty-six books? Who decided? Is a

---

4. The term *canon* has as its root meaning the Hebrew word for "reed." F. F. Bruce observes "the Greek word was probably borrowed from the Semitic word which appears in Hebrew as *qaneh*, 'reed, rod.' From the same origin come Latin *canna* and Eng. *cane*" (F. F. Bruce, *The Canon of Scripture* [Downers Grove, Ill.: InterVarsity, 1988], p. 17n.). Because the reed was a handy instrument for measurement (like our yardstick), other usages derived from the root word, such as "rule" (a literal measuring rod) and "standard" (the figurative usage). This latter usage is the idea behind biblical *canon*—the standard of faith. Another related (and valid) derivation usage is the idea of a "list"—e.g., of authoritative books.

THE CANON JESUS AFFIRMED

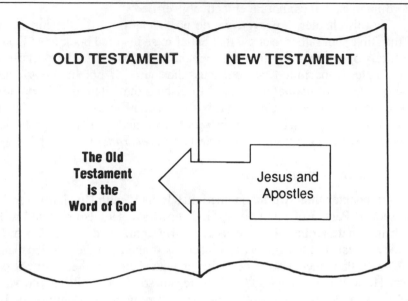

book authoritative because it is in the canon, or is it in the canon because it is authoritative?

Jesus' Bible

The Canon Jesus Affirmed. Jesus affirmed the exact Old Testament we have today in our Protestant canon as being the very Word of God. This is implied when He stated that the blood of all the prophets, *"from the blood of Abel to the blood of Zechariah . . . ,* shall be charged against this generation" (Luke 11:51, italics added). Jesus was alluding to the first martyrdom in the Bible (Gen. 4:8) and to the last martyrdom (2 Chron. 24:19-22). The Hebrew canon was ordered into three sections (the Law, the Prophets, and the Writings), although it included *exactly the same books* found in the Protestant Old Testament canon. Significantly, 2 Chronicles was the last book in the Writings. Thus "Abel's martyrdom is the first, and comes near the beginning of the first book of the canon; Zechariah's martyrdom is the last, and comes near the end of the last book. All the martyrdoms from Abel to Zechariah are therefore equivalent to all the martyrdoms from one end of the Jewish Bible to the other."[5] Thus

---

5. Roger Beckwith, *The Old Testament Canon of the New Testament Church* (Grand Rapids: Eerdmans, 1985), p. 215. For a brief but thorough study of possible interpretations of this passage, see pp. 212-22.

Jesus implicitly affirmed as His Bible the exact same thirty-nine books that make up our present Old Testament.

Past Authority. There are few subjects clearer than Jesus' attitude toward the authority of the thirty-nine Old Testament books. Jesus always assumed that both the "ordinary" and the miraculous events of the Old Testament took place historically—exactly as they were written—and used them as true illustrations to support His teaching.[6] Furthermore, He always assumed that all Old Testament prophecy must be fulfilled (in the present or the future) as it was written (in the past).

Present Authority. Jesus never corrected the Scriptures, nor did He rebuke His disciples or even His enemies for their adherence to Scripture, not only as truth but as a shared source of authority for faith and practice in the present. Indeed, He leaned on the Scriptures (Matt. 4). Further, He indicted the Jews (who prided themselves on their adherence to the letter of the law) because they were not loyal enough to the Scriptures or sufficiently biblical in their thinking (Matt. 22:23-28, John 5:45-47). He also rebuked them for adding their traditions to God's Word[7] and placing them on the same level of authority as the truth of God.

It is important to notice how Jesus quoted from Scripture. He labeled Moses' editorial comments as words from "the Creator" (Gen. 2:24; Matt. 19:4-5), because for Jesus, what Scripture says, God says. Jesus' vivid use of the present tense ("it says," "is saying") and the perfect tense ("it stands written")[8] reinforced the living and present authority of Scripture. By contrast, when men distorted Scripture by adding their traditions, Jesus did not use the introductory formulas above, but began, "You have heard it has been said."[9] This distinction is important because Jesus regarded Scripture, even though written down by human beings, as being the very Word of God—because the human writers were under the Spirit's control—whereas additions by other human beings distorted God's message.

---

6. E.g., creation, Adam and Eve, Noah and the Flood, the judgment of Sodom, the burning bush, manna in the wilderness, the bronze serpent, and even the "embarrassing" episode of Jonah's fish story. See Matt. 12:39-41; 16:4; 19:4; 24:37-39; Luke 11:32; 17:28-32; John 3:14; 6:31-51; and so forth.

7. For the objection that Jesus denied the Old Testament on occasion (e.g., Matt. 5: "it was said . . . but I say unto you . . . "), see John W. Wenham, "Christ's View of Scripture," in Norman L. Geisler, ed., *Inerrancy* (Grand Rapids: Zondervan, 1979), pp. 23-30. Jesus was actually stripping Old Testament commands of current misinterpretations and reinforcing greater reverence for Scripture.

8. *Legei, gegraptai*, and the perfect participle *gegrammenon* in the Greek. See Matt. 4:4, 6, 10; 11:10; 21:13; 26:24, 31; Mark 9:12, 13; 11:17; 14:21, 27; Luke 7:27; 19:46.

9. Matt. 5:21 (Ex. 20:13; Deut. 5:17); Matt. 5:27 (Ex. 20:14; Deut. 5:18); Matt. 5:33 (Ps. 50:14); Matt. 5:38 (Ex. 21:24; Lev. 24:20); Matt. 5:43 (Lev. 19:18). See Richard Longenecker, *Biblical Exegesis and the Apostolic Period* (Grand Rapids: Eerdmans, 1975), p. 60.

Future Authority. After Jesus' resurrection, He did not do away with the need for Scripture, but instead strongly reinforced it. For example, Jesus did not chide the two disciples on the road to Emmaus because they were slow to believe in the compelling circumstantial evidence regarding the resurrection, but rather because they were slow "to believe in all that the prophets have spoken" (Luke 24:25). After this, He "explained to them the things concerning Himself in all the Scriptures." When He appeared to the twelve, He "opened their minds to understand the Scriptures" (24:44-46). Rather than eliminating the need for the Old Testament, Jesus tethered their minds to the very words of Scripture—to equip them for the task ahead.

The Apostles' Bible

Did the apostles follow their Master in His dependency on the written Word of God? Yes, they did. After cataloging an extensive list of minor historical details found in the Old Testament, which are affirmed as authoritative in the New Testament, Grudem summarizes, "No detail is too insignificant to be used for the instruction of New Testament Christians."[10] A sampling of the two most prominent leaders in the early church will illustrate that the apostles did indeed assert the supreme authority of the Old Testament Scriptures.

Peter. Peter's "last will and testament" (2 Pet. 1:13-14) records the priority he placed on Scripture. According to Peter, the clearest apprehension of God's revelation is through His written Word. On the Mount of Transfiguration, Peter had been an eyewitness (1:16) of Jesus' majesty, and an earwitness (1:18) of the Father's voice. Peter's attitude toward this amazing and unique revelation is instructive: the written Scripture is more sure even than men's perception of God's immediate revelation.[11]

The clearest description of the process of inscripturation is found in verse 21: the prophetic spokesmen were "borne along" or "driven" (see the same term in Acts 27:15, 17) by the Holy Spirit. Michael Green observes, "The prophets raised their sails, so to speak (they were obedient and receptive), and the Holy Spirit filled them and carried their craft along in the direction He wished."[12] They did not only speak *about* God or *with* God, but *from* God. In other words, as they spoke, God spoke.

---

10. Wayne A. Grudem, "Scripture's Self-Attestation and the Problem of Formulating a Doctrine of Scripture," in D. A. Carson and John D. Woodbridge, eds., *Scripture and Truth* (Grand Rapids: Zondervan, 1983), p. 43.

11. The NASB incorrectly reverses the sense of the passage by inserting the italicized words "and *so* we have the prophetic word *made* more sure." But see Michael Green, *The Second Epistle of Peter and the Epistle of Jude* (Grand Rapids: Eerdmans, 1968), pp. 86-87.

12. Ibid., p. 91.

Paul. Although he came to Christ years after the ascension, Paul followed his Master in affirming that what Scripture says, God says (Rom. 9:17; Gal. 3:8). His "last will and testament" (2 Tim. 4:6-8) reveals the priority he placed on Scripture. Paul urged Timothy to be a diligent student of Scripture, "handling accurately the word of truth" (2:15). In the same epistle Paul states that all Scripture is *inspired* by God (3:16).[13] Whatever writings may be called "Scripture" are to be placed in this category.[14] Paul ends this section with the exhortation "Preach the Word" (4:2).

Both Peter and Paul placed the highest priority on the written Word of God. This was no innovative posture, but demonstrates their commitment to their Master who set their example by His reverence of God's authoritative Word.

THE CANON JESUS ANTICIPATED

OLD TESTAMENT

NEW TESTAMENT

The New Testament
is the
Word of God

Jesus and
Apostles

Our Bible

Whereas Jesus' view of the Old Testament is a matter of affirmation of what all Jews believed at the time, His view of the New Testament is a

13. Greek, *theopneustos*. For a complete discussion of this term, see B. B. Warfield, *The Inspiration and Authority of the Bible* (reprint; Philadelphia: Presby. & Ref., 1948), pp. 245-96.
14. This is the simplest form of logical relationship (the A-form categorical proposition), which means that "inspiration" is predicated to everything in the class "Scripture." If the class "Scripture" contains more than just the Old Testament, then inspiration would also be predicated to those writings.

matter of anticipation of future revelation. Although we would expect the evidence would be scanty (because the New Testament source document itself was not begun during Jesus' incarnation), some helpful indicators are present.

The Canon Jesus Anticipated. The Upper Room Discourse (John 13-17) records Jesus' "last will and testament" to His disciples prior to His crucifixion. Three facts are noteworthy. First, the things Jesus said were emphasized even more than usual by the refrain "these things I have spoken to you."[15] Second, Jesus is not addressing all Christians in this discourse, but the narrow group of the twelve. Third, Jesus promised another Comforter, who was to perform a future ministry in them.

Jesus told His disciples they were to keep His commandments (John 14:15-24). He then specified the future ministry of the Holy Spirit (John 14:26). Jesus promised that, although He had spoken many things to them while abiding with them (for more than three years), the Spirit would "bring to your remembrance all that I said to you." Most probably this refers to the Spirit's doing a work of enhanced memory and protection from errors of memory as the four gospels were penned.

Later in the discourse Jesus takes this promise further (John 16:12-15). Although He had more revelation to give the disciples, they did not have the spiritual enduement to receive it at that time. After the Holy Spirit came and indwelt them, "the Spirit of Truth will guide you into all the truth." In other words, there was more revelation to be received, but not until after the Spirit came (Acts 2).[16] This would refer to the revelation given in the chronicles of the apostolic church (Acts) and its apostolic teaching (the epistles and Revelation).[17]

Two further statements Jesus made are relevant. First, the disciples were promised that His words and the disciples' words are directly related in authority (John 15:20). Those who keep Jesus' words will keep the disciples' words. Second, Jesus prayed to the Father not only for the disciples, but "for those also who believe in Me through their word" (John 17:20). This includes modern readers if they have believed in Jesus through the Spirit-prompted and Spirit-protected apostolic testimony.

15. Greek, *Tauta lelaleka*—John 14:25; 15:11; 16:1, 4, 6, 25, 33. The use of the perfect tense may indicate the permanence of the things spoken of (cf. also 15:17).

16. The passage does not simply say that the Spirit "will guide into truth," but it refers to a specified agent ("the spirit of truth"), with specified objects ("you"), specified task ("show you . . . show you . . . show you . . . " — vv. 13, 14, 15), specified content ("the truth"), for a specified time ("all"—if all revelation was to be through these men [and their associates, as we shall see] then there must necessarily be a time limit)—all resulting in a specified purpose ("glorify me"—cf. v. 14; 17:3).

17. It is clear that this authority applied not only to oral teaching, but included written precepts (2 Thess. 2:15).

Jesus' remarks invite us to assign the same degree of reliability and canonical authority to the New Testament (which Jesus anticipated) as He assigned to the Old Testament Scriptures: absolute trust and authority. This is indeed the practice found throughout the New Testament. The apostles were given the authority to speak and write God's words (2 Pet. 3:2).

The Authority of the New Testament. Several pertinent observations may be made regarding the authority of the New Testament.

First, Jesus gave His associates authority to perform miracles (Matt. 10:1-2, 40), which power authenticated both the messenger and his message (e.g., Acts 2:22). Later Scripture refers to this ability as a "sign of an apostle" (2 Cor. 12:12; see Heb. 2:1-4).

Second, the authority of the apostles was recognized by the early church as unique among all believers (Acts 2:42-43; 5:1-13; 10:44; 14:3; 19:6).[18] "To lie to the apostles (Acts 5:2) is equivalent to lying to the Holy Spirit (Acts 5:3) and lying to God (Acts 5:4)."[19]

Third, we have said that Jesus specified a task the Holy Spirit would perform through the apostles: inscripturation (John 14:16, 25-26; 16:12-15; 17:17, 20).

Fourth, the apostles claimed divine authority for their own writings (1 Cor. 2:13; 4:14-21; 14:37-38; 1 Thess. 4:15; 2 Thess. 2:15; 3:14; 2 Pet. 3:2).

Fifth, not only did the apostles write authoritatively to specific churches, they expected their written words to be authoritative and applicable to all Christians in general.[20] It is clear that the intended readership of any given New Testament Scripture is broader than the immediate occasion and setting; whether or not a passage of Scripture is "to" us, it is certainly "for" us.

---

18. See Walter Chantry, *Signs of the Apostles*, 2d ed. (Carlisle, Pa.: Banner of Truth, 1976).

19. Wayne Grudem, *The Gift of Prophecy in the New Testament and Today* (Westchester, Ill.: Crossway, 1988), p. 284.

20. Although the epistles were "to" specific audiences (specified by either the address or the contents of the books), they were "for" the entire church. In Colossians 4:16 the Colossians were told to switch letters with the Laodicean church (though there is no evidence the church at Laodicea was troubled by "the Colossian heresy"). First Timothy 3:14-15 informs a general audience (all readers of all ages)—though specifically written to Timothy—that this book serves as a conduct manual for all churches. First Timothy 6:21 closes with "grace be with you [plural]." Likewise, 2 Timothy 4:22 ends with "The Lord be with your [singular] spirit. Grace be with you [plural]." Titus 3:15 closes, "Grace be with you all [plural]." The epistle to Philemon dealt with a personal matter between Paul and Philemon, but was also addressed to "the church in your house" (Philem. 2). After each of the seven specific addresses to single churches in Revelation 2-3, each "mini-epistle" closes with "He who has an ear, let him hear what the Spirit says to the churches [plural]."

Sixth, apparently the apostles also claimed this authority for the writings of other apostles. Peter classified Paul's writings with the "Scripture" (2 Pet. 3:15-16).

But what about non-apostolic authorship? Five New Testament books were written by associates of the apostles, and—even though it is true that they were within the apostolic circle—they were not a part of the twelve, nor were they specifically called apostles. These books are Mark, Luke, Acts, Hebrews, and Jude.[21] There is strong indication that the apostles extended their authority to their associates (see Acts 6:6 with 8:6-16), and even to the writings of their associates. For example, Paul classified Luke's writings as "Scripture"[22] (1 Tim. 5:18). This assumption about non-apostolic authorship has been the consensus of the church throughout history.

Canon and Authority

F. F. Bruce observed, "There is a distinction between the canonicity of the Bible and its authority. Its canonicity is dependent upon its authority."[23] History does not support the view that the books were authoritative because they were in the canon, but rather that they were in the canon because they were authoritative.[24] God's own people recognize the extent and authority of God's own Word ("my sheep hear my voice"), provided there are not personal distractions that hinder the process. However, the church does not ultimately stand over the canon; the canon stands over the church. We do not have an authoritative collection of books, but a collection of authoritative books.

We must remember, however, that the authority of the canon does not exclude faith in the providence of God, who guided the process. However, we have seen, in contrast to those who would claim otherwise and aim ridicule at believers, that this is not a "blind, unreasoning faith." There are reasons for believing these books are indeed God's Word. The

---

21. Grudem remarks concerning James, "James seems to be considered an apostle in Galatians 1:19 and 1 Corinthians 15:7. He also fulfills functions appropriate to an apostle in Acts 12:17; 15:13; 21:18; Galatians 2:9, 12; and perhaps Jude 1" (*The Gift of Prophecy*, p. 329n.).
22. Because in fifty out of fifty New Testament occurrences "scripture" is used of the divine Old Testament, Paul is putting Luke's writing (Luke-Acts) in the same category as the inspired Old Testament. (See Grudem, "Self-Attestation," p. 49.) We should add that, as Luke was Paul's associate, so Mark was the associate of Peter. Jude was the brother of James and Jesus. The authorship of Hebrews remains uncertain, but has long been deemed of apostolic authority.
23. F. F. Bruce, *The Books and the Parchments*, 3d ed. (Westwood, N.J.: Revell, 1963), pp. 95-96.
24. Ibid.

authority of the Bible is not some ad hoc external doctrine imposed upon the canon from without, but is a position affirmed within both the Old and New Testaments and ultimately anchored in the authority of Jesus.

Further tests for canonicity can be added to the Christological test. By putting the following approaches together we maximize the strengths of all and minimize the shortcomings of each. An attorney building his case step by step before a jury will certainly depend most heavily on his star witness, but he would be foolish to ignore other evidence that supports and strengthens his case.

THE SUBJECTIVE TEST

The question of canon may be approached subjectively, in which the intrinsic authority of the Bible is sufficient to validate itself and adequate to refute challenges.[25] There is a measure of truth to this approach. The canon of Scripture as it stands is majestic literature, and at the spiritual level the Bible does certainly "read me." Historically, however, Christians have differed on the canonical status of some books. This fact reveals that the subjective test is not adequate by itself to handle all the questions that arise. Therefore adding more objective tests is helpful.

THE "AUTHORITATIVE SPOKESMEN" TEST[26]

An extremely important test for canonical status of books in both testaments was whether or not the writer was an "authenticated spokesman" for God. This test could be applied progressively throughout Scripture.

Those who spoke for God in the Old Testament are simply called "prophets." In the Old Testament the authority of the prophet was not his own, but was the authority of the one who sent him. God placed His words in the mouth of the prophet, who often spoke for God in the first person. When God told His prophets to write down the words of their prophecy,[27] their written words were regarded as authoritative as their

---

25. Isaiah 55:11; this seems to be the approach of M. R. James, ed. and trans., *The Apocryphal New Testament* (Oxford: Clarendon, 1924), pp. xi-xiii.

26. For full development of this important argument, see R. Laird Harris, *Inspiration and Canonicity of the Bible* (Grand Rapids: Zondervan, 1957), pp. 154-79, 219-35.

27. E.g., Ex. 17:14; 24:4; 34:27; Num. 33:2; Deut. 31:22, 24 (see Josh. 24:26; 1 Sam. 10:25; 1 Chron. 29:29; 2 Chron. 9:29; 12:15; 13:22; 20:34; 26:22; 32:32).

spoken words.[28] Prophetic spokesmen continued in Israel from Abraham (Gen. 20:7) to Malachi.[29]

This criterion was clearly recognized and applied by the Jews. For example, "Thus says the Lord," which occurs more than two thousand times in the Old Testament, is totally absent from the Apocrypha.[30] Further, the writer of the Apocryphal book of 1 Maccabees (written between 140-104 B.C.) states that prophets had ceased in Israel (9:27), and 1 Maccabees 4:46 implies that no revelation was being given because there were no more prophets. The Dead Sea Scrolls, the Talmud, Josephus, and the Jewish philosopher Philo agree.[31]

This is precisely the position adopted by the New Testament.[32] At one point the entire Old Testament is alluded to as "the Scriptures of the prophets" (Matt. 26:56). God's speech through the prophets is regarded in the same way as God's speech through Christ (Heb. 1:1-2).[33]

Whereas God's spokesmen in the Old Testament were "prophets," those who spoke for God in the New Testament were called "apostles." Malachi 4:5 seems to be "an indication that the prophetic witness would end with Malachi and not begin again until the coming of an Elijah-type prophet in the person of John the Baptist (Matt. 17:11-12)."[34] We have maintained that the *authority* of Jesus was passed to the apostolic circle. The miracles the apostles performed were called "signs of an apostle."[35] The authority of the apostles was recognized as unique by all believers in

---

28. When Moses read the book of the covenant, the people responded, "all that the Lord has spoken we will do" (Ex. 24:7). See Grudem, "Self-Attestation," in *Scripture and Truth*, p. 27, and 2 Kings 14:6; 2 Chron. 25:4; Neh. 8:14; Mal. 4:4.

29. Because anyone could claim to speak for God as His prophet, there were certain tests of prophetic message, whether oral or written. See Norman L. Geisler, *Signs and Wonders* (Wheaton, Ill.: Tyndale House, 1988), pp. 133-36.

30. Bruce M. Metzger, "Introduction to the Apocrypha," in *The Oxford Annotated Apocrypha*, rev. ed. (New York: Oxford, 1977), p. xiv. Metzger continues, "From first to last the apocryphal books bear testimony to the assertion of the Jewish historian Josephus, that 'the exact succession of the prophets' had been broken after the close of the Hebrew canon of the Old Testament. . . . When a writer imitates the prophet character, as in the book of Baruch, he repeats with slight modifications the language of the older prophets." But he does *not* use the formula "Thus says the Lord."

31. See citations in Harris, *Canonicity*, pp. 169, 171-72, and Grudem, "Self-Attestation," in *Scripture and Truth*, p. 37.

32. That which prophets wrote is referred to as what *God said* (Matt. 1:22; Mark 7:9-13; Luke 1:70; 24:25-27; Acts 1:16; 2:16-17; 3:18, 21; 4:25; 13:47; 28:25; Rom. 1:2 [cf. 3:2]; 2 Pet. 1:21).

33. Harris calls prophetic authorship "a practical and reasonable test of canonicity that could have been applied by all the generations of the Jews and, except for a few places where evidence now is more slender, can be readily applied even today. What was prophetic was regarded as the Word of God. What was not prophetic was . . . not regarded as the Word of God" (*Canonicity*, p. 174).

34. Charles Ryrie, *Basic Theology* (Wheaton, Ill.: Victor, 1987), p. 106.

35. See Walter J. Chantry, *Signs of the Apostles,* 2d ed. (Carlisle, Pa.: Banner of Truth, 1976), and 2 Cor. 12:12; Matt. 10:1-2, 40; Acts 2:22; Heb. 2:1-4.

the early church[36] and (as with the Old Testament prophets) their authority extended to their writings.[37] External evidence that such a criterion was in force comes from Ignatius (martyred before A.D. 117), who said, "I do not, as Paul and Peter, issue commandments unto you. They were apostles; I am but a condemned man."[38]

A "thumbnail sketch" of the canon of Scripture, which assumes the criterion of authoritative spokesmen, may be found in 2 Peter 3:2. Peter stresses that in both his epistles he desires to arouse the minds of his readers "that you should remember the words spoken beforehand *by the holy prophets* and the commandment of the Lord and Savior spoken *by your apostles*" (italics added).

THE CONVERGENCE/COHERENCE TESTS

Two tests that would exclude material from Scripture (and thus would be negative tests) are the tests of *convergence* and *coherence*. Both assume that God is a God of consistent truth. Any document that does not cohere (internally) with itself, but rather has internal contradictions, would not qualify as Scripture.

Similarly, any document that does not converge (externally) with previously revealed and recognized canon, would not qualify as Scripture. In Galatians 1:8-9, Paul insists that any message contrary to what the Galatians had received is false, even if it were to come from Paul himself. The previous revelation (the accepted canon) was the standard and authority for judging the reliability of subsequent revelation—even when the human author was the same person (see 2 Thess. 2:5, 15; 3:4, 6).

THE "PRIMARY TESTIMONY" TEST

Certain tests for apostolic genuineness had to be applied early because of false teachers within the church. Some false doctrine was difficult to detect because it went beyond current Scripture so that the other tests, such as convergence, could not be clearly invoked. Furthermore, some false teachers were actually signing Paul's name to letters as though they had his authority (2 Thess. 2:2).

Because samples of Paul's writings were available, Paul could give them an immediate test of his own (primary) testimony: his distinctive signature. Thus Paul writes in 2 Thessalonians, "I, Paul, write this greet-

36. Acts 2:42-43; 5:1-10; 5:11; 8:6, 13-16; 10:44; 14:3; 19:6.
37. 1 Cor. 2:13; 4:14-21; 14:37-38; 1 Thess. 4:15; 2 Thess. 3:14; 2 Pet. 3:2 (see also 1 Tim. 5:18 and 2 Pet. 3:15-16).
38. Cited by Harris, *Canonicity*, p. 237.

ing with my own hand, and this is a distinguishing mark in every letter; this is the way I write'' (3:17). Because it was unlikely that the false teachers had firsthand samples of Paul's signature to forge, this would serve as a certain test for the Thessalonian Christians.[39]

Of course, the test of "immediate testimony" was capable of being used only on a limited basis. However, after the original autographs of Paul's letters were lost, the test was usable in a secondary sense: it gave further confidence in the discernment of the early church, which preserved the apostolic Scriptures.

CONCLUSION

To all the above tests we must add a word about the providence of God in history, which was at work in the canonical process. In about A.D. 90 a rabbinical council was held at Jamnia (Jabneh, north of Ashdod near the Mediterranean). A common misconception is that the Hebrew canon was set at Jamnia. Actually, the canonical discussions were limited to Ecclesiastes and the Song of Songs, and the verdict was to confirm what the Jews had practiced all along: that these books remained *with their companions* in a canon that came from God.

As far as the New Testament is concerned, the church Fathers recognized all the books which we now have as "Scripture." The Council of Carthage (A.D. 397) served the same function as did Jamnia for the Old Testament: it confirmed the twenty-seven New Testament books that were *already recognized* as from God and *were already in use*.

IS THE TEXT AUTHENTIC?: HISTORICITY

TESTS FOR TEXTUAL HISTORICITY

Are the actual texts of the Bible, which have gone through centuries of transmission, accurate to the original writings? Do we actually have the writings of Paul, Peter, and John, or have they been altered through centuries of transmission? There are three standard criteria by which the authenticity and integrity of ancient texts may be judged:

Quantity—   How many ancient manuscripts are there? Sheer volume helps, provided the second criterion is added.

39. See also 1 Cor. 16:21 ("The greeting is in my own hand—Paul"), Gal. 6:11 ("See with what large letters I am writing to you with my own hand"), Col. 4:18 ("I, Paul, write this greeting with my own hand"), and (perhaps less so) Philem. 19 ("I, Paul, am writing this with my own hand, I will repay it").

Quality—	How good are the manuscripts we do have? If they are few in number, are they of good quality?
Time Interval—	How much time elapsed between the original writing and the manuscript(s) we have? (Generally, the shorter the interval, the higher the reliability.)

We shall apply these three tests first to the Old Testament text, and then to the New Testament text. We shall also draw analogies with texts from other ancient literature.

THE OLD TESTAMENT TEXT[40]

As far as *quantity* is concerned, there are relatively few entire ancient manuscripts of the Hebrew Old Testament.[41] There are several reasons for this lack of manuscripts. First, the Jews wrote the Old Testament on animal skins, which did not last as long as clay tablets. Second, they were a migrant people who were also under political subjugation for a large portion of their history.[42] Certainly conditions were not friendly to the survival of manuscripts over a period of two or three thousand years. A third factor is not a negative but a positive one. Because of their very reverence for the Old Testament text, worn or flawed manuscripts were destroyed or buried by Hebrew scribes. Thus fewer manuscripts would be available for discovery.

The *quality* of the Old Testament manuscripts, however, should silence critical historians. This quality is the result of work done by a group called the Masoretes—Jewish scribal scholars of the fifth through the ninth centuries A.D., whose main work was copying and standardizing the text of the Old Testament. Geisler and Nix describe the care taken by the Masoretes in copying:

> According to the Talmud, there were specifications not only for the kind of skins to be used and the size of the columns, but there was even a religious ritual necessary for the scribe to perform before writing the name of God. Rules governed the kind of ink they were to use, the spacing of words, and also forbade their writing anything from memory. The lines, and even the letters, were counted methodically. If a manuscript was found to contain

40. See F. F. Bruce, "Transmission and Translation of the Bible" and Bruce K. Waltke, "The Textual Criticism of the Old Testament," both in Frank E. Gaebelein, ed., *The Expositor's Bible Commentary*, vol. 1 (Grand Rapids: Zondervan, 1979).
41. Rudolf Kittel's *Biblia Hebraica* was based on four manuscripts. Later notable manuscript finds include the Cairo Genizeh and the Dead Sea Scrolls.
42. Norman L. Geisler and William E. Nix, *A General Introduction to the Bible* (Chicago: Moody, 1968), p. 251, comment, "The city of Jerusalem was conquered forty-seven times between 1800 B.C. and A.D. 1948."

even one mistake, it was discarded and destroyed. This scribal formalism was responsible, at least in part, for the extreme care exercised in copying the Scriptures.[43]

As far as *time interval* is concerned, the scene has changed rapidly because of a landmark archaeological discovery. The Dead Sea Scrolls, discovered beginning in 1947, closed the time interval between the manuscripts we had and our earliest copies by a thousand years. More than one hundred copies of books of the Old Testament were found,[44] which have been dated from 200 B.C. to A.D. 68. Did the scrolls confirm the previous faith the scholarly community had placed in the Masoretes? Millar Burrows, textual scholar at Yale University, wrote, "It is a matter of wonder that through something like a thousand years the text underwent so little alteration. . . . [The chief importance of the find is in] supporting the fidelity of the Masoretic tradition."[45] Kenneth Boa's and Larry Moody's conclusion is certainly warranted: "the quality of manuscripts of the Hebrew Bible surpasses all other ancient manuscripts."[46]

Before considering the New Testament manuscripts, one final observation should be noted. The authority of Jesus Christ is paramount for the believer's reliance on the text of the Old Testament. Jesus assumed that the Old Testament text was reliable enough for Him to base arguments on the very words of a *translation of a copy* of the Hebrew Old Testament. He assumed that copies, and a translation of a copy, were tethered to the original autographs accurately enough for them to bear the arguments He put forth.

THE NEW TESTAMENT TEXT

There is just as much cause for confidence in the textual reliability of the New Testament as there is for the Old Testament. As far as *quantity* of manuscripts, there are more than five thousand Greek manuscripts and fragments. To this can be added about eight thousand Latin manuscripts and more than one thousand early translations (from Coptic, Syriac, etc.).

43. Geisler and Nix, *General Introduction*, rev. ed. (Chicago: Moody, 1986), p. 380. See also F. F. Bruce, *The Books and the Parchments*, p. 117ff. For comparisons of Old Testament Masoretic Text vs. Septuagintal quotes within the New Testament, see Gleason Archer and G. C. Chirichigno, *Old Testament Quotations in the New Testament: A Complete Survey* (Chicago: Moody, 1983).

44. Some books were repeated, and others were in various stages of completeness due to decomposition. They are now still being catalogued.

45. Millar Burrows, *The Dead Sea Scrolls* (New York: Viking, 1955), p. 304, cited by Geisler and Nix, rev. ed., p. 367. For additional details on textual comparisons see F. F. Bruce, *Second Thoughts on the Dead Sea Scrolls*, 2d ed. (Grand Rapids: Eerdmans, 1961).

46. Kenneth Boa and Larry Moody, *I'm Glad You Asked* (Wheaton, Ill.: Victor, 1982), p. 77.

The church Fathers offer the converging evidence of tens of thousands of citations from the New Testament.[47]

It is true, however, that the *quality* of New Testament manuscripts is less than that of the Old Testament ones. More variant readings do exist, although these are usually matters of spelling or word order, not matters of doctrine. However, because there are so many manuscripts of the New Testament available, by comparing the readings the original can be reconstructed. The result of the science of textual criticism is an almost pure text, and most of the remaining textual problems have reasonably sure answers.

The *time interval* for the New Testament manuscripts is unusually short for an ancient document. Some manuscripts are from the third and fourth centuries.[48] We have other manuscripts of the New Testament that date from within one hundred fifty years of their originals, and papyri that are within twenty-five years. Sir Fredric Kenyon, late director of the British Museum, stated,

> The interval, then, between the dates of original composition and the earliest extant evidence becomes so small as to be in fact negligible, and the last foundation for any doubt that the Scriptures have come down to us substantially as they were written has now been removed. Both the authenticity and the general integrity of the books of the New Testament may be regarded as finally established.[49]

For a broader perspective, we can compare the manuscript evidence for the New Testament with similar manuscript evidence from other ancient documents, which the scholarly community does *not* question. First, consider the criterion of *quantity* of manuscripts:

> It is sufficient to remember that while there are only 643 manuscripts by which the *Iliad* is reconstructed, nine or ten good ones for Caesar's *Gallic War*, twenty manuscripts of note for Livy's *History of Rome,* and only twenty by which Tacitus is known, yet there are more than fifty-three hundred Greek manuscripts to attest the New Testament.[50]

---

47. See F. F. Bruce, *The New Testament Documents: Are They Reliable?*, 5th rev. ed. (Grand Rapids: Eerdmans, 1960); Josh McDowell, *Evidence That Demands a Verdict* (San Bernardino, Calif.: Campus Crusade, 1972), pp. 53-54.
48. Some fragments are earlier still, which offers further proof of first-century authorship. For details on all the major Greek manuscripts, their condition, and their dates, see Bruce M. Metzger, *The Text of the New Testament*, 2d ed. (New York: Oxford, 1968).
49. Sir Fredric Kenyon, *The Bible and Archaeology* (New York: Harper & Row, 1940), pp. 288-89, cited in John W. Montgomery, *History and Christianity* (Downers Grove, Ill.: InterVarsity, 1964), p. 28.
50. Geisler and Nix, rev. ed., p. 408. To the many Greek manuscripts we may add the church Fathers (from which the New Testament can be reconstructed) and the thousands of early translations.

When considering the *quality* of manuscripts, there are far fewer variants in the New Testament documents (taken in proportion) than there are among those ancient secular writings. This is reasonable because New Testament copyists revered Scripture—an attitude that would motivate accurate transmission.[51]

Finally, the *time interval* between the actual writing and our earliest copies of *Gallic Wars* is nine hundred years; for the two manuscripts of Tacitus, eight hundred and a thousand years respectively; for Thucydides and Herodotus, thirteen hundred years; for Sophocles, Aeschylus, and Aristophanes, fourteen hundred years; for Plato, thirteen hundred years; for Demosthenes, twelve hundred years; for Euripides, sixteen hundred years; and so forth.[52] Clearly, the relatively short time interval between Greek manuscripts and the original Scripture writings further enhances our appreciation for the New Testament text by comparison.

Montgomery's verdict is well-founded: "To be skeptical of the resultant text of the New Testament books is to allow all of classical antiquity to slip into obscurity, for no documents of the ancient period are as well attested bibliographically as the New Testament."[53] In conclusion, the reliability of the historical documents that constitute the Bible is not a matter of subjective faith, but of public, objective fact.

ARE THE WORDS DEPENDABLE?: INERRANCY

We have considered the dependability of the manuscripts of both the Old and New Testaments, which deals with what Scripture actually *is*, and concluded that we may be confident that we have *Scripture* in our hands. But what about the reliability of its message? Just how trustworthy is what Scripture *says*? *Inerrancy* is a term that describes the degree to which Scripture is trustworthy, and it is commonly used by most Bible believers today. The Evangelical Theological Society requires its members to sign annually a doctrinal statement, which reads in part: "the Bible alone, and the Bible in its entirety, is the Word of God written and is therefore *inerrant in the autographs*"(italics added).[54]

Is inerrancy simply a matter of placement past a certain "inerrancy cut-off point" on a spectrum of trustworthiness, with those writings be-

---

51. Clark Pinnock, *Set Forth Your Case* (Chicago: Moody, 1971), pp. 78-79.

52. Cited by Geisler and Nix, rev. ed., p. 408, and Montgomery, p. 27. Actual details for further comparison may be found in "Ms. Authorities for the Text of the Chief Classical Writers," in F. W. Hall, *Companion to Classical Texts* (Oxford: Clarendon, 1913).

53. Montgomery, p. 29.

54. This statement is printed inside each issue of *The Journal of the Evangelical Theological Society*. The restriction of inerrancy to the original manuscripts ("autographs") is itself a biblical distinction; see Greg L. Bahnsen, "The Inerrancy of the Autographa," in Geisler, *Inerrancy*, pp. 151-93.

ANCIENT TEXTS AND THE NEW TESTAMENT

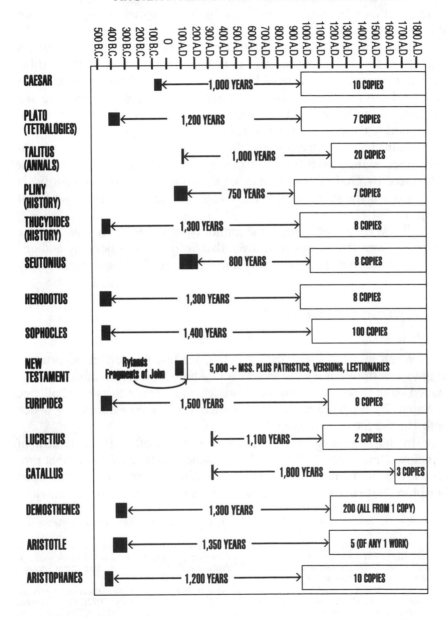

low the point being error-ridden and those fortunate writings above the point being error-free? Not at all. As Kathleen Boone rightly observes, "Inerrancy is . . . a non-relative term. Like *unique* or *black*, it ought not to admit of modification."[55] Having said this, however, it ought to admit of careful definition.

Inerrancy describes the *product* of inspiration: Scripture. It means that "Scripture is without error or fault in all its teaching."[56] If the Bible were not inerrant, then it would be like most other books: a mixture of truth and error. The *purpose* for inspiration includes (1) directing the thoughts of the human authors (the assertive purpose; 2 Pet. 1:21), and (2) rendering them incapable of error (the protective purpose).

Mathematics textbooks may be without error, but no one derives theological significance from this fact because no mathematics textbook is inspired by God. The inerrancy of the Bible would not be significant apart from inspiration, which lends authority to the inerrant words of Scripture.

As we have said before, the authority of the Bible is rooted in the claims of Jesus Christ. Jesus believed that Scripture was not only authoritative, but inerrant. Inerrancy was stated both explicitly and implicitly by Him.

JESUS' EXPLICIT TEACHING[57]

Matthew 4:4

When Jesus was tempted by Satan, He had the perfect opportunity to ignore Scripture if it were simply a psychological crutch human beings leaned on in times of weakness. However, in response to every challenge of Satan, Jesus cited Scripture as a source of common authority by which both He and Satan were bound.

In the beginning of His temptation, Jesus offered a statement of principle: "man shall not live by bread alone, but by every word that proceeds from the mouth of God." Not only did Jesus rest His defense upon Scripture, but He reinforced the *verbal* nature of inspiration: the individu-

---

55. Kathleen C. Boone, *The Bible Tells Them So: The Discourse of Protestant Fundamentalism* (Albany, N.Y.: State U. of New York, 1989), p. 26.

56. For the most complete recent definition of inerrancy (from which the above-quoted statement is taken), see *The Chicago Statement on Biblical Inerrancy*, reprinted in various theological journals in late 1978. Its nineteen articles of "Affirmation and Denial" and an "Exposition" section are reproduced in Geisler, *Inerrancy*, pp. 493-502.

57. Many fine books include discussions of Jesus' view of Scripture. Three excellent treatments are John Wenham, *Christ and the Bible* (Downers Grove, Ill.: InterVarsity, 1972); R. T. France, *Jesus and the Old Testament* (London: Tyndale, 1971); and Robert P. Lightner, *The Savior and the Scriptures* (Philadelphia: Presby. & Ref., 1966).

al words of Scripture, not just the message or ideas, are trustworthy. Furthermore, this reliability is *plenary,* because it extends to every word of Scripture.[58]

Matthew 5:17-20

In the midst of the Sermon on the Mount, Jesus made a graphic and sweeping statement about Scripture's trustworthiness. Scripture is accurate down to the very "jot" and "tittle" (KJV), "iota" and "dot" (RSV).[59] The "jot" refers to the smallest letter of the Hebrew alphabet, about the size of our apostrophe. The very letters of Scripture are inerrant. The "tittle" refers to the slight stroke of a pen, which could make a difference between two letters; this refers to something even more minute than single letters. For example, in English add one "tittle" to the word *Fun* and you get *Pun.* Add another and you get *Run;* still another will give you *Bun.*[60] Jesus is solemnly claiming that Scripture is reliable even to the most minute detail.

John 10:35

Jesus made the startling claim that He is God incarnate. In answer to His opposition, He supported His claim by pointing to two prongs of evidence: His words and His works (miracles).[61] In the midst of His defense of His deity, Jesus quoted from Psalm 82 and reinforced His quotation with the comment "And the scripture cannot be broken."

Jesus based His claim to be God on the reliability of a single word ("gods") found in an obscure psalm; it is not even a Davidic or a messianic psalm. His rationale for such dependence is that "the Scripture" (even *this* Scripture) partakes of the quality of all Scripture: it cannot be broken. "He rightly assumed that He could count on any part of the Bible and any word in any part."[62] On this word He was basing (immediately) His defense of His life, and (eternally) His claim to be God incarnate. Al-

---

58. This is well illustrated in the second temptation, where Satan distorts the meaning of Psalm 91. The psalm teaches that God will keep the righteous on their journeys, not that He will preserve them when they take needless risks, which was exactly what Satan had proposed to Christ. The Lord replied that to rely on part of a verse is to distort the verse; it would be to tempt God. Instead "Jesus would rely on every word that came from God, including every word of Psalm 91:11-12" (Charles C. Ryrie, *What You Should Know About Inerrancy* [Chicago: Moody, 1981], p. 77).

59. Greek, *iota* and *keraia.* The smallest letter in Hebrew is the *yodh,* which was represented in Greek by the *iota* (the smallest letter in the Greek alphabet).

60. Ryrie, p. 60.

61. For a detailed analysis of the logic of the argument, see W. Gary Phillips, "John 10:34-36: An Apologetic Study," *Bibliotheca Sacra* (September-December 1989).

62. Ryrie, p. 62.

though His critics objected violently to His divine claim, they did *not* criticize His use of, or appeal to, Scripture.

John 17:17

Jesus' declaration in John 17:17 is one of the Bible's most unique statements about God's Word, yet is one of the most neglected. At first glance, the statement "Thy Word is truth" seems rather innocuous, or at least so general as to be bland. Actually, it is contained within Jesus' "High Priestly Prayer." We are eavesdropping on a unique conversation between God the Son and God the Father in which the subject of God's own Word is addressed. Two of the most important words in John's gospel—*word* and *truth*—are placed in the simplest of logical relations to each other.

Truth is a crucial theme in John's writings—more than half the New Testament usages of the words for truth occur in his books. Here in John 17 Jesus asks the Father, in a private moment, to sanctify those who belong to Jesus by means of God's Word, which is truth. The grammatical emphasis in the sentence is on the attribute of truth.[63] God's Word is that which corresponds to reality, which is the biblical meaning of truth in John.[64] In other words, the Bible corresponds with facts, whether scientific and historical (verifiable) facts, or spiritual (unverifiable) facts. Only truth corresponds with facts; error does not.

JESUS' IMPLICIT TEACHING

Jesus rests His case at times on a word,[65] a tense,[66] and even a suffix.[67] These arguments assume that such things as words, forms of words

---

63. The predicate nominative (Greek, *alethia*, "truth") precedes the verb, a practice that lays stress on *truth*. John does the same in 1:14 ("the word *flesh* became"), 5:30 ("my judgment *righteous* is"), and in 1 John 4:16 ("God *love* is"). See F. Blass and A. Debrunner, *A Greek Grammar of the New Testament and Other Early Christian Literature*, trans. R. W. Funk (Chicago: U. of Chicago, 1961), p. 428.

64. For a study on the biblical meaning of "truth" see Roger Nicole, "The Biblical Concept of Truth," in D. A. Carson and John D. Woodbridge, eds., *Scripture and Truth* (Grand Rapids: Zondervan, 1983); for a *philosophical* study, see Norman L. Geisler, "The Concept of Truth in the Inerrancy Debate," *The Evangelical Review of Theology* 5:2 (October 1981), pp. 185-97. Both Nicole and Geisler support the "correspondence" view of truth.

65. John 10:34-35: "God." For an argument dependent upon singular vs. plural, see Galatians 3:16.

66. Matthew 22:32: present tense, "I am."

67. Matthew 22:43-45. This argument hinges on David's calling the Messiah "my Lord." In Hebrew, possessives ("my") are expressed in suffixes. Wayne Grudem comments, "The word my is signified by only one letter [very much like our apostrophe] in the consonantal Hebrew text. . . . A slight lengthening of the final consonant [to the length of our letter 'l'] would make 'his Lord'; a bit more lengthening . . . would make 'your lord,' in either case the argument would no longer work. Here Jesus' argument depends on the reliability of one letter of the written Old Testament" (Grudem, "Scripture's Self-Attestation," in *Scripture and Truth*, pp. 40-41).

(tense, number), and parts of words (suffixes) are reliable enough to bear the arguments they support. This degree of reliability is an important element in the definition of inerrancy.

ARGUMENTS AGAINST INERRANCY[68]

Adequate treatments of phenomena that diverge from inerrancy are found in many places, including Gleason Archer, *The Encyclopedia of Bible Difficulties* (Grand Rapids: Zondervan, 1982); Charles Ryrie, *What You Should Know About Inerrancy* (Chicago: Moody, 1981), pp. 81-100; John W. Haley, *Alleged Discrepancies of the Bible* (Nashville: Gospel Advocate Co., 1974 reprint); Everett F. Harrison, "The Phenomena of Scripture," in Carl F. H. Henry, ed., *Revelation and the Bible* (Grand Rapids: Baker, 1959), pp. 235-50.

Counter arguments certainly can challenge any faith position. If the Bible were error-ridden, then the above discussion would be worthless. That both detractors from and advocates for inerrancy exist indicates that the discussion may well depend less on the evidence analyzed and more on the worldview of the analyst.

However, three common theoretical objections have been raised against the idea of inerrancy. First, with such a large number of human authors (more than forty) who had different writing styles, in what sense can the Bible truly be God's Word? Second, by what reasoning should the rare claims for infallibility, made by particular Scriptures, be extended to include the whole of Scripture? Third, why make such a point of arguing for this teaching when inerrancy is not even a prominent theme within the Bible itself?

Question 1: What About Human Authorship?

Many have argued that divine and human authorship working together would necessarily pollute the process of inspiration. It is true that careful students of the Bible notice different styles and vocabularies. Paul tended to employ long sentences with involved grammar (and was fond of illustrations from the world of sports), whereas John used short, simple sentences. Luke the physician occasionally employed medical terminology. But certain perspectives help us understand what inspiration does and does not mean.

---

68. Errantists find errors; inerrantists do not. Theological experience has shown that interpretation of these details reflects whether or not the interpreter has committed a priori to inerrancy (see Norman L. Geisler, "Philosophical Presupposition of Biblical Errancy," in *Inerrancy*, pp. 307-34). Other inductive data includes the *phenomena* of Scripture, or the myriad details of the biblical text that converge with or diverge from inerrancy.

First, inspiration does not mean dictation. There was still room for individual personalities not only to remain but to be used to write God's truth while the Holy Spirit superintended the process (2 Pet. 1:21).

Second, it is true that "to err is human." But this cliché is not a tautology that can be reversed to read "to be human is (necessarily) to err." Error is not a defining characteristic of humanity, or else Jesus Christ was not fully human and glorified man will not be fully human in heaven.

Third, God is sovereign. Scripture says He providentially worked in the lives of the human authors, controlling genetics, education, and circumstances (Gal. 1:15; Jer. 1:4, 5, 7, 9) so that the resulting personalities were precisely who God wanted to use. Thus we have a man like Paul, with his precise legal mind, writing the book of Romans, and we have David, the shepherd-king who spent his youth among God's creation, writing psalms of nature. Thus the fact of human authorship is not in itself a valid objection to inerrancy.

Fourth, although human authorship is discernible throughout the biblical writings, it is a non-sequitur to assume that the Spirit could not overcome human limitations in knowledge to communicate His truth to mankind. Such work of the Spirit is precisely what inspiration means.

Fifth, the authority with which the Bible speaks assumes that human personalities do not pollute the integrity of the message. It was Jesus who claimed that what David said was actually spoken by David "in the Spirit" (Matt. 22:43).

Question 2: What About the Fallacy of Generalizing?

A critic might object, "By what logic do you claim inspiration for the entire Bible, when only a few passages even claim it themselves?" However, when Jesus said, "Scripture cannot be broken," He did not mean just that Scripture but "Scripture as a whole." That Scripture in particular cannot be broken because it partakes of the characteristics of the whole, which cannot be broken. When Paul claimed inspiration for Scripture, it was explicitly inclusive: "all Scripture is inspired."

We have already seen that Scripture was considered authoritative in all its parts. The evidence supporting the doctrine of inerrancy is representative and may be enlarged to include all of Scripture. In other words, Scriptures that are not explicitly given Jesus' imprimatur also partake implicitly of the same characteristic of authority. A scientist checking a pond for purity does not have to test every drop; a sample is sufficient because what is true of the parts reflects what is true of the whole.

Question 3: Isn't This Majoring on Minors?

Obviously, the attribute of inerrancy does not guarantee that a book bears the imprimatur of God. A railway schedule can be free from error. The Bible is not the Word of God because it is inerrant; rather, the Bible is inerrant because it is the Word of God. That is, not all inerrant books are God's Word, but any book that is inspired by God will be inerrant.

One primary reason for affirming inerrancy is that it is a crucial theme of Scripture. It was not asserted more often because all biblical writers assumed this degree of integrity (I have never read in any book a formal argument for the proposition that "paper exists"). The burden of proof would rest squarely on anyone who would assert otherwise.

Because of the authority of the Bible and its teachings on inerrancy, we conclude that anyone who is tempted to embrace an "errant" Bible should consider the following.

First, when confronted by a skeptic with an "error" in Scripture, we should make sure that a problem truly exists. Often problems disappear when the details of a passage are studied carefully and in context.

Second, is the problem we are wrestling with a conflict between the Bible and some external authority (e.g., archaeology), or is it a problem internal to the Bible? If external, then we may give the Bible the benefit of the doubt. This procedure has been vindicated repeatedly throughout history. If internal, it is wise to analyze the conflict logically. We may, for example, distinguish between a *contradictory* (error) and a *contrary* (problem of harmonization). A contrary would be a problem wherein two propositions require harmonization (e.g., this page contains the color white, this page contains the color black; in reality both propositions are true). A contradictory is a problem wherein two propositions seem to be irreconcilable (e.g., this is a book, this is not a book).

Most specific internal objections to inerrancy are contraries and await further study. But before leaving any problem unresolved—as a contradictory—we should make sure that all terms have the same definitions in both propositions (for example, "this is a table; this is not a table" may not be contradictory propositions if one is making a statement about a piece of furniture, while the other is referring to the water level).

Third, in this world we see reality in limited perspective; we do not have all the answers (1 Cor. 13:9-12). In fact, there is no doctrine of our faith that does not confront us with problems at some level. We recognize that God is infinite and man is finite, and therefore we should not be upset if we cannot work out all troublesome details immediately.

The contention for the factual, historical inerrancy of Scripture is motivated beyond the concern for the specific details under review. There would be no point in having mere inspired history. Inerrancy is intended to assure the authority also of the spiritual claims of the Bible, which make us "wise unto salvation."

Conversely, if the factual accuracy of Scripture is not absolutely trustworthy—even if it be established as "generally reliable" rather than absolutely reliable—then we have a problem of knowing just what is or is not God's Word,[69] and we have no reason to trust the Bible's spiritual truth. If the Bible proves unreliable in those areas we can verify, by what logic should we ask people to take a leap of faith to trust the Bible in areas they cannot verify—the spiritual claims on which they base their eternal destinies?[70]

CONCLUSION

In contrast to the common slogan "seeing is believing," Jesus said "believing is seeing" (John 11:40; 20:24-29). The Bible presents a view of reality that includes the empirical world, but its view extends beyond the limitations of scientific method (2 Cor. 4:18; 2 Kings 6:15-17). Therefore for believers to know things truly, they must view them through God's eyes. We believe that the lens of God's written Word gives the clearest vista of reality.

The most crucial consideration for the Christian is whether or not to accept the authority of Jesus Christ. The historical gospels present Jesus' claims accurately enough to induce belief in Him as the incarnate Son. These are the same records in which Jesus makes statements and implications about the absolute authority of the Bible, the extent of the Bible, and the dependability of the Bible. Surely it is inconsistent to accept Jesus' words about the one and reject His words about the other. Our convictions about the written Word are anchored in the incarnate Word.

But does belief in the Bible yield a coherent and consistent worldview? Two challenges face any worldview: the problem of evil and the problem of pluralism. How does a biblical worldview answer these challenges? This question shall be addressed in the next two chapters.

69. It is a dangerous thing to edit God. There is no higher authority by which Scripture can be authenticated than by Scripture itself (cf. Heb. 6:13).
70. Francis Schaeffer, *No Final Conflict* (Downers Grove, Ill.: InterVarsity, 1972), pp. 33-34. See 1 Corinthians 11:8.

CASE STUDY: Inerrancy: A "Fundamentalist" Concoction?

Influential philosopher and process theologian Charles Hartshorne severely criticizes as absurd any belief in the inerrancy of the Bible. Not only is the *idea* ridiculous to Hartshorne, but he maintains that the Bible makes no such claims. He states,

> Of all the claims to infallibility, those made by fundamentalist Christians seem the most extreme. Certainly they are the most complex in their implications. With the religion of Islam, for instance, one only has to believe in the divine inspiration of one man as absolutely reliable. But with Christianity there are, for instance, the four authors of the Gospels, none of whom, as I recall, explicitly claims infallibility, several writers of Epistles, the author of the Acts of the Apostles, and many authors of the Old Testament. All must be supposed infallible, though again they do not clearly claim this status for themselves, so far as I can see.[71]

"Fundamentalist Christians"—by which term Hartshorne means anyone who believes in the integrity of the Bible—do maintain that inerrancy is the internal claim of Scripture, established both deductively and inductively.

CASE STUDY: Self-Contradictions in the Bible?

The year 1859 saw significant attacks against the Christian faith. Not only did Charles Darwin publish *On the Origin of Species*, but the infamous *Self-Contradictions of the Bible* was published anonymously. The author was William Henry Burr, a newspaper reporter who was also an enthusiastic follower of Darwin.

The book simply listed 144 opposing propositions ("contradictions"), printed with the King James Version of the Bible texts that were said to be in tension. One review of the period described it as "a vilely composed and wretchedly printed attempt to destroy the faith of the civilized world in the Christian Religion."[72]

71. Charles Hartshorne, *Omnipotence and Other Theological Mistakes* (Albany, N.Y.: State U. of New York, 1984), pp. 40-41. Hartshorne has oversimplified the Islamic view of inspiration. Muslims do not believe Muhammad wrote the Koran but that the *suras* (chapters) were written down (inerrantly) by his followers. Some Islamic scholars question whether or not Muhammad was literate.
72. Cited by R. Joseph Hoffman in William Henry Burr, *Self-Contradictions of the Bible* (reprint; New York: Prometheus, 1987), pp. 9-10.

Recently Burr's book has been reissued by Prometheus Press, publishers of *Humanist Manifestos I and II*. R. Joseph Hoffman begins the new edition with this statement: "Sometimes old diseases demand old cures."[73] Thus the book was published to counter "the resurgence of fundamentalism."[74]

In his preface Hoffman makes a fascinating statement—or admission—about Burr's first edition: "[Burr's] failure to invoke context or linguistic usage to explain away any of the contradictions is precisely what made [the work] the threat that it was."[75] Christians, however, would indeed invoke context and linguistic usage to find promising resolutions to problems such as those listed below.

Burr divided his 144 "contradictions" in the Bible into four categories: theological doctrines (1-23), moral precepts (24-57), historical facts (58-107), and speculative doctrines (108-144). Following are the *first* entries within each of these successive categories.

(1) God is satisfied with His works: "And God saw everything that he had made, and behold it was *very good.*" (Gen. 1:31).

God is dissatisfied with His works: "And it *repented* the Lord that he had *made man* on the earth, and it *grieved* him at his heart." (Gen. 6:6).

(24) Robbery commanded: " When ye go, ye shall not go empty; but every woman shall *borrow* of her neighbor, and of her that sojourneth in her house, jewels of silver and jewels of gold, and raiment; and ye shall put them under your sons, and upon your daughters; and ye shall *spoil the Egyptians*" (Ex. 3:21, 22). "And they *borrowed of the Egyptians* jewels of silver, and jewels of gold, and raiment. . . . And they *spoiled* the Egyptians" (Ex. 12:35, 36).

Robbery forbidden: "Thou shalt not defraud thy neighbor, *neither rob* him" (Lev. 19:13). "Thou shalt not steal" (Ex. 20:15).

(58) Man was created after the other animals: "And God made the *beast* of the earth after his kind, and the *cattle* after their kind. . . . And God said, Let us make *man*. . . . So God *created man* in his own image" (Gen. 1:25, 26, 27).

Man was created before the other animals: "And the Lord God said it is not good that *man* should be *alone*; I will make a help-meet for him. And out of the ground the Lord God formed *every beast* of the field, and *every fowl* of the air, and *brought them unto Adam* to see what he would call them" (Gen. 8:22).

73. Ibid., p. 7.
74. Ibid.
75. Ibid., p. 10.

(108) Christ is equal with God: "I and my Father are *one*" (John 10:30). "Who, being in the form of God, thought it not robbery to be *equal with God*" (Phil. 2:5).

Christ is not equal with God: "My father is *greater* than I" (John 14:28). "Of that day and hour knoweth no man, not the angels of heaven, but my *Father only*" (Matt. 24:36).

DISCUSSION QUESTIONS

1. Can you *prove* to a skeptic that the Bible is inerrant? Why or why not?
2. You give the checkout clerk a five dollar bill. The change she gives you is for a ten dollar bill. Describe how the authority of the Bible should affect what you would do. (A question for your heart: *Would* it?)
3. Your best friend comes home from college, and the two of you get together. She begins by saying, "I don't believe the Bible anymore. It's full of contradictions. Besides, it was written too long ago to have any meaning for today." Dissect the objection, and describe how you would respond to each point.
4. A new Christian comes to you with a question: "I grew up in the Catholic church. My priest says that the Apocrypha is supposed to be in the Bible, but you don't have it in yours. Why do you say the Apocrypha is *not* God's Word?" How would you respond?
5. Summarize Jesus' view on the following topics, with two Scriptures supporting each point:
   The *authority* of the Bible
   The *dependability* (inerrancy) of the Bible
   The *extent* (canon) of the Bible.
6. You are a university student in 1930. Your professor has just told the class that Moses could not have written the first five books of the Bible, because writing had not yet been invented. This is in obvious contradiction with the Bible. What kind of "contradiction" is it? How would you answer it?

FURTHER READING

Archer, Gleason. *The Encyclopedia of Bible Difficulties*. Grand Rapids: Zondervan, 1982.

Beckwith, Roger. *The Old Testament Canon of the New Testament Church*. Grand Rapids: Eerdmans, 1985.

Bruce, F. F. *The New Testament Documents: Are They Reliable?* 5th rev. ed. Grand Rapids: Eerdmans, 1972.

Geisler, Norman L., and William E. Nix. *A General Introduction to the Bible*. Rev. ed. Chicago: Moody, 1986.

Harris, R. Laird. *Inspiration and Canonicity of the Bible*. Grand Rapids: Zondervan, 1957.

Henry, Carl F. H. *God, Revelation and Authority*. 4 vol. Waco, Tex.: Word, 1976-79.

Metzger, Bruce M. *The Canon of the New Testament: Its Origin, Development and Significance*. Oxford: Oxford U., 1987.

Warfield, B. B. *The Inspiration and Authority of the Bible*. Philadelphia: Presby. & Ref., 1948.

Wenham, John. *Christ and the Bible*. Downers Grove, Ill.: InterVarsity, 1972.

5

WHAT'S WRONG?:
THE PROBLEM OF EVIL

What Are the Problems?
    The Logical Problem: God Is Great, God Is Good?
    The Emotional Problem: When Bad Things Happen . . . to Me!
The Bad News
    What Problem? (Fideism)
    What Evil? (Illusionism)
    Is God "Great"? (Finitism)
    Is God "Good"? (Transmoralism)
The Good News
    The Problem of Suffering
        A View of the Past: Free Will and Possible Worlds
        A View of the Future: The Factor of Time
        A View for the Present: The Suffering of Jesus
    The Problem of Goodness

We were praying with the family in the emergency waiting room, desperately beseeching God that their lovely eighteen-year-old daughter would live through the night. The wreck had left all the other teenagers unharmed. The vigil was over when the doctor announced that their daughter would survive. After a few moments, joy slowly dissolved as the parents grimly wondered what life would be like as they cared for their daughter who was now severely brain-damaged. The father asked, *Why, Lord, did this happen to my daughter?*

It was Sunday morning in Lisbon, Portugal. The devout were dutifully worshiping in their churches when the earthquake struck. Thousands were killed. The European world of the Enlightenment noted that the pious who were going to church were more likely to be killed than the atheists who were still in their beds, many sleeping off their drunkenness. *Why would God allow a tragedy that punished the pious, but spared the guilty?*[1]

Elie Wiesel catalogs the horrors of the Holocaust in his book *Night*. Weisel observed small children and women humiliated and babies pitchforked, as well as the other horrors of Auschwitz. A child was hanged for taking bread, and Wiesel overheard someone groan, "Where is God? Where is He? Where can He be now?"[2]

The problem of evil is the shadow that falls across the biblical teaching about God's character. Why does an all-good and all-powerful God allow evil in His creation? How do we reconcile the pain in the world, and the pain in our own lives, with the character of the God we see in the Bible? The question simply will not be reduced by the admission that we are dealing with incomplete evidence. Something more must be said, for we are also dealing with God's goodness and His love—qualities foundational to Christian theology. Philosopher Ronald Nash summarizes the impact of the dilemma in this way:

> Objections to theism come and go. Arguments many philosophers thought cogent twenty-five years ago have disappeared from view. A few other problems continue to get a sympathetic hearing from one constituency or another. But every philosopher I know believes that the most serious challenge to theism was, is, and will continue to be the problem of evil. I share the view that the most serious intellectual obstacle that stands between many people and faith is uncertainty about the existence of evil.[3]

Stephen Davis concurs: "The problem of evil, in my opinion and in the opinion of many others, is the most serious intellectual difficulty that Christians and other theists face."[4] Jaroslav Pelikan observes, "Every answer to that question [of evil] has been fraught with danger to one or another central affirmation of the Christian faith—or to several of them at the same time."[5]

The problem of evil is universal. The problem does not arise only because some people have been victims of evil. Even people whose lives have been untouched by personal tragedies can envision a better world with less suffering.

1. Robert C. Solomon, *Introducing Philosophy*, 4th ed. (New York: Harcourt Brace Jovanovich, 1989), p. 318.
2. Elie Wiesel, *Night* (New York: Avon Books, 1969), p. 9.
3. Ronald Nash, *Faith and Reason* (Grand Rapids: Zondervan, 1988), p. 177.
4. Stephen Davis, *Logic and the Nature of God* (Grand Rapids: Eerdmans, 1983), p. 93.
5. Jaroslav Pelikan, *The Melody of Theology* (Cambridge, Mass.: Harvard U., 1988), p. 84.

How are we to approach the problem of evil from a biblical world-view? The problem is not merely a philosophical one to be analyzed by the test of coherence (whether or not the existence of evil fits with my theistic worldview). My answer must also correspond to what I know the world to be. Further, my answer should pass the test of experience: Can my worldview provide a response (beyond the answers of armchair philosophers) to the emotional turmoil that senseless evil evokes?

WHAT ARE THE PROBLEMS?

Often problems can be resolved simply by clarifying the terms used by opposing sides. Although the dilemma of evil is not so easily settled, much excess baggage can be jettisoned when we clearly understand what we do and do not mean by the term *evil*. Some things we call evil are simply things that displease us because they hinder the fulfillment of our inflated desires. For example, it may be that "we desire to do something—to play tennis, let us say—and we count it an evil that the weather does not cooperate. Much of our muttering about evil is nothing more than the tantrum behavior of God's spoiled children."[6] Clearly, however, deprivation of desire and/or fulfillment is not what is normally meant by "evil."

By "evil" we mean both moral evil and natural evil. The term *moral evil* refers to the evil choices made by free human agents.[7] If I choose to rob a bank, or to overeat, or to beat my dog, I am making a free moral choice. *Natural evil* does not involve human willing or acting, nor does it necessarily reflect any observable, intelligent purpose. The tragedies of Mt. St. Helens, of Hurricane Gilbert, of the 1989 San Francisco earthquake, or of famine and drought are examples of natural evil. Some see the occurrence of natural evil as the greater problem for theists to explain. When moral evil occurs there is an intermediate agent between God and the evil so that the "blame" is in some sense diffused. But with natural evil God is more immediately involved. No human being caused the earthquake in Portugal. In a case such as that, some argue, God may not delegate the blame so easily.

At times when a free choice results in natural evil, the two categories overlap into what some call *mixed evil*. My friend's free decision (moral choice) to smoke may result in the ravages of cancer (natural evil). If lightning destroys a building, the contractor who bribed the fire-safety

---

6. William H. Halverson, *A Concise Introduction to Philosophy*, 3d ed. (New York: Random House, 1967), p. 164.
7. Other personal, moral agents, such as angels, are not in view in this discussion.

inspector to certify that standards had been met is not exonerated from blame simply because he did not cause the lightning.[8]

Some further distinctions are important. First, the problem of evil is compounded when we consider the sheer quantity of evil in the world. If God uses pain to make some kind of point, does the quantity of suffering (such as took place in the Nazi holocaust) justify the point He is making? Second, the quality or intensity of senseless evil that exists is also a problem. Does God have morally sufficient reasons for permitting senseless evil, such as the slow, painful death of a child? This is sometimes called *gratuitous evil* and is the most difficult kind of evil for theists to resolve on the personal (and particularly emotional) level.

Third, some have tried to narrow the problem by pointing out that good results occur from pain, results that presumably would not otherwise occur and that justify the amount of evil suffered to produce the "good." An athlete might say, "No pain, no gain." The pain of bodily surgery or dental drilling may be necessary for a healthy body. At the spiritual level, for example, patience can be seen as a "good" that comes through enduring hardship.

But, we may ask, aren't we still left with the question of why God created a world in which these good results could have come about *in no other way*? Couldn't God think of a better way? Therefore, good results do not necessarily mean that evil is no longer bad. Furthermore, the problem of evil remains, because at times the quantity of evil far exceeds the quantity of good that may result.

In seeking to understand more clearly the overall problem of evil we shall first discuss the *logical problem* of evil. We shall then turn to the personal and *emotional problem* of individual evil. We believe a biblical worldview offers a response that is coherent, that corresponds with the real world and its problems, and that satisfies our emotional need to manage our pain.

THE LOGICAL PROBLEM: GOD IS GREAT, GOD IS GOOD?

A common prayer a child would utter begins, "God is great, God is good." This juxtaposition of two of God's attributes creates a problem when those attributes are viewed through the lens of evil in this world. If God is all good (omnibenevolent) and all powerful (omnipotent), why did He make a world with so much suffering? If He is all knowing (omniscient), then certainly He knew who would suffer as the victims of sense-

8. Halverson, p. 171.

less evil. Why did He even allow them to be born? If He created all things that exist, and evil exists, does it not follow that He created evil? The very character of God is at stake. J. L. Mackie states the case with flair: "If you are prepared to say that God is not wholly good, or not quite omnipotent, or that evil does not exist, or that good is not opposed to the kind of evil that exists, or that there are limits to what an omnipotent Being can do, then the problem of evil will not arise for you."[9]

The problem of evil is complex and needs to be carefully unraveled before we give in to the temptation to offer simplistic answers. David Hume, H. G. Wells, and Bertrand Russell formulated the problem into a dilemma similar to this one:[10]

1. Both God and evil are realities that truly exist.

2. If God were all-powerful, He could destroy evil.

3. If God were all-good, He would destroy evil.

4. Evil has not been destroyed.

5. Therefore, there is no all-good, all-powerful God.

The three great theistic worldviews of Christianity, Judaism, and Islam traditionally affirm propositions 1-4 and therefore are faced with the dilemma of the problem of evil. For many insightful people, the problem of evil does not *necessarily* disprove logically that there is a God.[11] However, they would argue that the presence of unexplained evil offers a good reason for not believing in such a God. In other words, although the problem of evil may no longer be a logical reason for *disproving* God, it does offer a personal reason for *disbelieving* in Him.

THE EMOTIONAL PROBLEM: WHEN BAD THINGS HAPPEN . . . TO ME!

My relatives were numb. Everyone around them was silent. The tiny casket made no sense at all. Cancer and car wrecks at least are somewhat understandable. But their toddler was not the victim of cancer or a drunk driver. The baby had simply climbed out of the crib in the middle

9. J. L. Mackie, "Evil and Omnipotence," in *Philosophy of Religion: Selected Readings*, ed. William Rowe and William Wainwright (New York: Harcourt Brace Jovanovich, 1989), p. 224.

10. D. Hume, *Dialogues Concerning Natural Religion*, pt. 10; see also *The Encyclopedia of Philosophy*, vol. 3 (New York: Macmillan, 1967), s.v. "Evil, The Problem of," by John Hick (included is a valuable chronological bibliography).

11. This includes most current philosophers of religion, according to Rowe and Wainwright, *Philosophy of Religion*, p. 193.

of the night—on the wrong side. Strangulation. Between the wall and the crib railing. *Why would God allow such a senseless evil?*

The death of a child is, understandably, often cited as a test case for proposed resolutions to the problem of evil, both in Western and Eastern cultures. Hindu texts cite the death of a young child as an illustration of the problem of extraordinary evil.[12] Dostoevsky used it to draw out the agony of the problem of evil as a reason for disbelief in God in *The Brothers Karamazov.*[13] Job lost all of his children through divinely permitted tragedy. Job believed in the sovereignty of God. But Job's faith in God's sovereignty did not relieve his anguish; it *caused* it. Job was not tempted to disbelieve the *sovereignty of God,* but to disbelieve the *goodness of God.*

The problem of individual evil is more accurately the problem of individual suffering. A coherent worldview must provide a consistent and realistic framework from which to manage the pain of personal suffering. It is one thing to deal with suffering in the abstract and discuss philosophical issues relating to the problem of evil. It is quite another thing to try to offer yourself or people you love carefully reasoned solutions to the logical problem of evil, when what is needed is comfort.

THE BAD NEWS

Because all religions must deal with the problem of evil at both the logical and the personal level, it is not surprising that many responses have appeared.[14] Some views ignore the problem, others redefine "evil," and some even redefine "God." The standard by which the Christian must measure all responses is the Bible. Therefore we shall now consider four representative answers to the problem of evil: fideism, illusionism, finitism, and transmoralism.

WHAT PROBLEM? (FIDEISM)[15]

The first approach considers the problem of evil a dilemma that human beings will never resolve. Some have argued that "God works in

---

12. D. Carmody and J. Carmody, *Ways to the Center* (Belmont, Calif.: Wadsworth, 1989), p. 109.

13. Fyodor Dostoevsky, *The Brothers Karamazov,* trans. C. Garnett (New York: Macmillan, 1923), chapter on "Rebellion."

14. Many helpful insights for this chapter were found in Millard Erickson, *Christian Theology* (Grand Rapids: Baker, 1983), 1:411-32, and in Ronald Nash, *Faith and Reason* (Grand Rapids: Zondervan, 1988), chaps. 13-19.

15. The term *fideism* is thrown about freely in apologetics debates and therefore needs to be defined. By fideism we mean that God's ways are beyond comprehension and reason, and therefore consideration of the problem of evil leads us necessarily into logical contradictions. Only through a nonreasonable (or anti-reasonable) leap of faith can we maintain our faith in God's power and goodness in the face of real evil.

EXPLANATIONS OF PERSONAL SUFFERING

View	Description	Redefines...
FIDEISM	God's mysterious ways are beyond man's comprehension.	Man's ability to understand God.
ILLUSIONISM	1) Everything is neutral, there is no good or bad, and hence no real evil. 2) The physical world does not exist, hence physical evil is an illusion.	1) Evil 2) World
FINITISM	Evil is something outside God's control, hence He is not responsible for evil.	God's Power
TRANSMORALISM	God is beyond morality; whatever He does (including what man calls "evil") is "good" by necessity.	God's Goodness

mysterious ways, and therefore we cannot understand His purposes in allowing evil. This view is not simply saying that we *cannot* understand God's ways but that we should not even *try* to understand them.[16] Whenever we try to resolve the logical problem of evil, our closely reasoned arguments seem to backfire and actually compound our problem—we then have both the problem of suffering and the problem of doubt. Therefore, victims of evil should simply do their best to manage their pain (most would add: with God's help) and not probe too deeply into mysteries that are not their ultimate concern.

Certainly it is difficult for thoughtful people to maintain such a position in the face of admitted paradoxes. We may admire the "faith" that prompts this response to the problem.[17] Rather than giving up on God's goodness, or God's power, or denying the reality of evil, persons who believe this way have given up any personal claim to grasp a solution to the problem—they have given up on themselves.

However, we believe that this solution to the problem is too costly. It seems more an indictment of God than a defense. Biblical belief in God's all-good and all-powerful nature and in the reality of evil is established and maintained as a matter of *rational* belief. To retreat at the point of tension into nonrationality (or anti-rationality) while still holding to the other beliefs is inconsistent. Further, once fideism is adopted as an operating principle, it cannot be invoked merely for difficult problems. Assurance of understanding *anything* rationally about our faith has then been abandoned.

Biblically, God has made us as image-bearers who have self-consciousness and who engage in thought processes. Further, He has made Himself known to us. It is through the reasoned apprehension of revelation that we know that God is good. "God's goodness implies He would provide us with at least some understanding of His purposes. These considerations suggest that the theist should be able to provide fairly plausible accounts of at least some significant kinds of evil even if he or she cannot adequately explain all kinds (animal suffering, for example) or account for the quantity of evil."[18]

Further, revelation assumes that man's reason is the filter through which all thought about God should occur. Whenever special revelation

---

16. Given propositions A and B (teachings of my faith), there is a difference between saying that I do not understand how proposition A and B fit together and saying that proposition A and B are logically contradictory (i.e., B = non-A). The latter is what is proposed by the fideistic position.

17. E.g., the eighteenth-century philosopher Pierre Bayle, "Paulicians," in *Introducing Philosophy*, 4th ed., ed. Robert C. Solomon (New York: Harcourt Brace Jovanovich, 1989), pp. 318-22.

18. Rowe and Wainwright, p. 195.

took place, God assumed that the recipients were to follow His reasoning, which at times was quite detailed and logical. Christians are told to love God with their *minds* (Matt. 22:37). Jesus regularly presented arguments, all the while assuming the validity, ability, and necessity of man's reason as one component used in knowing Him. Paul rebuked the Corinthian Christians because they were adopting a form of worship that excluded their minds (1 Cor. 14:12-19).

Some cite Isaiah 55:8-9 as support for emphasizing the gap between God's thoughts and our thoughts, and God's ways and our ways. In its context, however, the statement is not emphasizing a finite/infinite cognitive gap in which we may take comfort, but is an indictment that the Israelites *should be* thinking God's thoughts and following God's ways.

This does not mean that believers know *all* truth exhaustively, but it does mean that we may know certain things truly, and that our true understanding is broad enough to embrace the problem of evil sufficiently without resorting to fideism.

WHAT EVIL? (ILLUSIONISM)

One simple way to deal with evil is to claim that it is not real: "Evil is an illusion of the human mind. It is just an emotional reaction to events that are otherwise without objective value."[19] This is the position of most transcendental worldviews. For example, advocates of Vedanta Hinduism teach that this world, including the appearance of evil, is *maya*, or illusion.

Western philosopher Benedict Spinoza's pantheistic approach affirms that whatever exists, exists eternally as one substance. There is no ultimate separation between Creator and creation. Appearances of distinction (as between myself and my computer) are not true reflections of reality. Therefore when people refer to "evil," the term is a mere convention that obscures the fact that evil is a part of the one (neutral) substance which is called "God."

John Hick adds that "a confused echo of this doctrine is heard in contemporary Western Christian Science."[20] Mary Baker Eddy writes in *Science and Health*, "The Christianly scientific real is the sensuous unreal. Sin, disease, whatever seems real to material sense, is unreal in divine

---

19. Peter Facione, *A Student's Guide to Philosophy* (Mountain View, Calif.: Mayfield, 1988), p. 142.
20. Hick, "Evil," in *Encyclopedia of Philosophy*, 3:136.

Science.''[21] She continues, ''Evil is but an illusion, and it has no real basis. Evil is a false belief.''[22]

The attractiveness of this view is that ''evil'' becomes redefined in such a way as to relieve the problem of its ''existence.'' Because reality is not material and the senses are a source of error, then suffering and even death are simply phases in the process of the total illusion.

Problems with the illusory view far outweigh its single advantage. First, evil is redefined in a way that does not square with the overwhelming biblical picture of evil as real and, at times, personal.[23] The Bible does not describe evil as an illusion, but as a reality inexorably tied to a material world. The only way to avoid contact with the world is to leave it (1 Cor. 5:10).

Second, this view does not fit with actual experience of the world, or of evil. Although my experience is not necessarily the final criterion for determining whether or not a physical view of reality is true, the burden of proof would certainly rest on those who would deny material reality. I may argue verbosely that words do not convey meaning, or shout at the top of my lungs, ''Vocal chords do not exist!'' but neither is convincing. An illusionist suffers no less from the illusion of a toothache than he or she would from a real toothache.

Third, our entire view of reality (not just evil) is of course at stake in this refutation. All ''knowledge'' from our senses would be held in tension; daily living would involve second-by-second denial of impressions of the external world. The meanings of such terms as *flesh*, *resurrection*, and even *God* and *Christ* would have to be totally redefined, as Mary Baker Eddy does.[24] Further, once such redefinition of terms is accepted, then evangelism and dialogue become impossible because, essentially, two different languages are being spoken.

Finally, and very important, the problem of evil is not answered by this view. It has simply been shifted to a different level. The origin of the illusion of evil requires just as cogent an explanation as real evil does. Instead of asking, ''Whence evil?'' we ask, ''Whence the illusion of evil?'' The second question is just as significant a challenge as the first one. Further, whenever evil seems to be properly dealt with, who is to say that the satisfaction of seeing justice triumph over evil is not also an illusion?

21. Mary Baker Eddy, *Science and Health* (Boston: Trustees of the Will of Mary Baker G. Eddy, 1875), p. 353.
22. Ibid., p. 480.
23. John Wenham, *The Enigma of Evil* (Grand Rapids: Zondervan, 1985), p. 7.
24. Eddy, pp. 579-99 (glossary).

IS GOD "GREAT"? (FINITISM)

Another way to deal with evil is to redefine God's sovereignty: God is attempting to overcome evil, but He is unable to do so by Himself.[25] Many claim that God is somehow finite, subject to "laws" higher than Himself. These laws may be considered coeternal with God. Because God is not all powerful, there is no certainty of the final result; man must work *with* God to overcome evil. Thus this view maintains God's goodness at the expense of God's power.

Finitism is not new. It existed in various forms of ancient *dualism* (such as Zoroastrianism and Platonism). In more modern times it has been embraced by John Stuart Mill, Edgar S. Brightman,[26] and has become quite well known through Rabbi Harold S. Kushner's best seller *When Bad Things Happen to Good People.*[27]

In some ways, this approach solves the problem of evil. God is not at all responsible for evil, because He is unable to overcome it by Himself. In a sense God is also a victim of evil—His plan is victimized to the extent that it is contingent.

But again, finitism must be embraced at too high a price. If an exterminator tells you, "I got rid of your termites—I burned down your house!" you may feel that the solution is of little real help, because it creates even greater problems. This view relieves God from the moral responsibility for evil, but the origin of evil remains a mystery. In other words, this view solves *the problem of the problem of evil,* but not *the problem of evil.*

Finitism must redefine God's omnipotence by claiming that God is not sovereign over all creation. However, because God's attributes are being redefined, it follows that the term *God* itself is being redefined. God now becomes understood as a finite being. But because finite beings are conditioned by forces beyond their control, should those forces now be called "God"?

When we turn to the Bible, however, there is no doubt that God's power is total, including His power over evil (Ps. 147:4; Matt. 10:29-30; John 19:11; Eph. 1:11). There are no accidents in the universe outside God's knowledge or control. Job 1-2 clearly illustrates the control God

25. Edgar S. Brightman, *A Philosophy of Religion* (New York: Prentice-Hall, 1940), pp. 285-303.
26. Ibid., pp. 240-340. For a critique of Brightman's position, see Gordon Clark, *A Christian View of Men and Things* (Grand Rapids: Eerdmans, 1952), pp. 267-81.
27. Harold S. Kushner, *When Bad Things Happen to Good People* (New York: Avon, 1981). See especially the chapter entitled "God Can't Do Everything, But He Can Do Some Important Things."

exercises over moral and natural evil; God holds the reins of Satan, who can engage in evil only by God's permission.

IS GOD "GOOD"? (TRANSMORALISM)

Whereas the previous view affirms God's goodness at the expense of His omnipotence, transmoralism affirms God's omnipotence at the expense of His goodness. God is not really good in the way man usually understands goodness. That is, the traditional definitions of God's goodness must be reconsidered, primarily by placing God's "goodness" into different theological perspectives in which God transcends morality. In the Hindu *Upanishads* the gods are either inadequate (finitism) or actively malevolent (transmoralism).[28]

The first theological perspective that may be used to redefine God's goodness is His absolute sovereignty. God is beneath no law or standard (even of "goodness") to which He must conform. After all, does not the Bible quote God saying, "I . . . create evil" (Isa. 45:7, KJV)? Accountability determines morality. Because He is accountable to no one, God's character defines what is meant by "good." The view can be stated simply:

> Major Premise: Whatever happens is caused by God.
> Minor Premise: Whatever is caused by God is good.
> Conclusion: Whatever happens (including evil) is good.

Gordon Clark cites specific examples of apparent evils that are also "good." "The crucifixion of Christ—was it good or evil? To Judas and the Pharisees it was a crime productive only of evil and of the greatest of evils. To the disciples on the other hand it was productive of the greatest of goods."[29] Clark also maintains that Saul's persecution of Christians was "both good and evil, in different respects and to different persons; yet Christ met him on the road to Damascus and eliminated that evil."[30]

Pantheism provides a second form this view may adopt. If God is the world, then God is identified with the evil in the world. Both illusionism and transmoralism may be seen in the comment of one Hindu leader who said he would bow before women who represent both pure mother-

28. Carmody and Carmody, *Ways to the Center*, p. 110.
29. Clark, *Christian View*, p. 272.
30. Ibid., p. 273.

hood and prostitution. He reasoned that because good and evil are all a part of the same illusory world (which is God), good and evil are one.[31]

Many problems attend both forms of transmoralism. In a sense, it is *psychologically* difficult to accept, because labeling evil "good" does not make it so. What is at issue is not whether or not specific events may have mixed value to different people, but whether as an explanation transmoralism can account for *all* specific cases of evil. The explanation wears thin when trying to account for the occultic flaying of a baby or the horrors of a Nazi extermination camp.

Biblically, it does not follow from its supposed scriptural support. When the Bible quotes God as saying "I . . . create evil" (Isa. 45:7, KJV), the Hebrew parallelism makes it clear that God visits with calamity when He acts in judgment, not that He originates evil.[32]

Theologically, it is troublesome because in essence God can do with moral impunity what men are sent to jail for doing. But this view is also difficult to live with *practically,* because any words describing God's character lose their meaning and we are plunged into a sea of theological equivocation. "God does good" and "man does good" become so dissimilar that we no longer have a guarantee that a clear idea exists of what they mean. Yet God has given some of His attributes as models for His children to live by. Because He is holy, we are to be holy (1 Pet. 1:16); because He is truth, we are to speak truth (Eph. 4:21-25). In other words, we are to "be imitators of God" (Eph. 5:1). God assumes that we are able to understand these qualities enough to reproduce them in our own lives.

THE GOOD NEWS

We have dealt with several inadequate solutions to the problem of evil. Their inadequacies arise because they are internally unbiblical, inconsistent and/or emotionally unsatisfactory. Answers to tough problems are rarely simple. Not all of the evidence is in yet. Further, we are interpreting our world (which is affected by sin) with our minds (also affected by sin). Consequently, we may expect to wrestle deeply with questions for which we do not, at present, have all the information. Still, a biblical worldview contributes scriptural perspectives that not only explain the presence of evil but offer realistic hope for the future.

31. Wenham, *Enigma of Evil*, p. 190.
32. R. C. Sproul, *Knowing Scripture* (Downers Grove, Ill.: InterVarsity, 1977), pp. 86-87.

THE PROBLEM OF SUFFERING

Suffering is easiest to understand when it comes as the direct result of a moral choice to sin. When David sinned by committing both adultery and murder, the judgment that befell him did not cause him theological anguish. He knew that God is both just and loving. However, not all suffering can be described as having an immediate cause/effect relationship with sin. Jesus' disciples were wide of the mark when they made this assumption, as were Job's friends centuries earlier (Job 42:7; John 9:1-2).

Suffering is also understandable when it can be seen to promote greater good. James 1 offers encouragement to believers who endure trials because James knew of the spiritual fruit that results from suffering. Paul's chronic suffering from his "thorn" was for a similar purpose (2 Cor. 12:7-9). When Joseph was enslaved, he certainly did not view what happened as good, yet later in his life comforted his brothers, "You meant evil against me, but God meant it for good in order to bring about this present result, to preserve many people alive" (Gen. 50:20).

It is always possible that God may view as ultimately good what we view as immediately evil. His perspective is eternal, His knowledge is infinite, and His judgments include all variables. Our judgments, by contrast, are based on incomplete data.

At times we try to superimpose a rationale for present suffering by positing some future "greater good"—from "God must be teaching me patience" to "God must want me to counsel others who also have lost a child." Even so, we know there is more to the matter and feel uneasy that we have simply accepted a contrived solution in order to make the pain more manageable; we have not been honest with our own minds. Further, in many cases the victim of evil would just as soon have done without the greater good and therefore without the accompanying pain. Rabbi Kushner admits,

> I am a more sensitive person, a more effective pastor, a more sympathetic counselor because of Aaron's life and death than I would ever have been without it. And I would give up all of those gains in a second if I could have my son back. If I could choose, I would forgo all the spiritual growth and depth which has come my way because of our experiences, and be what I was fifteen years ago, an average rabbi, an indifferent counselor, helping some people and unable to help others, and the father of a bright, happy boy. But I cannot choose.[33]

---

33. Kushner, pp. 133-34. Aaron Kushner died of progeria at the age of fifteen.

I appreciate Kushner's honesty and candor. Christians wrestle with similar problems. What should Christians think about those cases where there is *no observable good reason* for their suffering? Three components of the dilemma, which have so far been ignored, are *free will, time,* and *the suffering of Jesus.* Each of these has something to contribute to the biblical perspective on evil.

A View of the Past: Free Will and Possible Worlds

When creating man, God could have made him morally perfect, either with choice or without choice. However, man without free choice would not be man. God chose to make *man,* not an android.[34] Man's will, like other aspects of God's creation (e.g., water, fire), has the capacity to be used for good or evil. "God did not create sin. He merely provided the options necessary for human freedom."[35]

The "Free Will Defense" was originally put forth by Augustine and recently meticulously defended by Alvin Plantinga.[36] It answers many of the questions of moral evil: free human agents decide whether or not to sin. But could God not have done it differently? Have we not simply redefined the problem on a different level so that we must now ask, Why did God make a plan like this? Consider the following propositions.

We know only *this* (actual) world.

We can conceive of other *possible* worlds (including one with less evil) but not *all* possible worlds, because we are finite.

God (who is infinite) knows *all* possible worlds.[37]

This world is not (at this time) the best of all possible worlds (even that we can think of).

When we stand in our Lord's presence and enter eternity, the Bible says we will be in the best of all possible worlds (John 14:1-6; 1 Thess. 4:13-18; Rev. 21-22; etc.).

Therefore, although this is not (now) the best of all possible worlds, a world of man's free choice (even to do evil) is the best way to achieve the best of all possible worlds.

---

34. Wenham, *Enigma of Evil*, p. 54.
35. Erickson, *Christian Theology*, p. 429.
36. Alvin Plantinga, *God, Freedom, and Evil* (Grand Rapids: Eerdmans, 1974).
37. For example, in Matthew 11:20-24 Jesus indicates that if He had performed certain miracles in Tyre and Sidon, they would have repented. See William Lane Craig, *The Only Wise God* (Grand Rapids: Baker, 1987), p. 132.

Stephen Davis summarizes this approach: "What the Free Will Defense must insist on is, first, that the amount of evil that in the end will exist will be outweighed by the great goods that will then exist; and second, that this favourable balance of good over evil was obtainable by God in no other way that was within his control."[38]This position includes faith commitments arising from a biblical worldview. Knowing all possible worlds, God knew this was the best possible way to result in the best possible world. Thus the defense becomes a "best way" instead of a "best world" position. In this way, God achieves the greatest good.[39]

Biblically, natural evil in the world is a consequence of the decision by man to do moral evil. When Adam sinned, this world became the domain of Satan and his minions (Gen. 3:17ff.; see also Rom. 8:19-22, where the creation awaits its restoration to a pristine state). Yet God's power maintains control over both moral and natural evil, as a study of Job 1-2 reveals. In this sense God may be considered the *ultimate* cause of evil (in that He is the *Author* of the *author* [Satan] of sin); this does not, however, require that He is the *blameworthy* cause of sin. Thus, "although not without its problems (such as the riddle of evil *ex nihilo),* this affirmation of the traditional notion of the Genesis 3 fall accounts for both natural and moral evil."[40]

A View of the Future: The Factor of Time

The component of time is crucial to a biblical worldview of evil (Rom. 8:18). One day, God will wipe away all tears from our eyes (Rev. 21:4). Until then, even saints in the Lord's presence wail "How long, O Lord?" as they anticipate cosmic restoration (Rev. 6:10).

Let us reconsider our original propositions:

Both God and evil are realities that truly exist.

If God were all-powerful, He could destroy evil.

If God were all-good, He would destroy evil.

Evil has not been destroyed.

38. Davis, *Logic and the Nature of God*, p. 100.
39. See Norman Geisler, *Philosphy of Religion* (Grand Rapids: Zondervan, 1974), pp. 349-79. For counter-arguments see Davis, p. 99.
40. Daniel Clendenin, "Security But No Certainty: Toward a Christian Theodicy," *Journal of the Evangelical Theological Society* 31:3 (September 1988), p. 326.

Before drawing the conclusion, the last proposition should be re-worded to fit with our biblical worldview. This is how it should read: Evil has not *yet* been destroyed. Thus we may draw a new conclusion: Evil *will be* destroyed by an all-good, all-powerful God.

This is logically coherent and is precisely what the Bible claims. Although we do not yet have enough data to answer why each individual act of suffering takes place, we have a reasonable perspective within which to deal with our pain. Is our biblical worldview large enough to trust God with our remaining uncertainties?

In the realm of science, for example, physicists cannot logically harmonize the wave and particle nature of light. Lack of certainty in this area, however, does not render modern physics impossible. The assumption is made that the answer will be forthcoming, and in the meantime scientists go on about their work. Thus, the presence of unsolved dilemmas does not falsify a worldview. We assume God knows all possible worlds, and that we do not. We also assume He is good, loving, and just. May we not trust His judgment and know that His reasons are compelling and sufficient?

There is a startling biblical symmetry between sin's entrance into the world (Gen. 1-3) and its exit from the world (Rev. 20-22). A brief perusal is enough to convince us that the tragedy that was inaugurated in the beginning will be completely dealt with before we enter the eternal state.

Genesis 1-3[41]	*Revelation 20-22*
"In the day you eat from it, you shall surely die" (2:17)	"There shall no longer be any death" (21:4)
Satan appears as deceiver (3:1)	Satan removed forever (20:10)
"I will greatly multiply your pain" (3:16)	"There shall no longer be any mourning, or crying, or pain" (21:4)
"Cursed is the ground because of you" (3:17)	"There shall no longer be any curse" (22:3)
First paradise closed (3:23)	New paradise opened (21:25)
They were driven from God's presence (3:24)	"They shall see His face" (22:4)

41. Adapted from Kenneth Boa, *Talk Thru the New Testament* (Wheaton, Ill.: Tyndale House, 1981), p. 225.

In the meantime, however, those who belong to Jesus have been told to anticipate that they will follow their Lord in suffering (John 15:20-27; Rom. 8:17), realizing that Jesus has overcome the world (John 16:33). Therefore, we can take comfort in the fact "that the sufferings of this present time are not worthy to be compared with the glory that is to be revealed in us" (Rom. 8:18).

A View for the Present: The Suffering of Jesus

This "best world" apologetic may not, however, resolve our personal dilemma in dealing with private suffering. It is one thing to say in the abstract that this is a logical and biblically consistent solution. It is quite another thing to comfort yourself that this is the best of all possible worlds when you are facing terminal cancer. As one philosopher put it, "the happy phrase 'best of all possible worlds' may warm our hearts in the comfort of a church or a seminar room, but it quickly becomes cold when confronting real tragedy."[42]

On the other hand, this world in which we live, and in which evil seems to flourish, serves as an object lesson of need: "The existence of suffering on this earth is, I believe, a scream to all of us that something is wrong."[43] The presence of evil and our lack of acceptance of injustice or pain is an indication to believer and unbeliever alike that this world is not as it should be—or as it came from the hand of God.

Suffering and Jesus' Ministry. Although others may offer no hope, false hope, or illusory hope, the Bible offers realistic hope because of the work of our compassionate Savior. In Jesus' high priestly role God became man and thus understands experientially what our sufferings are like. We are exhorted to remember that "we do not have a high priest who cannot sympathize with our weakness" (Heb. 4:15). Isaiah reminds us that in the life of the Messiah He would become "acquainted with grief" (Isa. 53:3). He is now the head of His Body, and when members of His Body hurt, He hurts (Acts 9:4-5).

Our Lord does not ask His own to ignore pain. Jesus wept in the presence of death (John 11:35). Even though Paul referred to his own death as "gain" (entrance into the immediate presence of Christ—Phil. 1:21), he referred to the potential death of one of his friends as "sorrow upon sorrow" (Phil. 2:27). Believers should expect suffering if they follow Christ (Mark 8:34; John 15:20) and thus can in a sense rejoice in

---

42. Solomon, *Introducing Philosophy*, p. 323.
43. Philip Yancey, "Pain: The Tool of the Wounded Surgeon," *Christianity Today*, 24 March 1978, p. 14.

those sufferings, which are for Christ's sake (2 Cor. 4:17-18; 7:4; Phil. 3:10; 1 Pet. 4:13).

Suffering and Jesus' Death. From a biblical worldview, the ultimate apologetic for the problem of evil is God's action (through Christ) in becoming the victim of maximum evil. God took the punishment of sin upon Himself. He became man, and in that form He—and He alone— suffered the entire composite of human evil and misery. Not only did He bear our sins, He bore our emotional pain (Isa. 53:4).

Although components of the problem of evil may remain a present mystery, a more amazing mystery is that God allowed sin to occur at all, knowing that He would become its ultimate victim. Furthermore, the worst of all possible evils (the death of Christ—history's only absolutely sinless man) was not only permitted, but decreed from eternity past (Acts 2:23). "By taking it on himself, Jesus in a sense dignified pain. Of all the lives He could have lived, he chose a suffering one."[44]

Though this analogy is not technically a solution to the personal problem of suffering, I believe it is a resolution. And it is unique among the religions of the world.

THE PROBLEM OF GOODNESS

A final perspective is important. Theists must wrestle with the problem of evil. Naturalists and pantheists, however, have twice the problem. Not only must they account for evil, they must account for good (and why they define it as such). R. C. Sproul observes, "We can account for the origin of good but not of evil. The pagan can account for the origin of neither."[45] Prager and Telushkin aptly note, "The believer in God must explain one thing, the existence of sufferings; the nonbeliever, however, must explain the existence of everything else."[46] Harry Emerson Fosdick said it well, "The mystery of evil is very difficult when we believe in a good God, but the problem of goodness seems to us impossible when we do not."[47]

The existence of evil is a disturbing dilemma but in no way does it disallow a biblical worldview. The Bible does not ignore the reality of evil, it meets it squarely, describes its origins and its power—and its ultimate demise.

---

44. Ibid., p. 15.
45. R. C. Sproul, *Reason to Believe* (Grand Rapids: Zondervan, 1982), p. 128. John Mackie recognizes the strength of this argument also (cited by Rowe and Wainwright, p. 224).
46. Dennis Prager and Joseph Talushkin, *The Nine Questions People Ask About Judaism*, quoted in *Reader's Digest*, October 1988, p. 158.
47. Harry Emerson Fosdick, quoted in Clendenin, "Security But No Certainty," p. 325.

CASE STUDY: *Evil and the Presence of God*

For some, the presence of evil is a weapon used to reject the existence of an all-knowing, all-caring God. For others, personal evil casts a shadow of doubt over God's involvement in the world.

As an example of the first, Christian writer Terry Muck attended the tenth world congress of the International Humanist and Ethical Union (IHEU) held in Buffalo, New York, during August of 1988. The passionate atheistic tenor of the conference dominated the speeches. Muck recorded the presentation and response of humanist Frank Miosi:

> "If God is all powerful, then why does evil exist?" The audience snickered knowingly. "If God is all wise, why does he bind himself and limit his effectiveness?" (snicker). "Why does God allow young children to die, earthquakes to destroy cities, famine to ravage villages, thalidomide babies to be born?" (angry snort). "Why would a real God allow 747s full of innocent people to be shot down?" (outraged laughter).[48]

An example of the second dilemma is seen in the life of Elie Wiesel, winner of the 1986 Nobel Peace Prize. As a teenager in Hungary during the Second World War, Wiesel suffered greatly at the hands of the Nazis. Brutally treated and hustled away with his family to Auschwitz, the horrors that greeted him seared his devout Jewish faith. One of his first sights at the death camp was a burning ditch, flames leaping into the night air. As his group was marched closer, he saw that the ditch was full of babies. He writes,

> Never shall I forget that night, the first night in camp, which turned my life into one long night, seven times cursed and seven times sealed. Never shall I forget that smoke. Never shall I forget the little faces of the children, whose bodies I saw turned into wreaths of smoke beneath a silent blue sky.
> Never shall I forget those flames which consumed my faith forever.
> Never shall I forget those moments which murdered my God and my soul and turned my dreams to dust.[49]

CASE STUDY: *Evil and the Pilgrimage*

Many Christians struggle deeply with the emotional problem of suffering. And no problem tugs at the heart more strongly than the suffering

48. Terry C. Muck, "God and Man in Buffalo," *Christianity Today*, 13 January 1989, pp. 22-23.
49. Elie Wiesel, *The Night Trilogy* (New York: Hill and Wang, 1960, 1972, 1985), p. 43.

of a child. Below is the story of Gerald Oosterveen, a chaplain whose stark emotions test any simplistic treatments to the problems of evil and suffering.[50]

I tramp through the loose, swirling snow. Where the wind has whipped it into drifts, I sink in deep and struggle to get through. My boots are not tall enough; snow seeps around my feet and they are getting cold. A bitter wind from the Dakotas, maybe all the way from Canada, quickly erases my footprints and turns my face stiff like the faces of those who lie below the snow. The wind chill is forty-five below zero. Of all the days to visit this little Northwest Iowa cemetery! I hope no one sees me. I want to be alone here. I am alone.

The graves are easily visible in the old section where the headstones stand tall and close together, faithful sentinels keeping their eternal and silent watch. But where I want to be they use smaller markers which today are hidden by the snow. I trip over one such unseen stone and hurt my ankle. Fortunately, I have only a short way to go.

At last I find the place. I grope around for the marker. When I have brushed away the snow from the cold granite I see the inscription I already know by heart. Just three short lines—his name, the years of birth and death, a testimony: "At Home with Jesus." I sink onto the frozen ground. It was frigid like this the first time I was here too. And like then, the weather does not really matter now. I think about my son.

He was our first child, first son, born before we had really planned to have children. I remember the pride I felt when he came, pride because he was a new generation destined to carry on our family name, pride also because he was such a beautiful child, happy and healthy. When, later, he rode in his stroller, total strangers were attracted by his friendly smile. Still later his intelligence showed as he became inquisitive, full of questions, never satisfied until he knew how something worked or came apart and back together. Life was exciting for him, challenging and adventurous. For hours he could be an engineer who with his bulldozer created endlessly winding roads on the gravel driveway; then he'd become a race driver who zipped his cars through twists and turns.

I think of the times I punished him, remembering with a twinge of guilt that the punishment too often reflected my impatience or lack of humor rather than his misbehavior. I subdue the sudden wish that those years could be relived differently, better. How quickly they passed! Those nine years he lived with us were for him a lifetime drawn out even then almost beyond his endurance. For us they were too short. If only I had taken a bit more time to understand my young son as a person, to know his feelings and his fears. If only. . . . But now it is too late.

He was not even six when the cancer came, first as foreboding suspicion, then as crushing certainty, and almost always with the sharp pain that

50. Gerald Oosterveen, "Pilgrimage," *The Sunday Digest*, 1 February 1981. Used by permission.

swept into oblivion the good years that were. Long since have I forgotten what that doctor looked like who with just a few words exploded our hopes and dreams. But always I will remember the small, shiny basin with the red tumor tissue which left no doubt that our son would die. "Reticulum cell carcinoma," the doctor called it. Death it was, death not more than six months hence. Had he died then, in surgery, my pain could not have been more severe.

I remember weeping. I remember also the range of fury and frustration at my helplessness and the unfairness of it all.

"Why," I asked the nun who tried to bring words of comfort, "why this beautiful child who has a lifetime of living yet to do? Why not, if we must give up a child, our retarded second son who will need supervision all his life?"

"God must love you very much," she gently replied while my anger boiled over, "to ask so much of you."

"Love like that I can do without." The words echo through my mind still, but they bring no peace.

Perhaps some parents find comfort in shared grief—husband and wife drawn together through common pain. But my pain was so intense and overwhelming that no room was left for my wife's feelings. Was that selfishness, I wonder, a sign that I did not love her then as I should? Was that normal, that I let my hurt overshadow hers? Or was it simply an instinctive reaction, a spontaneous withdrawal into the self while every other stimulus is blocked out in a feeble, frantic attempt to prevent sorrow from piling upon sorrow?

Cancer, that horrible dreaded furtive killer. How does it come? From where? Can it be defeated? I never expected a cure for my son. Yet, when the six predicted months were up, he still lived. It was even as if the cancer was gone, except for the visits to the clinic every few weeks. The boy only knew he had a serious disease, for we had kept the death sentence from him for the time being. As before, he seemed so healthy. He was active again and thankful that the pain was gone.

It was like that for more than a year. The doctor had been wrong about the time period; did that mean he was wrong about the outcome too? Against reason, we hoped. And prayed, knowing our friends were praying also.

"Lord, come down, my son is ill. If you but speak, he will be healed."

And then the cancer came back. With the pain. Dare I ever again let my heart rule over reason?

I remember the subtle, slow, persistent progress of the disease, like an invisible but irresistible snake swallowing up my vivacious son, draining away the luster of his complexion, hollowing out his cheeks, attacking muscles and nerves. First the legs. Walking became a chore, running impossible, climbing trees out of the question. Always he wanted a new bike to replace his old, secondhand one. We kept stalling, then gently helped him realize he would never get better again, never more ride a bike. One day he rode anyway, as if to prove he was invincible. His school friends, in a spontaneous outpouring of love and encouragement, that same day raised enough money for a new bike. At a program already planned for that night there was an additional agenda item when the bike was given. I remember my son's face, radiating speechless joy. I recall my struggle to keep back tears. He only rode his bike three times, with my help, less than a mile altogether.

A wheelchair came, then a special bed in the family room, where we turned his now paralyzed, emaciated, twisted body from one side to the other every few hours. Losing sensation and control, he needed diapers —to him the epitomy of shame and disgrace. Occasionally he was rebellious, or cried.

"Why do I have to die now?" My explanation was less than convincing. I did not know either.

But he kept fighting. While his arms still functioned, he glued together tall towers of spaghetti. Finally even that became too much. The snake had almost reached the head. And always that pain, that excruciating pain. At times the massive doses of analgesics made him a bit delirious, but most of the time he was alert, thinking about the future, the little time left here and eternity beyond. He became a philosopher, wise beyond his years.

"Dad, when I was a kid, I never realized kids can die too."

Drawing on what he had learned in church and Sunday school, he was a theologian searching for meaning behind illness, and for hope.

"Isn't that amazing that Jesus should be preparing a place for me in his Father's house? He loves me!"

When I wished we had more money to pay the mounting medical bills, he functioned as my teacher and gently rebuked me.

"Don't say we're poor, Dad. Christians are never poor. When you've got faith, you're rich."

The words of Jesus come to my mind, and somehow they seem spoken to me: "Unless you become like one of these little ones, you shall not enter the kingdom of God."

He willed himself to live at least until he could see the baby his mother was expecting. Then, that last wish fulfilled, he just as deliberately prepared for death. His shiny, barely used bike he donated to a school for the mentally impaired. His money he divided, then told us to buy presents with it that would perpetuate his memory, a watch or rings. He left instructions that his brother and brand-new sister not have their gifts until they were fifteen at least, and would value them. Also a note for his sister. With Christmas approaching, he was ready.

"Don't buy me any presents. I don't have pain anymore, and Jesus will soon come for me to take me to my new home."

Three days later, expectantly, he closed his eyes for good. He had lived nine years, three months, two days. The predicted six months had become a precious thirty-nine.

Perhaps I have been weeping, perhaps it is the cold, but my face is wet. I look at the stone again. "At Home with Jesus," it reads and so I believe him to be. But I still miss him. I try to imagine what heaven is like. Do people there remember us, I wonder, or miss us? Some day, I reflect, I must die and will see my son again. But when my time comes, will I have conquered my fears as he did and go out in faith? Can I ever hope to become so trusting, believing as a child, as this *my* child?

Suddenly, I feel proud to have been, even if for such a short time, father of this remarkable child. He enjoyed life so much, yet was so ready to give it up because he believed in God and in Jesus as his Savior. I thank God for the memories I have, for the lessons my son taught me, for the faith that sustained him then and me now, for love, God's love, that surrounds us in the darkest hours.

I get up. I will not visit this place again.

DISCUSSION QUESTIONS

1. Is the presence of evil in the world a problem for an atheist? For a materialist? For a pantheist? For an agnostic? For a Christian?

2. A friend to whom you are witnessing says to you, "My mom has had a hard life since Dad left us, and last week she just found out she has cancer. I wish I could believe what you say about God loving me and Jesus dying for me and all that, but I just can't believe in a God of love anymore." What would you say?

3. Your neighbor is a member of the Christian Science movement and has told you that his or her family does not believe that physical pain exists. What would you say?

4. Your marriage engagement has just been broken because your sweetheart has decided he or she does not love you. Your roommate pats you on the back and says, "Well, Romans 8:28 — all things work together for good!" What should your attitude be toward your fiance? Toward your roommate?

5. Read Lamentations 3. What was going on when Jeremiah penned these words? Can you detect a change within Jeremiah's attitude as the chapter progresses? If so, why? (Do the same for Habakkuk 3.)

6. How can the suffering of Jesus be used to evangelize people who are struggling with the problem of evil? How can the suffering of Jesus be used in counseling the bereaved?

FURTHER READING

Boa, Kenneth, and Larry Moody. *I'm Glad You Asked*. Wheaton, Ill.: Victor, 1982. See chapter 7.

Clark, Ralph W. *Introduction to Philosophical Thinking: Readings and Commentary*. New York: West, 1987. See chapter 4.

Feinberg, John S. *Theologies and Evil*. Washington, D.C.: University Press of America, 1979.

Geisler, Norman L. *Philosophy of Religion*. Grand Rapids: Zondervan, 1974. See chapters 14-17.

Lewis, C. S. *The Problem of Pain*. London: Geoffrey Bles, 1940.

Nash, Ronald. *Faith and Reason*. Grand Rapids: Zondervan, 1988. See chapters 13-15.

Plantinga, Alvin C. *God, Freedom, and Evil*. Grand Rapids: Eerdmans, 1974.

Solomon, Robert C. *Introducing Philosophy: A Text with Integrated Readings*. 4th ed. New York: Harcourt Brace Jovanovich, 1989. Pages 312-27.

Wenham, John W. *The Enigma of Evil*. Grand Rapids: Zondervan, 1985.

Yancey, Philip. *Where Is God When It Hurts?* Grand Rapids: Zondervan, 1977.

————. *Disappointment with God: Questions Nobody Asks Aloud*. Grand Rapids: Zondervan, 1988.

6

WHO'S RIGHT?:
THE PROBLEM OF PLURALISM

James kept probing. The conversation had occurred many times before, but with different people.

"How can you believe in a God who would condemn anybody to hell? Many people have lived moral lives and been faithful in their religion! Are they damned simply because that religion was not Christianity?!

"And furthermore," he continued, "what about those who have never heard about Christ? Are they condemned too?" He warmed to the topic, sensing the weakness of an Achilles' heel.

"And how do you explain the fact that in a Christian country, most people are Christians, in a Muslim country, most people follow Islam, and in a Buddhist country, most people are Buddhists? That doesn't sound like any God is at work, it sounds more like sociology to me!"

His face showed that he believed his triumph was complete.

PLURALISM DESCRIBED

Edward Gibbon, in *The Decline and Fall of the Roman Empire*, stated that during the decline of the Empire all religions were regarded by the people as equally true, by the philosophers as equally false, and by the politicians as equally useful![1] People react in different ways when the subject of other religions (the question of pluralism) is raised. For some, the topic is an interesting intellectual question; for many, pluralism is a deeply emotional issue.

Although discussions of pluralism are not new, all the relevant questions need to be carefully considered. What is God like? Is God a personal being or an impersonal force? Is man's destiny one of continued self-conscious existence, or reabsorption into the matrix of the cosmos? What is heaven—a real place or simply a state of consciousness? Is salvation heightened awareness of other beings, or redemption from sin? Is salvation attained by works, by meditation, or by faith? If Christianity is true, does it necessarily follow that all other religions are wrong? Can so many be wrong, or are all religions equally valid? Could it be that some are more valid than others, while those that fall short may be at least adequate for God's purpose of salvation?

The fact of a pluralistic world has required religious thinkers to adopt positions regarding believers in other religions. Several different approaches have been adopted.[2]

Selectivism says that other religions have elements of truth, but only one (the religion of the selectivist) is totally true. A selectivist enjoys the religious cafeteria approach: even though there is one main course, he may take what he likes and discard what he dislikes from each religion. The resulting religious fare will be acceptable to God.

Inclusivism says there is only one true religion through which salvation may be obtained (the religion of the inclusivist). But God may impute salvation to the sincere worshiper of false gods. Although those in other religions may refuse to partake from (or not know about) the proper religious diet, God will not let them starve.

---

1. Cited in James Montgomery Boice, *The Minor Prophets* (Grand Rapids: Zondervan, 1986), 2:124.
2. Different worldviews give different answers to these basic questions. Consequently, *religious pluralism* is difficult to define because one must assume a common understanding of such concepts as "salvation," "heaven," and even "God." Furthermore, not all worldviews are explicitly religious, and of those that *are* religious, not all mean the same things by these terms. The definitions given here are *stipulative*—that is, this is what we mean by these terms.

Exclusivism maintains that there is one true God, and that other truth-claims that conflict with the religion of the exclusivist are therefore false. All other positions lead to spiritual anorexia.

Universalism says (positively) all worldviews can be valid avenues of salvation and (negatively) exclusivism is wrong. Because all religions are equally true, we should toss all religious truth claims into one huge melting-pot and enjoy religious stew. The undergirding assumption of universalism is that we have no access to ultimate reality for deciding which worldview is true. We are left with diversity but no unity; particulars but no universals; relatives but no absolutes.[3]

PLURALISM DEFENDED

I was shocked when I looked closely at the newspaper. There, with saffron robe and shaved head, sat one of my old friends—in lotus position, no less. The picture and its story told of my high school classmate who had gone on to Princeton and, earning a Rhodes Scholarship, on to England for further study. There he encountered the teachings of Buddhism and became a Buddhist priest. He described himself now as a "Christian Buddhist." I would expect intense exposure to the worldview of Buddhism if he had gone to south Asia— but England?

Seventy-five percent of the world, though mostly theistic or pantheistic, is non-Christian. Hinduism claims 700 million followers (670 million are in India),[4] and there are now 180 million Buddhists worldwide. The growth of Islam in particular is significant, because Muslims are becoming more aggressive—there are currently 600 mosques in the United States. Islam is now the eighth-largest religious denomination in the U.S. (larger now than both the Episcopal Church and the Assemblies of God).[5] Today there are 900 million Muslims worldwide.[6] George Fry observes that, all things being equal, by the year 2001 Islam will be world's largest religion.[7]

3. R. C. Sproul, *Lifeviews* (Old Tappan, N.J.: Revell, 1986), p. 114. All the above positions (except universalism) affirm that at least *some* will not be saved. Universalism says that everyone will be saved; hell will be ultimately unpopulated.

4. Some of the information to follow, particularly current statistics, are taken from *SIM Now 43* (January 1989).

5. Terry Muck, "The Mosque Next Door," *Christianity Today*, 19 February 1988, p. 15.

6. The Western world, 9.9 million (1.6 percent of population); Eastern Europe, 54.1 million (13 percent); Bangladesh, 95.3 million (87 percent); Pakistan, 103.9 million (96.6 percent); India, 96.4 million (11.8 percent). (*SIM Now*, p. 5.) Approximately 75 percent of Muslims do not speak Arabic, which is the exclusive mode of their religious orthodoxy, according to Lamin Sanneh, "Pluralism and Christian Commitment," *Theology Today* 45:1 (April 1988), p. 23.

7. George Fry, "Coming to Grips with Islam," *Fides et Historia* (5 August 1987): 68.

Our global village is shrinking. Until recently, evangelizing a Muslim meant going across the ocean. Today, it means going across the driveway to have coffee with your next-door neighbor. Now more than ever, Christians need to be able to respond to the challenges of other worldviews (both religious and nonreligious). First, if Christianity is right, are all others wrong? Second, are those who do not believe in Christ, but warmly embrace another religion, bound for an eternity in hell? Third, what about the eternal destinies of those who have never had the chance even to hear of Jesus Christ?

PLURALISM DISPUTED

"Christians are religious bigots. You think you are right and everybody else is wrong!" The lady's complaint could just as easily have been directed to a Muslim. Our survey of the options among theistic and non-theistic worldviews should make it clear that worldviews are mutually exclusive; they cannot all be right. If theism is true, then naturalism and transcendentalism are false. If Christian theism is true, then Islam and Judaism are wrong, and vice versa.

Christians do *not* think they are morally better than people in other religions. Because Christianity does not teach salvation by works but salvation by grace through faith, all boasting is excluded (Rom. 3:27). The central issue for a biblical worldview, however, is what the Bible claims about salvation through Jesus Christ. Is it exclusive? The following premises make a tight case.

PREMISE A: JESUS CLAIMED TO BE THE ONLY WAY OF SALVATION

He taught the multitudes that salvation was not by works but by believing in "Him whom He [God] has sent" (John 6:22-36, especially v. 29). This salvation to eternal life is a gift from Jesus (v. 27). In John 14:6 Jesus made both positive and negative statements. Positively, He claimed to be *the* way, *the* truth, and *the* life. Jesus did not simply claim to be *a* way of access to the Father.[8] The definite article preceding each noun emphasizes uniqueness. Negatively, Jesus claimed that *no one*[9] is able to

---

8. Indeed, all Jesus needed to say to establish His point was that He was *the way*. By adding the other two terms, which emerge throughout the book as significant themes, the argument is strengthened all the more. It is noteworthy that the first name by which the early Christians designated themselves was "the way" (e.g., Acts 19:9, 23; 22:4; 24:14, 22; see also 9:2, 16:17; 18:25-26).

9. The fact that, in the Greek, *oudeis* is placed first in the sentence may indicate emphasis.

come to the Father except through Him. It is difficult to imagine a clearer or more forceful statement of uniqueness.[10]

PREMISE B: JESUS' FOLLOWERS CLAIMED
THAT HE IS THE ONLY WAY OF SALVATION

The exclusive nature of Jesus' message became an integral part of the apostles' preaching. In Acts 4:12 Peter made two negative statements to his Jewish audience: first, there is salvation in no other *person* but Jesus; second, God has made no *provision* for salvation other than through Jesus. Here (as in premise A) salvation is linked with the *name* of Jesus— specific content his listeners needed to know so that they might be saved (see v. 10). Later, when speaking to a Gentile audience (Acts 10:43), Peter anchored their thoughts to the truth of the Old Testament and pointed out that (through His *name)* everyone who believes in Jesus the Nazarene (v. 38) receives forgiveness of sins.

Paul's claims were no less pointed. When asked by a pagan jailer in a pagan culture how to receive salvation, Paul did not encourage him to "be diligent in your religion, whatever it may be," or comfort him that his sincerity had already made him acceptable before God, but rather told him to fulfill a specific condition in order to be saved: "Believe on the Lord Jesus" (Acts 16:31).

In Romans 10:9-17 the condition for salvation is confession with the mouth that "Jesus is Lord" and belief that God raised him from the dead.[11] This message is to be taken to all people: both Jew and Greek (v. 12). Again, however, those who would be saved must call on the name of the Lord Jesus (v. 13—see v. 9 where "Lord" is specified). Therefore, there is great urgency in mission (vv. 14-15) so that the word of Christ (v. 17) will be proclaimed to all peoples.[12]

PREMISE C: JESUS CLAIMED THAT
OTHER WAYS OF SALVATION ARE FALSE

In other words, Jesus was not claiming to be merely *a* way of salvation (premise A), but that all other ways were dead ends. John 3:18 indi-

---

10. The point at which Jesus stopped speaking to Nicodemus and John continued commenting (if indeed John commented at all) in John 3:18-21 is unclear. If Jesus uttered these words, we may add these verses to this premise; if the passage is John's comment, then this point fits under premise B.

11. Paul is reflecting Moses' order (quoting Deut. 30:14 in Rom. 10:8); the presence of Hebrew synonymous parallelism indicates that no distinction should be made between "confessing" and "believing" (as there is no difference between the imputed "righteousness" and "salvation" in verse 10).

12. See also Rom. 6:23; Gal. 1:8; 1 Tim. 2:5.

cates that people do not fall under the condemnation of God because they have actively rejected Christ, but because they have not accepted Him ("because he has not believed in the name of the only Son of God").

John 8 is filled with statements regarding the spiritual condition of the most religious men of the day: the Jewish leaders. In verse 19 Jesus said that because they had no relationship with Jesus, they had no relationship at all with the Father. In verse 24 Jesus applied to Himself one of the Old Testament self-designations of God, and told His audience that they would die in their sins *(not* "in their ignorance") "unless you believe that I AM." In 8:41-42 Jesus corrected the misconception of the Jewish leaders. They claimed to be children of God, and Jesus rebuked them. If God were truly their Father, He said, then they would love Jesus. Because they did not love Jesus, then they had no relationship with God the Father. Indeed, their true "father" was the devil (v. 44). The reason they did not believe in Jesus (hear the words of God) is because they were "not of God" (v. 47).

PREMISE D: JESUS' FOLLOWERS CLAIMED
THAT OTHER WAYS OF SALVATION ARE FALSE

As before (premise B), the apostles continued to claim the restrictive nature of God's plan of salvation. On the first missionary journey, Paul addressed the Jews and the Gentile converts to Judaism in the synagogue at Pisidian Antioch. He declared that the means of salvation embraced by the Jews—the keeping of the law—did not bring about forgiveness of sins (Acts 13:38-39).

When speaking to a sophisticated Gentile audience in Athens, Paul told the philosophers of the Areopagus that they must repent (Acts 17:30). Previously, they had been worshiping deity in images of "gold, or silver, or stone" (v. 29)—which Paul refered to as "ignorance" (v. 30). Although it is true that God is "not far from each of us" (v. 27), the condition of repentance must be met to avoid judgment (v. 31). The significance of this confrontation is that Paul had an ideal opportunity to express the unity of all religions as legitimate means of salvation, but instead told his audience that their religious systems did not bring salvation.

In Acts 26:17-18 Paul described to King Agrippa his commission from the mouth of God as "opening their eyes." Furthermore, those who were not Christians were described as being in darkness (not light), in the power of Satan (not God), and without forgiveness. First Corinthians 8:4-6 clearly denied that the polytheistic practices of the Corinthians led to salvation—indeed, Paul claimed that sacrifices offered to such idols were in reality offered "to demons and not to God" (10:20; 12:2; 1 Thess. 1:9). Other passages abound.

CONCLUSION: JESUS IS THE ONLY WAY OF SALVATION

The conclusion of these premises can be stated both positively and negatively: Jesus is the only way of salvation (positive); other ways of salvation are false (negative). Salvation consistently is linked with Jesus' *name, person,* and *lordship.* Jesus is both the ontological basis and the epistemological basis for salvation.

Christian mission is not to supplement, complement, or add to other faiths, but to *displace* them. We may either accept or reject what the Bible says on this point. One option we do not have is to deny that this is indeed what the Bible says.

PLURALISM DISARMED

THOSE WHO HAVE HEARD: THE QUESTION OF TRUTH

There are indeed similarities between the world religions. First, most believe in God or gods and in the unseen but real world. This is in contrast with a materialistic or naturalistic worldview. Second, most religions have an ecclesiastical hierarchy and a fellowship of faithful believers. Third, most religions have a code of ethical conduct that devotees are to follow.[13]

The point is, however, that all religions cannot be true. There are significant differences between them, which include crucial foundational issues. The nature of God, of matter, and of man are all defined differently by various religious systems. Therefore, when man confronts God, nature, and self, the worldviews that arise will be different. Is life after death a new sphere or level of personal existence, or are we simply absorbed into transcendental impersonal force? How do we come to know God? Is it through asceticism (purposely living a life of discomfort), through mysticism (meditation and focus on paradoxes), through the works of self-discipline, or by grace through faith?

What about Jesus Christ? Is Jesus an eternal being, or was He a created being? Was He truly God and truly man, or was He exclusively human? Did He die for the sins of mankind (Christianity), did He die a disillusioned and misunderstood itinerant rabbi (Judaism), or was He tak-

13. J. N. D. Anderson, "Do All Religions Lead to God?" *Radix* (May-June 1983), p. 4.

en up into heaven without dying at all—and therefore is not a Savior (Islam)?

The Problem Described

The goal of every person is to discover truth about God, not to be found in error or to be self-deceived. The question of truth, however, is not how we might *want* things to be, but how things actually *are*. Truth and sincere faith are an ideal combination. However, it is possible to have sincere faith without truth. Those who work in coal mines may have sincere faith in the struts and bankments that protect them, but if the laws of geophysics are violated, their sincerity will not save them. It does not matter how sincerely a skater believes that the ice is two feet thick; if its thickness is really only a quarter of an inch, she is going to get wet. Those who embraced Adolf Hitler's doctrine of Aryan supremacy, or those who followed Jim Jones to Guyana, were sincere in their faith but were tragically wrong. In other words, faith has no intrinsic value; one may sincerely believe that which is false. The validity of faith depends not on the *sincerity* of the *subject* (who is believing) but rather derives from the *truth* of its *object*.

Truth is absolute; if not, then nothing is true. If truth were relative, the statement "truth is relative" would itself be relative. All guarantee of meaning and communication would disappear. In both the physical and spiritual realms truth is truth, no matter how "narrow" it may be perceived to be. "Christians believe this [teaching of salvation exclusively through Jesus Christ], not because they have made it their rule, but because Jesus Christ our Lord taught it. A Christian cannot be faithful to his lord and affirm anything else. He is faced with the problem of truth."[14]

A Biblical Response

The Christian exclusivist is classified by some as a bigot. Wilfred Cantwell Smith stated bluntly, "Religious diversity poses a general human problem, because it disrupts community."[15] He would be rid of all religious teachings in which one religion takes issue with the doctrines of another. Particularly abhorrent are evangelistic religions that seek converts out of other religious systems.

It is true that belief in Jesus Christ as God's exclusive way of salvation does motivate Christians to persuade those in other religions to aban-

---

14. Paul Little, *Know Why You Believe* (Wheaton, Ill.: Victor, 1967), p. 119.
15. Wilfred Cantwell Smith, "The Christian in a Religiously Plural World" in *Christianity and Other Religions*, ed. John Hick and B. Hebblethaite (Philadelphia: Fortress, 1980), p. 94.

don their religion and embrace Christ.[16] The exclusive claim of Christianity has always been challenged from the outside. Recently, however, Christian exclusivism has been challenged from within. For example, one of this century's best-known Christian writers, C. S. Lewis, stated that those who reject Christ can be finally saved when "divine Grace has guided them to concentrate solely on the true elements in their own religion."[17] Is this a position for a consistent Christian to embrace? This question concerns thoughtful believers, for there are many morally upright people who do not believe in Jesus but choose to serve another god instead—or no god at all.

The laws of reason affirm that two mutually exclusive propositions can both be false, but cannot both be true. If I say I am a husband, a father, a teacher, and a bank robber, these are not contradictory statements; they may not be true, but they are not necessarily contradictory. For example, if I say Jesus is God and Jesus is man, these are not necessarily two contradictory statements.[18] However, consider the following propositions:

Jesus did die on the cross (Christianity).

Jesus did not die on the cross (Islam).

If I affirm both propositions (without equivocating terms), then I would be affirming that which would be contradictory. The Koran says Jesus did not die on the cross, but the Bible says He did. They cannot *both* be true.[19]

Consider two other basic Christian truths: (1) the Person of Jesus Christ, and (2) the way of salvation. The focus of Christianity includes both: the uniqueness of Jesus Christ as God's way of salvation. One may meditate on the great religious leaders of world history, but none of those claimed to be God, none of those claimed to make payment for the sins of

16. *The Encyclopedia of Religion*, s.v. "Religious Pluralism," by John Hick (New York: Macmillan, 1987), p. 331.
17. From a letter to Bede Griffiths, cited by Richard Purtill, *C. S. Lewis's Case for the Christian Faith* (New York: Harper & Row, 1981), p. 81. Although Lewis was not necessarily trying to promote this position, it is illustrated in Lewis's *The Last Battle* (New York: Macmillan, 1956), where Emeth, the virtuous soldier who has served the false god Tash (and consciously rejected Aslan), is accepted by Aslan because "all the service thou hast done to Tash, I account as service done to me" (p. 295). Lewis was not a universalist, however.
18. Indeed their harmonization is the point of the words of both Jesus (Matt. 22) and Paul (Phil. 2). To show that these were mutually exclusive concepts, I would have to demonstrate that deity and humanity cannot coexist in one person/Person. See S. Morris Engel, *With Good Reason*, 3d ed. (New York: St. Martin's, 1986), pp. 135-36, for the distinction between *contrary* and *contradictory*.
19. J. N. D. Anderson, *Christianity & Comparative Religion* (Downers Grove, Ill.: InterVarsity, 1970), p. 93.

the world, and none were resurrected.[20] Other religions may tip their hats to Jesus as a wonderful human being, but they all deny that He is God come in the flesh. If they are correct, Christianity is false; if Christianity is true, they are in error.

Furthermore, almost every religion has the ethical equivalent of the Golden Rule; but the Bible makes clear that because of sin, no one can fulfill even the Golden Rule (Rom. 3:10-23). Other religions offer means by which man earns his salvation. Biblically, the only thing man can earn is spiritual death (Rom. 6:23*a*). "In a sense, other religious systems are sets of swimming instructions for a drowning man. Christianity is a life preserver."[21] Christianity promises eternal life, provided through the work of Christ on the cross (Rom 6:23*b*; 10:9-10).

If Jesus is who He said He was, then we are bound by His words— including His claims to be the only way of salvation—not only as true, but also as authoritative for how we are to think about other religions. In spite of the humanitarian appeal of nonexclusive positions, they will not work. The absolute nature of truth will not allow all religions to be true. To believe in everything is to believe in nothing.

THOSE WHO HAVEN'T HEARD: THE QUESTION OF JUSTICE

What about those who have not heard about Jesus? Few questions are asked more often than this one. Some ask out of a motivation to be contentious, some to redirect an attempt to witness to them, but others ask because they have sensitive spirits and are concerned about how God's justice fits with God's mercy. Christians also are concerned and want to be both biblical and honest as they deal with the question of God's justice. Is salvation limited to those who live in a culture where the gospel is heard?

The Problem Described

Cultural pluralism has led to cultural and social tolerance. The Christian doctrine of exclusive salvation through Christ and eternal damnation of the lost is regarded as a maximal example of social intolerance. A pluralistic society will not tolerate intolerance. It seems grossly unfair

---

20. See Romans 1:4. For information on the defense of the historical resurrection of Jesus, see Daniel Fuller, *Easter Faith and History* (Grand Rapids: Eerdmans, 1965); Gary Habermas, *The Resurrection of Jesus: An Apologetic* (Grand Rapids: Baker, 1980); Gary Habermas and Antony G. N. Flew, *Did Jesus Rise from the Dead? The Resurrection Debate*, ed. Terry L. Miethe (San Francisco: Harper & Row, 1987); Merrill Tenney, *The Reality of the Resurrection* (New York: Harper & Row, 1963). See also Pinchas Lapide, *The Resurrection of Jesus: A Jewish Perspective* (Minneapolis: Augsburg, 1983).

21. Little, p. 121.

WHO'S RIGHT?: THE PROBLEM OF PLURALISM   169

that those with easy access to the message of Christ seem to have, in effect, "redemptive privilege" (this is a charge against all "exclusivist" religions that have content that must be believed or obeyed for salvation). As with the problem of evil, the question of God's justice in a pluralistic world results in a personal problem. It serves as a gauge of the believer's emotional comfort in God's character: His love, justice, and fairness.

Traditionally, an overwhelming evangelical consensus has affirmed Christian exclusivism.[22] However, a recent survey of evangelical college and seminary students showed that almost one-third no longer hold to the traditional view. James Davidson Hunter observes, "The existence of such a sizable minority of Evangelicals maintaining this [new] stance represents a noteworthy shift away from the historical interpretations. . . . If historical precedent is instructive, it becomes clear that these tendencies will probably escalate."[23]

For example, evangelical spokesman Clark Pinnock confidently asserts, "Of one thing we can be certain: God will not abandon in hell those who have not known and therefore have not declined His offer of grace. Though He has not told us the nature of His arrangements, we cannot doubt the existence and goodness of them."[24] According to Pinnock and a growing number of evangelicals, ignorance does not disqualify grace.

Some Biblical Responses

The Responses Described. Does the Bible offer the same clear comfort that Pinnock and others have offered? We shall describe and evaluate the following options held within Christian circles (these are regarded as more or less coherent and consistent with biblical theology). Even those who have no opinion have adopted attitudes that may fall into one of the following options:[25] "Universal Light," "Designated Light," "Existing Light," "Greater Light," and "Later Light."

1. The *"Universal Light"* View. The view, sometimes called "universalism," teaches that ultimately all men will be saved. Jesus Christ is the light that "enlightens every man" (John 1:9), and He is present *incognito* in other religions. After all, did Jesus not say that he who is not against us is for us (Luke 9:50)?

22. James Davidson Hunter, *Evangelicalism: The Coming Generation* (Chicago: U. of Chicago, 1987), p. 34.
23. Ibid., pp. 38 and 49.
24. Clark Pinnock, "Why Is Jesus the Only Way?" *Eternity*, December 1976, p. 32.
25. All taxonomies may be judged by the criterion of utility: Do they adequately and fairly portray the options? Some may be more complete than others, but the intent here is to be representative of logically possible views, whether or not they are widely held.

Universalists support their position biblically by citing texts that they say: (1) teach that the cross ensured universal salvation (2 Cor. 5:19; Col. 1:20ff.; Titus 2:11; Heb. 2:9; 1 John 2:2); (2) teach that God intends universal salvation (1 Tim. 2:4; 2 Pet. 3:9); and (3) predict universal salvation explicitly (John 12:32; Acts 3:21; Romans 5:18-19; 1 Cor. 15:22-28; Phil. 2:9-11).[26]

The idea of an everlasting hell also motivates people toward universalism.[27] Many believe that biblical descriptions of God as just and loving would be contradicted by the existence of an eternal agony of punishment; in fact, because the redeemed would know about the ongoing torment of the damned, heaven would no longer be heaven for the redeemed. Universalists who claim a biblical basis for their positions affirm that, although hell is real, hell will be *finally* unpopulated.[28]

Even though all might wish this view were correct, we are again faced with the problem of truth. Scripture describes hell as a place not of annihilation, nor of emptiness, but of eternal destruction, conscious ruin, and endless pain (Matt. 25:46; Mark 9:43-48; Luke 16:24; 2 Thess. 1:9, 2:6-9).[29] Second, Christians who are embarrassed or offended by the biblical doctrine of hell lack a biblical perspective. "The thought of eternal judgment is the reverse of embarrassing to the Bible writers; on the contrary, it is fundamental to their theodicy, their gospel, and their knowledge of God."[30] Finally, universalism "condemns Christ Himself, who warned men to flee hell at all costs, as having been either *incompetent* (ignorant that all were finally going to be saved) or *immoral* (knowing but concealing it, so as to bluff people into the kingdom through fear)."[31]

---

26. J. I. Packer, "The Way of Salvation," *Bibliotheca Sacra* (January 1973), pp. 7-8. See Packer for critiques of these points.

27. See Paul Helm, "Universalism and the Threat of Hell," *Trinity Journal* 4 (1983), pp. 35-43.

28. For a discussion of this view, see John Wenham, *The Enigma of Evil* (Grand Rapids: Zondervan, 1985), pp. 34-41, and John Stott, *Evangelical Essentials* (Downers Grove, Ill.: InterVarsity, 1989), pp. 312-31. Standard critiques of universalism do not necessarily apply to "conditional immortality." Brunner spoke of this view as based on "evasion rather than exegesis" (Emil Brunner, *Eternal Hope,* trans. Harold Knight [London: 1954], p. 183, cited by Packer, "Way of Salvation," *Bibliotheca Sacra,* p. 7n.). For a critique of conditional immortality and annihilationism see Roger Nicole, "Universalism: Will Everyone Be Saved?" *Christianity Today,* 20 March 1987, pp. 32-39.

29. Packer, "Good Pagans and God's Kingdom," *Christianity Today,* 17 January 1986, pp. 22-23. It is noteworthy that in Matthew 25:46 the exact Greek word describing the duration of *both* heaven and hell is *aionios.*

30. Packer, "Way of Salvation," *Bibliotheca Sacra,* p. 6.

31. Packer, "Good Pagans," *Christianity Today,* p. 25, italics his. Packer states elsewhere, "Now if universalism [= all faiths are ways of salvation] is true, and the founders of Christianity did not know it, their preaching stands revealed as ignorant and incompetent; and if universalism is true, and they did know it, their preaching stands revealed as bluff, frightening people in the kingdom by holding before them unreal terrors" ("Way of Salvation," p. 10).

2. The *"Designated Light"* View. This view asserts that God has designated those who will have the light of the gospel, and therefore He has also designated those who will not. The rationale looks like this:

Because God knew from eternity past who will/will not be saved, and

Because God knew from eternity past where the gospel will/will not be preached,

Conclusion: God has those people who will be saved born into circumstances (including geography) in which the designated light will be effective, and by extension those who *will not respond* are born into circumstances (including geography) in which He knows the light will not shine.

Some would say that God's motivation is *justice*. God in effect has nailed the lid on the spiritual coffin of the spiritually dead. "God's judgment *settles* all moral problems. Specifically, it addresses the question as to how God can still be powerful and just if there is evil in the world. It sees this present life as an interim period at the end of which God will publicly vindicate his character. This vindication (which cannot be *vindictive . . .*) will set truth forever on the throne and error forever on the scaffold."[32]

Others would add that God's motivation may also be *mercy*. Those who are in circumstances to be exposed to the gospel, but who reject it, are in worse shape than those who God knows will reject it but who do not specifically turn their backs on Christ. Although they are still under God's judgment, their judgment is not compounded by overt rejection of God's Son. In this sense God protects them from further judgment; He does not let the non-elect hear because of His compassion.

It is true that the Bible clearly states God's sovereignty over the affairs of men (Rom. 8:29-30; 9:6-24), including circumstances that begin from birth (Jer. 1:5; Gal. 1:15). God's intention (for at least some individuals) was in place even before they were born—before they made any rational decisions or were conditioned by any environmental circumstances. Furthermore, Jesus specifically said He would not pray for the non-elect (John 17:1-11, esp. v. 9); presumably they are irredeemable. Finally, Paul reminds the Ephesians that Christ loved and gave Himself for the *church* (Eph. 5:25).

This view leaves some questions dangling, however. It does not explain why God does let some hear the gospel who He knows will reject it.

32. David F. Wells, "Everlasting Punishment," *Christianity Today*, 20 March 1987, p. 42. Wells does not necessarily hold to the view described above.

If part of His motivation is not to compound judgment of His creatures, why let them be exposed and thus become more accountable? Would it not make more sense for the gospel to be presented only to those who would accept it? In fact, why would God allow those who He knows will reject the gospel even to be born in the first place?

3. The *"Existing Light"* View. This view suggests that those who respond positively to the light they have can be saved without further light. God's revelation in creation (Rom. 1:20) and conscience (1:19; 2:15) makes people aware that they are guilty before their Creator. No one can live up even to his own internal standard, and consequently a person may cast himself upon God's mercy without knowing upon what basis that mercy was provided. In fact, because almost all religions lack a concept of man's depravity being overcome by God's grace and mercy, the untold would be saved not *because of,* but rather *in spite of,* their own religious system.[33]

This does not mean the untold persons have "lived up to the light they have." A salvation founded on that basis would be a form of salvation by works. But proponents of the existing light view affirm that salvation is by means of grace on the basis of Christ's cross work, through faith, although the content of what is believed is a response to the light of general revelation: that I cannot save myself and need help. Thus the *form* of the gospel is there, without the *content.*

Some of the early church Fathers believed that "those who lived by the logos present in the whole world were in reality Christians if their attitude was right."[34] Similarly, since 1963, Roman Catholic teaching has affirmed that (1) Protestants, (2) those in non-Christian religions (Judaism, Hinduism, Buddhism, Islam), and (3) those who are unreached may be saved outside the visible Catholic church.[35]

Spokesmen for this view do not necessarily maintain that all people will be saved. Intensely religious people like the Pharisees were pronounced doomed by Jesus because they had faith in themselves and their own abilities to attain salvation. However, they do mean that God may sovereignly save some via His mercy, because (through circumstances

---

33. J. N. D. Anderson, *Christianity and Comparative Religion* (Downers Grove, Ill.: InterVarsity, 1970), pp. 94, 109. For salvation, he contends, not knowledge but a right attitude toward God is essential; for *assurance,* however, knowledge is essential (p. 104).

34. Clark Pinnock, "Why Is Jesus the Only Way?", p. 15.

35. See Walter M. Abbott, ed., *The Documents of Vatican II*, trans. Joseph Gallagher (New York: America Press, 1966), "The Church," ii.16; "Decree on Ecumenism," i.3; "Declaration on the Relationship of the Church to Non-Christian Religions," i.2-4.

only He can weigh) those persons have not otherwise been exposed to the gospel.

Biblical support for various parts of the existing light view comes from Scriptures such as *The New Berkeley Version* of Acts 10:35, where Peter says, "In every nation he who reveres Him and practices righteousness is acceptable to Him." Paul says much the same thing in Acts 14:17. It also comes from the analogy with Old Testament characters: Melchizedek, Jethro, Job, Abimelech, Baalam, Naaman, the sailors in Jonah's boat, Cyrus, and Nebuchadnezzar all worshiped God and were accepted by Him. We are reminded that John describes the preincarnate Word as "the true light which *enlightens every man*" (John 1:9, italics added).

The existing light view fits nicely with the idea of progressive revelation. Abraham was saved by faith, although the content of what was believed was God's promise about his offspring (Gen. 15:6). Some may object that because Abraham had no other special revelation available to him at that time, the analogy is imperfect. Apollos, however, may perhaps serve as a better example. Apollos had believed "accurately" regarding Jesus, but knew only John's baptism (Acts 18:24-26). Other revelation was available at the time, but Apollos did not know it.[36] Thus it is possible that God judges the individual not by the criterion of what revelation has been given to all of mankind up to that time, but by the criterion of what is available to the individual.[37]

A recent variation of this view has been put forth by evangelicals Evert D. Osburn[38] and John E. Sanders.[39] Osburn maintains that there is indeed redemptive hope for the untold through both general revelation and special revelation (oral tradition, dreams, visions, etc.). The analogy is drawn from the Old Testament: because many of the Old Testament redeemed did not believe directly in Jesus Christ, they fall into the same category as the untold.[40]

---

36. The analogy is imperfect because Apollos did have special revelation, but the point may still hold.

37. Further support comes from passages such as Matthew 25:34-40 where some who are redeemed do not seem to know they have served Christ. Robert H. Gundry disagrees; see "Salvation According to the Scripture: No Middle Ground," *Christianity Today*, 9 December 1977, p. 14, and William Banks, "They Are Without Excuse," *Eternity*, March 1977, p. 91.

38. Evert D. Osburn, "Those Who Have Never Heard: Have They No Hope?" *Journal of the Evangelical Theological Society* 32:3 (September 1989): 367-72.

39. John E. Sanders, "Is Belief in Christ Necessary for Salvation?" *Evangelical Quarterly* 60 (1988): 241-59.

40. For a critique of Osburn's thesis, see W. Gary Phillips, "Evangelicals and Pluralism: Current Options," *Evangelical Quarterly* (forthcoming).

Also, suggests Osburn, some may be exposed by means of oral tradition to the basic themes of incarnation and salvation by grace through faith. At Pentecost "devout men from every nation under heaven" (Acts 2:5) may have taken the idea of the gospel back to their homelands.[41]

Five objections should be mentioned.

First, if oral tradition is invoked we must remember that any oral message becomes distorted through centuries of transmission by deletions and accretions. At some point a true message that is progressively distorted becomes untrue.

Second, although the theoretical possibility of coming to faith without special revelation should be considered, Paul's point in Romans 1-3 is that no one does (and from Romans 8:7-8, that no one *can*).[42]

Third, some have objected that this view could hinder missions efforts through lack of motivation. After all, if God were going to redeem His own anyway apart from specific knowledge of Christ, why fulfill the Great Commission?

Fourth, we have more warrant for believing that God gave direct special revelation in Old Testament times—particularly early in the progress of revelation—than we have for assuming that He does so today (Deut. 34:10; Heb. 1:1-2; 2:3-4).

Finally, the passages and illustrations that are used as support do not explicitly make the point they are supposed to sustain. We must be careful when declaring that Old Testament patterns for salvation (in which content varied due to the progress of revelation) are normative for the untold today.

4. The *"Greater Light"* View. The fourth view maintains that those who respond to the light they have will be given greater light. Cornelius's devotion to the Lord and seeking after the one true God was rewarded by the sending of a missionary (Peter) to share the good news for which Cornelius had been waiting. Modern illustrations from contemporary missionaries abound, which reinforce this possibility.[43] God rewards "those who diligently seek Him" (Heb. 11:6) with the special revelation of the

41. Osburn, p. 370.
42. Millard Erickson, *Christian Theology* (Grand Rapids: Baker, 1983), 1:173. Scripture describes the salvation of both Jews and pagans as the passage from *death* to *life*, not from less light to complete light.
43. Cf. Don Richardson, *Eternity in Their Hearts*, rev. ed. (Ventura, Calif.: Regal, 1984).

gospel. God will sovereignly intervene to make the gospel available to His sheep, no matter where they are located.

The greater light view is not salvation by works, nor salvation apart from the gospel content; salvation remains the same for all men. The redeemed will have believed on the Lord Jesus Christ for their salvation.

Still, there are problems. It is difficult to fit this view with the history of modern missions, which did not begin until the eighteenth and nineteenth centuries. Does this view contend that no pagan was sincere enough to receive greater light until recent history? Second, Cornelius is not an illustration of God's sending special revelation to follow acceptance of general revelation; he was a "God-fearer" (Acts 10:2), which meant that he had believed in the God of Abraham, Isaac, and Jacob (special revelation), and was sent more special revelation. Because of the uniqueness of the Gentile situation in Acts,[44] the analogy is not exact enough to validate the conclusions that are drawn.

5. The *"Later Light"* View. This view says God will allow those who have never heard of Christ a chance to hear the gospel and respond for or against Jesus at a future point—either after death, or at the second advent. In addition, it may be that God will allow those who heard about Christ the first time in adverse circumstances another chance to respond.[45] The assumption is that because "God has not told us what His arrangements with the unevangelized are,"[46] believers are free to speculate.

Again, this view is not advocating salvation by works. God's justice requires that He must judge sin, and therefore He cannot allow those without Christ's righteousness into heaven. Yet God's mercy requires that all men have a chance to receive Christ's righteousness. Thus Peter says Christ preached to those who had already vacated this life (1 Peter 3:18-20). To what purpose? Surely it was to evoke a decision for salvation, as was the rest of His preaching.[47]

---

44. Peter was exercising the authority Christ gave him to "unlock" the gospel (Matt. 16:19) to all categories of people—to the Jews (Acts 2), to the Samaritans (Acts 8), and to the Gentiles (Acts 10, the household of Cornelius).

45. Actually, though this is popularly called a "second chance," it is more accurately a *"first chance"* in second mode of existence. For those who heard in adverse circumstances (e.g., from those whose lives or mental abilities did not commend the gospel), this would genuinely be a second chance.

46. Pinnock, "Jesus the Only Way?" *Eternity*, p. 15.

47. Ibid.

Problems with this view abound. First, 1 Peter 3:18-20 does not clearly support the conclusions drawn from it.[48] Second, certain passages imply that choices made in this life are irrevocable (Luke 19:26; John 8:21, 24). Finally, the Bible states that "after death comes judgment" (Heb. 9:27), not second chances.

The Responses Evaluated. Several biblical facts bring perspective to this problem of pluralism and exclusivism/inclusivism. First, the *basis* of man's condemnation is not that he has rejected Christ, but that he is a sinner. If the basis were simply that he had rejected Christ, then we should tell no one about Jesus, so they will not reject Him. All men are "in Adam" (Rom. 5:12-21). "People are not lost because they have not heard. They are lost because they are sinners. We die because of disease, not because of ignorance of the proper cure."[49]

Many people assume that because man is ignorant of special revelation, therefore he is innocent. Actually, man's ignorance is not absolute, but relative. Man is not ignorant of the existence and certain attributes of God the Father, nor is he unaware of his own sinful condition. In the first century, the Roman philosopher Seneca wrote, "We are all wicked; what we blame in another each will find in his own bosom."[50] Man has knowledge of external revelation in creation (Ps. 19; Rom. 1:18-25), as well as the internal revelation of both conscience (Ps. 19; Rom. 1:19; 2:15) and finite creaturehood (Eccles. 3:11).

Paul's point is that mankind has rejected both external and internal revelation (Rom. 1:18-32; 2:1; 3:9-20). Thus, even though there may be relative ignorance, it is not to be considered excusable but inexcusable ignorance.

Second, the nature of man's condemnation is a real hell. It would be easier emotionally to accept that an unsaved person would simply be annihilated (which seems rather neutral by comparison) than it is to accept that my neighbor will spend an eternity in a conscious hell, especially if he never even heard of Jesus. If it were not for the doctrine of hell

---

48. First, the text does not say Christ preached to try to get persons in hell to respond, but merely that He proclaimed/announced something to them. Second, He preached to them *while* they were imprisoned—it does not say "*then* they were imprisoned"—their judgment seems already fixed. Third, verse 20 indicates these were individuals (possibly angels) from the days of Noah's pre-Flood world, not people who had never heard, and not ones who were in environments that were unfavorable to belief. Fourth, these "spirits" were "disobedient" spirits and most likely not disobedient to general revelation alone, but also special revelation through the preaching of Noah. Fifth, the "preaching" may refer figuratively to Jesus' preaching through Noah prior to the Flood. (See R. Gundry, "Salvation According to Scripture," *Christianity Today*, p. 15.)

49. Kenneth Boa and Larry Moody, *I'm Glad You Asked* (Wheaton, Ill.: Victor, 1982), p. 147.

50. Cited by Boa and Moody, p. 152.

(anchored to the authority of the Scriptures) there would be much less concern with the problem of justice.[51]

Finally, the Bible clearly says that God does not want any to perish (2 Pet. 3:9), and that God's way of salvation is by believing in Jesus Christ (John 3:18, 5:23-24, 14:6; Acts 4:12; Rom. 1:16; 10:14). Those in non-Christian religions are described as "having no hope, and without God in the world" (Eph. 2:12).

It is important to gain a perspective on "fairness" in inequities. It is true, from our perspective, that life is not fair. But ignorance is not life's only inequity. Other inequities can be added to ignorance of the gospel. Some may have heard the gospel from a parent or a pastor who committed adultery. Others may have been told about Christ from someone whose intellectual abilities did not recommend Christianity as a faith for thoughtful people. Still others may have heard about Christ's being sent by His Father who "so loved the world," but themselves could not abide the thought of a "heavenly father" because they had been sexually abused by their earthly father. Some may have the unfortunate circumstance of being born into (or worse, having earned) great wealth, which is a hindrance from coming to Christ in self-abnegation (Matt. 19:24).

Robert Gundry has observed, "Do the suggestions of salvation through general revelation and of conversion after death in fact do the apologetical job they were intended to do? No. If we demand equal treatment for people who have never heard the Gospel, others cry out for equal treatment too. The attempt to justify God's ways cannot stop with the ignorant heathen. . . . Given the complexities, we might not be able to recognize perfect equality."[52] As finite and fallen beings we cannot evaluate all the variables that will constitute final, absolute justice.

CONCLUSION

The problem of truth must be settled from within God's Word. If the way of salvation according to the Scriptures is true, then contradictory claims of other religions are false. Scripture is clear regarding the predicament of man and the requirements for salvation.

The problem of justice is more difficult for most Christians, because our emotions are torn as we attempt to harmonize God's justice with God's love. Scripture affirms that hell is a real state of eternal, destructive punishment, and that hell is a just state in which God inflicts punishment

51. See the interesting discussion in Kathleen Boone, *The Bible Tells Them So: The Discourse of Protestant Fundamentalism* (Albany, N.Y.: State U. of New York, 1989), chapter 7.
52. Gundry, "Salvation According to Scripture," *Christianity Today*, p. 16.

178 MAKING SENSE OF YOUR WORLD

on man for sinful deeds. Scripture also indicates that there will be degrees of placement in eternity (both in heaven and in hell), according to the light we have received and our response to it.[53]

Certainly all Christians would love to be "hopeful agnostics" about any provisions God would make for people in other religions, and especially for those who have not heard of Christ. Scripture does not say, however, that God makes such provisions. Any suggestions that people can be saved apart from clear faith in Christ are not from explicit statements of Scripture, but are implicit. Wise interpretation does not jettison clear revelation for secondary, possible inferences. Packer observes, "It might be true [that God could save someone apart from their direct knowledge of Christ], as it may well have been true for at least some of the Old Testament characters. . . . But we have no warrant to expect that God will act thus in any single case where the gospel is not known or understood. Therefore our missionary obligation is not one whit diminished by our entertaining this possibility."[54] If forced to adopt a view, it is wisest to *assume* that all who are in other religions, including those who have not heard, are under God's eternal judgment. As Nicole observes, "it is dangerous to be more generous than God has revealed himself to be!"[55]

Throughout this discussion we have focused on the dark side of the way of salvation. The focus of the Bible, however, is that the gospel is *good* news—cause for joy, not cause for despair. We may rest confident in the judgment of God who is the epitome of fairness, love, wisdom, knowledge, and discernment. He alone is described as the "righteous judge." We may be assured that no one will be in hell crying out, "I wanted to be saved and would have believed, but God did not give me the chance."

We know that in a culture that embraces pluralism, the offense of the cross can only become increasingly offensive. But whereas we have limited knowledge, incomplete data, and possibly distorted perceptions of fairness, the One who will judge all men (John 5:22, 27) is the same One who loves us so much that He would rather die than live without us. He comforts us with the assurance that "my judgment is just" (John 5:30). We have confidence that "the judge of all the earth will do right" (Gen. 18:25).

---

53. Matt. 11:21-24; Mark 12:40; Luke 12:47-48; 20:47; 2 Cor. 11:15; Heb. 10:29; Rev. 20:12-15; see also Mark 14:21; Rom. 2:5; Jude 15; Rev. 22:12.
54. Packer, "Good Pagans," *Christianity Today*, p. 25.
55. Nicole, "Universalism," *Christianity Today*, p. 38.

CASE STUDY: The Quest for Truth—Islam vs. Christianity

Christianity and Islam are both historic, revealed, exclusivistic religions with claims for inerrant scriptures. There the similarities end and the many contrasts begin.

First, there is a difference in the role of the mind in Christianity and Islam. "Christianity calls for reasonable service, Islam for blind obedience."[56] Islam is a religion of the emotions more than of the mind. Second, Islam expects divine vindication of the righteous in present history, whereas Christianity and Judaism often patiently wait for the end times.[57] Third, Islam inextricably entwines politics and faith; there is an urgency for faith to dominate the government. Although Christianity has implications for politics, Jesus distinguished between the two realms (Matt. 22:21). Fourth, in Islam Allah loves only those who love him, not those who do not (Koran 3:31-32). In Christianity, God's love is unconditional and is even given to God's avowed enemies (Rom. 5:8; 1 John 4:10).[58] Fifth, Islam places the Koran in the place of central veneration; although Christians revere the Bible as God's Word, Jesus Christ alone is central. Finally, Islam insists upon Arabic language and culture to worship Allah correctly. As a missionary religion, it has been described as *nontranslatable* (a term that refers to both culture and language). Christianity, in contrast, was shown from the birth of the church at Pentecost to be translatable (Acts 2:5-11) and hence transcultural.[59]

The contrasts between the founders of the two religions are even more striking. First, Muhammad's ministry was accompanied by success (by the end of his life his armies had spread Islam extensively), Jesus' ministry was accompanied by rejection. Second, Muhammad believed that, rather than suffer, he should escape Mecca and return later to rule. Jesus chose to suffer rather than to rule (rather than be proclaimed king after feeding the five thousand, He chose the cross). Third, Muhammad used force to extend Islam among neighboring peoples, establishing the Islamic empire. Jesus refused force, but rather told Peter to sheath his sword. Fourth, Muhammad saw the rule of God as imposed by applying divine law to all aspects of life. Jesus saw the limitations of law and insisted on transformation from within.

56. Fry, "Coming to Grips with Islam," *Fides et Historia*, 69.
57. Ibid., p. 71.
58. Most of these contrasts are extracted from J. Dudley Woodberry, "The Cross Within the Crescent," *Christianity Today*, 17 June 1988, pp. 32-33.
59. Lamin Sanneh, "Pluralism and Christian Commitment," *Theology Today* (April 1988): 23-24.

CASE STUDY: *Evangelicals and the Problem of Justice*

Could Jesus be present incognito in other religions? Could those who have not heard be redeemed apart from knowledge of Christ? Historically, Christians have said no. James Davison Hunter observes that to deny this is to deny orthodoxy (historically understood).[60] Yet Hunter also observes that evangelicals in the pew are shifting away from this position in sizeable numbers, and that this shift will escalate.[61] Unfortunately, evangelical scholars are also divided.[62]

There are three models currently being adopted by those who are moving away from Christian exclusivism, traditionally understood.

The *eschatological* model takes two forms. In both alternatives the perceived problem of eternal injustice is said to be relieved somewhat. The first says there will be opportunity for salvation *post mortem*, usually based on 1 Peter 3:18-22.[63] The second form redefines the nature of damnation—it is not eternal, conscious confinement in hell, but annihilation.[64]

The *election* model argues that because God knows all possible worlds, He knows whether any particular untold person *would have* believed had he been born in Grand Rapids, Michigan, rather than a remote village in rural south Asia. God elects the individual to salvation according to His knowledge of a potential world rather than according to choices made in this actual world.

The *exception* model borrows the analogy of Old Testament believers and maintains that because those individuals were clearly redeemed without knowledge of Christ, God will make—in some cases—divine exceptions of grace. God may even combine three elements: (1) His general revelation to all men, (2) truth passed down by oral tradition from people who returned from Pentecost (Acts 2:5, 8-11), and (3) special revelation

60. Hunter, *Evangelicalism*, p. 34.
61. Ibid., p. 35-40.
62. The 1989 annual meeting of the Evangelical Theological Society in San Diego devoted both plenary and parallel sessions to this issue. There was no clear consensus. See Evert D. Osburn, "Those Who Have Never Heard: Have They No Hope?"; John Sanders, "Is Belief in Christ Necessary for Salvation?"; Clark Pinnock, "The Finality of Jesus Christ in a World of Religions," in *Christian Faith and Practice in the Modern World*, ed. Mark Noll and David Wells (Grand Rapids: Eerdmans, 1988), pp. 152-68 (endnotes 318-20); the panel discussion entitled "Evangelical Megashift," *Christianity Today*, 19 February 1990, pp. 12-17; Colin Chapman, "The Riddle of Religions," *Christianity Today*, 14 May 1990.
63. Clark Pinnock refers to this view both in his article "Why Is Jesus the Only Way?" *Eternity* (December 1976) and in his chapter "The Finality of Jesus Christ in a World of Religions," in Noll and Wells (pp. 165-66).
64. Edward Fudge, "The Final End of the Wicked," *Journal of the Evangelical Theological Society* (September 1984).

given through dreams and/or visions to teach the untold enough about the way of salvation for their redemption.[65]

DISCUSSION QUESTIONS

1. You befriend a young man from Pakistan who has just accepted Jesus as his Savior. He has received word this morning that his grandfather, a devout Muslim, has suddenly died. He asks you, "Is my grandfather in hell?" What will you say?
2. Which of the "light" views seems the *weakest* to you? Why? Which of the "light" views seems the *strongest* to you? Why?
3. Evaluate the case for Jesus Christ as the only way to God. How strong is it? Do you think a Muslim would accept your reasons?
4. Read Acts 13:14-41. Was the worldview of Paul's audience closest to naturalism, transcendentalism, or theism? How did Paul approach his audience? (What knowledge could he assume they shared? Did he challenge their worldview?, etc.)
5. Read Acts 17:16-34. Was the worldview of Paul's audience closest to naturalism, transcendentalism, or theism? How did Paul approach his audience? (What knowledge could he assume they shared? Did he challenge their worldview?, etc.)
6. Consider the various "light" views and answer this question for each one: How motivated would *you* be to evangelize if you believed in this "light" view?

FURTHER READING

Anderson, J. N. D. *Christianity and Comparative Religion.* Downers Grove, Ill.: InterVarsity, 1970.

Carmody, Denise L., and John T. *Ways to the Center: An Introduction to World Religions.* Belmont, Calif.: Wadsworth, 1989.

Hick, John. *God Has Many Names.* Philadelphia: Westminster, 1982.

————, ed. *Truth and Dialogue in World Religions: Conflicting Truth-Claims.* Philadelphia: Westminster, 1974.

---

65. From the writings of Osburn, Sanders, Pinnock and the rest it is clear that they still hold to Jesus as the *ontological* basis of salvation; they are maintaining that Jesus is not necessarily the *epistemological* basis of salvation. Only in the eschatological model must Jesus remain the epistemological basis for salvation. For analysis and critique of these views, see W. Gary Phillips, "Evangelicals and Pluralism: Current Options," *Evangelical Quarterly* (forthcoming).

Kantzer, Kenneth, ed. "Universalism: Will Everyone Be Saved?" Christianity Today Institute, in *Christianity Today*. 20 March 1987.

Livingston, James C. *Anatomy of the Sacred: An Introduction To Religion*. New York: Macmillan, 1989.

Neill, Stephen. *Christian Faith and Other Faiths*. Downers Grove, Ill.: InterVarsity, 1984.

Newbegin, Lesslie. *The Gospel in a Pluralistic Society*. Grand Rapids: Eerdmans, 1989 (published jointly with the World Council of Churches).

Packer, J. I. "The Way of Salvation." *Bibliotheca Sacra*. April-June 1972 to April-June 1973.

Tucker, Ruth. *Another Gospel*. Grand Rapids: Zondervan, 1989.

PART 2:

A VIEW FOR THE WORLD

So what?

So we believe that the Bible gives a comprehensive and credible view of life and the world. So we can understand and articulate the essentials of a biblical worldview. So we have explored other worldviews and are able to defend the biblical perspective against its detractors.

So what?

Just because we can explain the world from a biblical framework does not necessarily mean that we possess a biblical worldview. Unfortunately, merely assenting to a particular worldview does not always lead to a specific philosophy of life. Possessing a biblical worldview—*truly possessing it so that we are convinced of its truth*—compels us to action. A biblical worldview is more than a means of interpreting and explaining the world. If it is true we will be driven to conform our personal thoughts and actions, and even the world around us, to the guidelines revealed in Scripture.

The active side of a worldview comprises the second half of our definition of a worldview given in chapter one: "A worldview is, first of all, *an explanation and interpretation of the world* and second, *an application of this view to life.*" Once we have a biblical view *of* the world we can use it to forge our biblical view *for* the world.

In light of our discussion of the different worldviews, it is important to explain that the enemy of a biblical worldview is *not* primarily naturalism or transcendentalism. Rather, the number one adversary is secular thinking. The secular mindset is devoid of any orientation toward the supernatural, any conscious acknowledgment of absolute values and ideas.

David Gill locates the most devastating form of secularism.

> The real problem with ideological secularism is not with some god-less congress or faculty, but with intellectually secular (though personally, or churchly pious) *Christians!* [These are] Christians who read the Bible and pray at breakfast (good so far!) but then go to class or the office and think and work exactly in the pattern and style of the surrounding world. Secular Christianity, not secular paganism, is the great enemy of the Christian mind and the gospel.[1]

The crucial message to Christians is that a biblical worldview is more than "believing the right things." The time has come for Christians to go beyond the "profession-of-faith" mentality. We may not live what we profess, but we will certainly live what we believe. What many Christians believe seems to provide the momentum for secularization to strangle the work of the church.

Secularization begins with the individual: with Westerners who think with their wallets; with teenagers who crave new experiences; or with professing Christians who are more deists than theists. From the secular mindset of the individual comes the secularization of society. Os Guiness describes secularization as "the process through which, starting from the center and moving outward, successive sectors of society and culture have been freed from the decisive influence of religious ideas and institutions."[2]

The individual mandate of a biblical worldview is the flip side of secularization. It is also a process that must begin with myself and then penetrate every area of my life and world with the truth of God. In Part 2 we will explore the implications of a biblical worldview through successive sectors of our world. We will begin with a biblical view for the self and then follow with the family, the church, and finally, the world.

1. David Gill, *The Opening of the Christian Mind* (Downers Grove, Ill.: InterVarsity, 1989), p. 41.
2. Os Guinness, *The Gravedigger File* (Downers Grove, Ill.: InterVarsity, 1983), p. 51.

7

A VIEW FOR THE SELF

A Biblical Self-View
    The View from Below
    The View from Above
        Man's Uniqueness: God's Special Creation
        Man's Sin: Diseased, Determined, or Depraved
        Man's Redemption: God's Grace and Glory
A Biblical Response
    The Response Toward God
    The Response Toward Others
    The Response Toward Myself

A BIBLICAL SELF-VIEW

Who am I?

The question seems simple enough. I would answer, "I am John," or, "I am Mary." But upon reflection, I must admit that I am not my name. My name, be it "Bill Brown," "Gary Phillips," or "Jane Doe," is merely a label that designates me. My name is certainly not unique. Many others have the same name, but they are not me. I could change my name, yet I would still be me.

At this moment, I am looking out the window at a body of water. Every day I see this placid, meandering river, which never seems to change. But it does change. For over a century its name—the Tennessee River—has remained the same. Yet its banks, bed, and water are never identical from one moment to the next. I am much like this river. My physical body, which now is typing these words, also changes constantly. The cells of my body are engaged in a ceaseless process of renewal. My name has remained the same, but my present physical body is not the

185

same body I had seven years ago. Therefore, I cannot be my body. There must be something else that is "me."

Maybe I am my mind. Maybe my mental functions, including the memories of experiences and thoughts of the past, constitute the "real me." But I know that I cannot be *totally* my mind, because my physical body sets much of the agenda for my emotions and thinking. Illness, pain, or accident can radically change how I view myself, how I think, how I feel. On the other hand, my mind can also affect the way I feel physically. I can be mentally scarred, depressed or manic, and it influences me—the real me.[1] What if my brain is transplanted into the body of another person? Am I the same person? Does my mind accompany my brain?[2]

Now I am beginning to feel uncomfortable. My name, my body, my mind—it seems that not one of these is capable of being called "me." I have come full circle and am less knowledgeable for the trip. Who am I? What am I? Why am I?

The harder we think about who and what we are, the more confusing the quest seems to become. For this reason many do not even try to think about such matters and just get on with the rigors of daily living. After all, as Albert Camus reminds us, "We get into the habit of living before acquiring the habit of thinking."[3] It might be easy to conclude that how I think of myself must not be important.

But it is important. In fact, coming to grips with who and what we are is not optional. We all develop a "self-concept"—thoughts and feelings about ourselves as being a particular type of person. This image becomes the fundamental motivation for our choices, values, and behavior. Living up to our self-concept is the primary goal of every individual. Psychologist Prescott Leckey claimed, "Every human's central mission in life is the preservation and enhancement of his concept of himself." S. I. Hayakawa agrees: "The primary goal of a human is not self-preservation but preservation of the symbolic self."[4] Both reflect the biblical truth "As he thinks within himself, so he is" (Proverbs 23:7).

What this means is that we must think correctly about ourselves if we are to understand our place in the world. The proper application of a

1. Among the most cogent arguments for the nonidentification of the "self" with the mind or the body is given by Richard Taylor in many of his works. See for example, "How to Bury the Mind-Body Problem," *American Philosophical Quarterly* 6 (April 1969):136-43.
2. For a lively dialogue on this subject, see Derek Parfit and Godfrey Vesey, "Brain Transplants and Personal Identity: A Dialogue," in Louis P. Pojman, *Philosophy: The Quest for Truth* (Belmont, Calif.: Wadsworth, 1989), pp. 219-24.
3. Albert Camus, *The Myth of Sisyphus and Other Essays* (New York: Alfred Knopf, 1969), p. 8.
4. Quoted in Jack M. Bickham, "The Core of Characterization," *Writer's Digest* (November 1989), p. 26.

biblical worldview begins with a proper application of that view to myself and then to my relationships to the people around me. It does not matter what view of ourselves makes us feel comfortable or happy or fulfilled. Our goal must be truth. Unless we have an accurate self-concept we will be living a lie. Contemporary attempts to understand the self have unfortunately been limited to a horizontal search with no regard for God's revelation from above. The results have been a dismal commentary on man's inability to make sense of his world.

THE VIEW FROM BELOW

"I see the face of god, and I raise this god over the earth, this god whom men have sought since man came into being, this god who will grant them joy and peace and pride. This god, this one word: 'I.'"[5] Ayn Rand's statement is the thesis of her many novels and writings. The major enemy of humanity, she claims, is collectivism, or "the group": government, mores, religion. Each person must be free, totally free, from any laws or restrictions that limit the full expression of the individual self.

Ayn Rand's philosophy may seem extreme to many,[6] but she is boldly proclaiming the prevailing truth that the self has become the "god" of modern culture.[7] Psychologist Eric Johnson agrees, "The self has become the ultimate arbiter of truth and value and in fact is the ultimate value for many in our day."[8] Self-enthronement has produced a society that cherishes the individual self above everything else. Charles Colson summarizes the societal results of this chilling truth as "a new dark age." He adds, "Having elevated the individual as the measure of all things, modern men and women are guided solely by their own dark passions; they have nothing above themselves to respect or obey, no principles to live or die for. Personal advancement, personal feeling, and personal autonomy are the only shrines at which they worship."[9]

Sociologist Robert Bellah's insightful evaluation of middle class Americans reveals a pervasive and growing trend toward blatant indivi-

5. Ayn Rand, *For the New Intellectual* (New York: Random House, 1961), p. 65. The statement is made by a character in Rand's novelette, *Anthem*.
6. To see the application of Rand's philosophy, see her *The Virtue of Selfishness: A New Concept of Egoism* (New York: Signet, 1961, 1964).
7. For an analysis of the religious aspects of secular culture and the worship of the self, see Paul Vitz, *Psychology as Religion: The Cult of Self-Worship* (Grand Rapids: Eerdmans, 1977).
8. Eric L. Johnson, "Self-Esteem in the Presence of God," *Journal of Psychology and Theology* 17:3 (1989): 226.
9. Charles Colson, *Against the Night: Living in the New Dark Ages* (Ann Arbor, Mich.: Servant Books, 1989), pp. 107-8.

dualism.[10] Bellah found that most Americans place value only in the interests of individual pursuits. Some seek meaning through the attainment of money or "things" (utilitarian individualists) while others live for personal experiences or relationships (expressive individualism). In both cases, the ultimate focus is myself and "what I can get out of life."

It is understandable that naturalism and transcendentalism focus on the self. In both of these worldviews there is no point of reference beyond the individual to provide a self-concept. Meaning and purpose must be self-derived because there is no hope except within the self in a society without a personal God. Stanford psychiatrist Irvin Yalom summarizes this view, "We can try very hard to put meaning into life, but we have to devise this meaning on our own."[11] This is life that is lived only at the horizontal level.

Naturalism locates the totality of the person in the physical processes of the body. For example, physicist and Nobel laureate I. I. Rabi stated simply, "The proper study of man is science."[12] The scientific study of the human body, it is thought, will give us complete knowledge of the nature of humanity. Transcendentalism, on the other hand, views the individual personality as unnatural, almost an embarrassment to the oneness of all things. Yet transcendentalism still calls for the individual to "look within" for all the answers to life's questions because we are "god"—the ultimate self-worship. Both approaches are intensely religious and place the self in the position of the theistic God. Pop psychologist Wayne Dyer claims, "Using yourself as a guide and not needing the approval of an outside force is the most religious experience you can have."[13]

What is most disconcerting is the manner in which a large segment of professing Christianity has bought into a form of self-glorification. The self has become the criterion by which all ministries are judged. If a particular ministry does not "meet my needs" then it is rendered unspiritual, unprofitable, or at least inappropriate for me. Faith in God is seen as a means by which I have my (financial, emotional, social, or family) needs met. Loving and accepting myself have become central parts of a message that is touted as "the new reformation."[14]

10. Robert Bellah, *Habits of the Heart* (Berkeley, Calif.: U. of California, 1985).
11. Irvin D. Yalom, "Exploring Psychic Interiors," *U.S. News and World Report* 107:17 (October 30, 1989), p. 67.
12. I. I. Rabi, interview with Jeremy Bernstein, *The New Yorker*, 20 October 1975).
13. Wayne Dyer, *Your Erroneous Zones* (New York: Avon, 1976), p. 68.
14. Robert H. Schuller, *Self-Esteem: The New Reformation* (Waco, Tex.: Word, 1982).

But self-centered and self-serving approaches are destined for self-delusion and despair.[15] Scrutinizing myself will never allow me to understand myself. A scientific, sociological, or psychological study of man will provide us with a great deal of facts about man's behavior, but such an endeavor only gives us "symptoms of real humanity, not real humanity itself."[16] All attempts to understand myself at the horizontal level are empty and tortuously tend toward despair.

The Bible recognizes man's agonizing search to make sense of his life at the horizontal level. For example, Job acknowledges the difficulties present in man's attempt to understand himself (Job 14:1-6, NIV):

> Man born of woman
> is of few days and full of trouble.
> He springs up like a flower and withers away;
> like a fleeting shadow, he does not endure.
> Do you fix your eye on such a one?
> Will you bring him before you for judgment?
> Who can bring what is pure from the unpure?
> No one!
> Man's days are determined;
> you have decreed the number of his months
> and have set limits he cannot exceed.
> So look away from him and let him alone,
> till he has put in his time like a hired man.

Man's life appears meaningless and empty to the writer of Ecclesiastes (Eccl. 1:1), who moans that even hard work produces nothing significant for a man: "And this is also a grievous evil—exactly as a man is born, thus will he die. So, what is the advantage to him who toils for the wind? Throughout his life he also eats in darkness with great vexation, sickness and anger" (5:16-17). Such is life "under the sun." The horizontal search for personal identity and meaning produces only despair. Again, we need help from the outside. The Grand Artist must be allowed to explain His creation.

THE VIEW FROM ABOVE

I remember the story of a fine arts professor who eloquently described the features of a classic painting to his class. The artist was Rem-

15. For an analysis of how people form and sustain false beliefs about themselves, see David G. Myers, *The Inflated Self: Human Illusions and the Biblical Call to Hope* (New York: Seabury, 1981), pp. 43-111.
16. Karl Barth, *Church Dogmatics* (Edinburgh: T. and T. Clark, 1936), vol. 3, pt. 2, p. 200.

brandt, he explained, and this work of art poignantly revealed a great deal of Rembrandt's character: the shadows illustrated the artist's dark moods, the brush strokes his vigor for life, the colors his ideal view of humanity. At the conclusion of his moving narrative, one of the students politely noted that the painting was not by Rembrandt but by Monet. "Oh, my," the professor cried, "that changes everything!" whereupon he began a new interpretation of the work.

By itself, an artistic creation has the potential of any number of interpretations, but the true meaning of the work must begin with the artist. In fact, the more one knows the artist, the more one will understand his creations. In the same way, since God is the creator of man, our view of the self *must* begin with God. His character and revelation must guide us to the true meaning of His "works of art."

A biblical view of the self may be summarized as follows. "We are orginally good and special creatures (made in God's image); yet we are sinful and worthy of damnation; and in Christ we may become God's children."[17] We will take these three themes—creation, depravity, and redemption—as a springboard for our view for the self.

Man's Uniqueness: God's Special Creation

In light of the awesomeness of the created world, humanity seems an insignificant speck. Yet, there is an awareness that we are the special object of divine creation and concern. The psalmist lifts his eyes to God to ponder the unique place of man in creation (Psalm 8, NIV):

> When I consider your heavens,
> the work of your fingers,
> the moon and the stars,
> which you have set in place,
> what is man that you are mindful of him,
> the son of man that you care for him?
> You have made him a little lower than the heavenly beings
> and crowned him with glory and honor.
> You made him ruler over the works of your hands;
> you put everything under his feet:
> all flocks and herds,
> and the beasts of the field,
> the birds of the air,
> and the fish of the sea,
> all that swim the paths of the seas.
> O Lord, our Lord,
> how majestic is your name in all the earth!

17. Eric Johnson, "Self-Esteem," p. 228.

The Bible is clear that man is the result of a special act of God's creation. The first man was made alive by the breath of God (Gen. 2:7). There is no human life (or any life for that matter) that is apart from the free creative act of God: "In Him was life" (John 1:4). Our being is thus rooted in the purpose and will of God.

Because of this special creation, man has a unique place in God's order. This is further amplified by the truth that man is created "in God's image" (see chapter 3). Three times in the Old Testament (Gen. 1:26; 5:1; 9:6) and twice in the New Testament (1 Cor. 11:7; James 3:9) the biblical writers affirm man's inherent nature as the "image of God." What this actually means is a matter of great discussion; however, it is certain that humanity's position in creation was intended by God to be unparalleled. Theologian John Gerstner summarizes the implications of this truth, "Man is a creature superior to all other creatures in this world —and therefore having rule over them—by virtue of his ability to know and love his Creator. This ability to know (mind) and love (will) is the *imago Dei* because in so knowng and loving God, man knows and does in finite measure what God does in infinite measure.[18]

Once I understand the nature of myself as God's special work of art I must also conclude that whatever value I have as a person is derived from God's purpose for the creation. I reflect His glory and His will. Therefore, self-actualization and self-realization are wrongly directed if they are not rooted in the utter dependency of the self to God. A biblical worldview affirms the significance of the individual but denies the misdirected focus of individualism.

Man's Sin: Diseased, Determined, or Depraved?

The fact that man was created originally good and holds a special place in God's creation is marred by the reality of man's sinfulness. Regardless of one's view of humanity, the evil present in our world cannot be ignored. Even a casual observer recognizes that sin in the world is not rooted in society but in the individual heart. Albert Einstein, in a 1948 lecture, remarked, "The true problem lies in the hearts and thoughts of men. It is not a physical one. . . . What terrifies us is not the explosive force of the atomic bomb, but the power of the wickedness of the human heart."[19]

---

18. John H. Gerstner, "The Origin and Nature of Man: Imago Dei," in *Basic Christian Doctrines*, ed. Carl F. H. Henry (Grand Rapids: Baker, 1962), p. 89.

19. Quoted in *Illustrations for Biblical Preaching*, ed. Michael P. Green (Grand Rapids: Baker, 1989), pp. 102-3.

Many naturalists, of course, believe that evil behavior is a *disease*, a condition that results from physical and environmental influences. Like a cold or the mumps, "evil" is hard to cure and takes the right prescription of counseling and behavior modification to overcome.

In light of the daily incidence of crime, such a diagnosis of the sin problem is difficult to accept. For example, in April of 1989, a group of boys between the ages of fourteen and seventeen raped, beat, and stabbed a young woman who had been jogging through New York's Central Park. The boys were not members of a gang but "normal," middle-class youths. Their attitude toward the victim and their crime was disdain. Even after their arrest, one of the assailants said of the victim, "She was nothing."

The overwhelming sense of revulsion at this incident is countered by a secular mindset that blames society for infecting these boys with the desire to commit such a horrible deed. Chuck Colson quotes "experts" who analyze the boys' behavior: "Forensic psychologist Shawn Johnston explained the boys are 'damaged . . . in pain inside . . . acting out their pain on innocent victims.' As Harvard educator Alvin Poussaint put it, 'They're letting out anger. There's a lot of free-floating anger and rage among a lot of youth.' And psychologist Richard Majors summed up, 'We have to be honest. Society has not been nice to these boys.' "[20]

The "disease" explanation for this terrible crime rings hollow. Such evil acts are the responsibility of those who perpetrate them. Yet the motivation arises not from societal influences but from within. The Bible is clear that every person, *by nature*, possesses a sinful disposition:

> There is none righteous, not even one;
> There is none who understands,
> There is none who seeks for God (Rom. 3:10-11);
>
> And you were dead in your trespasses and sins, . . .
> and were by nature children of wrath (Eph. 2:1, 3);
>
> The heart is more deceitful than all else
> And is desperately sick;
> Who can understand it? (Jer. 17:9);
>
> Furthermore, the hearts of the sons of men are full
> of evil, and insanity is in their hearts throughout
> their lives. Afterwards they go to the dead (Eccl. 9:3);
>
> But the Scripture has shut up all men under sin . . . (Gal. 3:22);
>
> For all have sinned and fall short of the glory of God (Rom. 3:23).

20. Charles Colson, "You Can't Cure the Wilding Sickness," *Christianity Today*, 8 September, 1989, p. 80.

Others reject the biblical view of sin by concluding that all behavior is *determined*. Every action, from the most heinous crime to the slightest mistake, is predestined to occur. There is no free will, there is no choice. Therefore, we are not responsible for our actions no matter how despicable they may be.

The well-known atheist and attorney Clarence Darrow shared the following sentiments with the prisoners at the Cook County jail: "There is no such thing as a crime as the word is generally understood. . . . The people here can no more help being here than the people on the outside can avoid being outside. . . . There are a great many people here who have done some of these things (murder, theft, etc.) who really do not know themselves why they did them. It looked to you at the time as if you had a chance to do them or not, as you saw fit; but still, after all you had no choice."[21]

Biblically, such a deterministic view of behavior is in error. Our free will to choose our actions is not merely an illusion. God holds us accountable for our behavior (e.g., Rom. 2:6; 2 Cor. 5:10), and future judgment is based on the decisions we make in this life (John 5:22-29).

The "disease" and "determined" explanations for sin are an attempt to remove blame and guilt for a person's behavior. If this can be successfully accomplished, then an individual will sense no need to find forgiveness for sin. Anna Russell expresses this view in her humorous "Psychiatric Folksong:"

> At three I had a feeling of
> Ambivalence toward my brothers,
> And so it follows naturally,
> I poisoned all my lovers.
>
> But now I'm happy; I have learned
> The lesson this has taught;
> That everything I do that's wrong
> Is someone else's fault.[22]

Man's rebellious desire to be independent of God is rooted in the very fabric of his spiritual nature, an inheritance from the first man and woman (Gen. 3:1-7; Rom. 5:12-21). What person is there who does not harbor evil thoughts and intentions that no one ever sees? These hidden

21. Quoted in Ed L. Miller, *Questions that Matter: An Invitation to Philosophy*, 2d ed. (New York: McGraw-Hill, 1987), pp. 410-11.
22. Anna Russell quoted by O. H. Mowrer in "Sin, the Lesser of Two Evils," *American Psychologist* 15:(1960):301.

thoughts are internal evidences of man's sinfulness. Mark Twain once noted, "Every man is like the moon: he has a dark side that no one sees."

The external evidences of man's depravity are just as clear. Everywhere man's selfish exploitation of the people and things around him is even acknowledged by secularists as a reflection of "human nature." For example, the widespread looting in the Virgin Islands that occurred in the aftermath of the 1989 hurricane Hugo was seen as a "normal" human reaction. University of South Carolina psychology professor Robert Heckel agreed that the frenzied stealing was not surprising. "It's human nature to take advantage of a situation life this," he said.[23]

However, in spite of sin's pervasiveness, it is popular to deny personal depravity and its consequences. Television mogul Ted Turner boldly claimed, "Christianity is a religion for losers. I don't want anybody to die for me. I've had a few drinks and a few girlfriends, and if that's gonna put me in hell, then so be it."[24] Denying sin, giving it a different label, or limiting it to external influences do not change the destructive tendencies present in every heart. To deny that we are sinful is the ultimate self-deceit (1 John 1:8-10) because it takes away the possibility of ever truly dealing with that part of our nature which alienates us from ourselves, others, and God. Recognizing our sinfulness and accepting responsibility for it is the foundation for a truly biblical view of the self.

Man's Redemption: God's Grace and Glory

In spite of man's sin, the Scriptures are clear that God has purposed to rescue man from the consequences of his depravity. Jesus' mission was "to save His people from their sins" (Matt. 1:21); "to take away the sin of the world" (John 1:29); and "to seek and save that which was lost" (Luke 19:10). God's love and mercy directed toward man is the motivation to save (Eph. 2:4-5; Titus 3:4-5). The death of Jesus Christ is the means by which the judgment for every person's sin was accomplished. When any person responds in faith toward the offer of full forgiveness from sin, he becomes a child of God (John 1:12-13).

The need for redemption is a universal need. Whereas cultures differ in what behavior is expected, man's sinfulness remains the same. Worldviews may explain life differently, but the outworking of man's sin is evident: evil, suffering, pain, and death are shared by all men. The anxiety caused by these elements of human life is the driving force behind

---

23. Quoted by Steve Marshall, "Looting Spree: 'There's No Law and Order,'" *USA Today*, 21 September 1989, p. 5A.
24. Quoted in *World* 4:24 (November 11, 1989), p. 4.

man's quest to find peace and purpose. True salvation reverses the terrible consequences of sin.

When a person comes to Christ, he is not completely transformed; that is, there remains an element of his redemption that is yet to come. No Christian is guaranteed a preservation from sickness or suffering in this life, or deliverance from death (2 Tim. 3:12). There may be individual events of healing and deliverance (the Scriptures are full of these wonderful stories), but the reality that even the godly suffer cannot be ignored. Further, no Christian is promised total freedom from error. We see through a glass darkly in this present life (1 Cor. 13:12), and a clear vision of all reality is yet to be seen. The perfections secured by salvation are received in part in this life and more fully in the life to come.

There will come a day when all things will be made right, when truth will reign, when the final enemy, death, will be destroyed (1 Cor. 15:26). Man's future is an existence with God that stretches endlessly beyond the grave (Matt. 25:34, 46; 1 Thess. 4:17). This is the final solution to man's predicament in the world. We know our ultimate future, so we may have hope in this life.

A BIBLICAL RESPONSE

The biblical view of the self contrasts radically with the perspectives of human nature given by naturalism or transcendentalism. I am a special creation of God, intended to reflect His image. Yet, I am sinful, and naturally tend toward independence of God. God has taken the initiative to reconcile me to Himself, and when I respond to His offer of forgiveness and redemption I become His eternal child.

In light of this view of myself, how should I live? What characteristic lifestyle should accompany my biblical self-view? Let's briefly explore the implications of this view from three areas of response: toward God, toward others, and toward myself.

THE RESPONSE TOWARD GOD

When asked which of the many commandments were the most important, Jesus responded by quoting the fundamental Old Testament admonition, "Love the Lord your God with all your heart, soul, mind and strength" (Mark 12:30). From the creation of the first human, this has been God's desire for man: that he devote his entire being to love his Creator. A biblical view of the self makes the benefits of loving God clear. Our existence, self-concept, and self-esteem are not discovered within ourselves but are derived from God.

What is involved in loving God? We could list attitudes and actions such as obedience, fear, devotion, honor, and commitment. However, let us focus on two areas of personal thinking and living which may be seen to summarize the others: *knowing God* and *worshiping God*.

Knowing God

The Scriptures describe knowing God as the highest of all attainments. For example, the apostle Paul proclaimed, "But whatever things were gain to me, those have I counted as loss for the sake of Christ. More than that, I count all things to be loss in view of the surpassing value of *knowing Christ Jesus my Lord,* for whom I have suffered the loss of all things, and count them but rubbish in order that I may gain Christ, . . . *that I may know Him* (Phil. 3:7-8, 10, emphasis added).

In His prayer before His death, Jesus summarized the realization of eternal life as the knowledge of God, "This is eternal life, *that they may know Thee the only true God, and Jesus Christ whom Thou hast sent*" (John 17:3, emphasis added). The apostle Peter adds, "Seeing that His divine power has granted us everything pertaining to life and godliness, *through the knowledge of Him* who called us by His glory and excellence" (2 Pet. 1:3, italics added).

It is important to understand that the knowledge of God spoken of in the Scriptures is the reflection of an intimate, personal relationship. Such knowledge is not achieved in a momentary rush of spiritual insight or a conversion experience. We grow in our knowledge of God just as we grow in our knowledge of another person: by intimate communication over a period of time. Thus, Scripture reading and prayer are not ends in themselves but means through which we know our Lord better. The Lord does not keep track of the number of times I pray or study His word, any more than my wife maintains a record of the amount of time we spend talking. However, if communication is not a priority, the relationship suffers and the fellowship is strained.

Knowing about God is a fundamental step in knowing Him, and *doing things for the Lord* is an outgrowth of our devotion to Him, but neither can take the place of a true knowledge of Him that begins with a faith commitment and continues in a growing relationship with Him. Knowing God should be the most cherished relationship is our lives. Nothing this world offers can match the joy, peace, and excitement that comes from knowing Him. Knowing God thus becomes the goal of every person— above every measure of personal gain or glory:

Thus says the Lord, "Let not a wise man boast of his wisdom, and let not a mighty man boast of his might, let not a rich man boast of his riches; but let him who boasts boast in this, *that he understands and knows Me,* that I am the Lord who exercises lovingkindness, justice, and righteousness on earth; for I delight in these things," declares the Lord. (Jer. 9:23-24, italics added)

A practical question may be asked, How do I know that I know Him? The answer, of course, is that such assurance is based upon the character of God as revealed in the Scriptures. He desires to be known and reveals the means of knowing Him through Jesus Christ. There is also an intangible sense of assurance that comes from the Holy Spirit, "The Spirit Himself bears witness with our spirit that we are children of God" (Rom. 8:16). As we grow in our knowledge of God, our assurance and security in the relationship also grows. Further, we must not forget that "we become like what we love." The longer our affections are set on Him, the more our life will reflect the fruit of His righteousness.

Practically, a biblical self-view draws our deepest emotions upward toward God. Prayer, study, and meditation become privileges, not duties. Our lives become God-centered rather than self-centered. As C. S. Lewis summarizes it, living for the Lord "means that every single act and feeling, every experience, whether pleasant or unpleasant, must be referred to God. It means looking at everything as something that comes from Him, and always looking to Him and asking His will first, and saying, 'How would He wish me to deal with this?'"[25]

Even our leisure time becomes an ultimate concern in light of God's presence. J. I. Packer astutely reminds us, "Living becomes an awesome business when you realise that you spend every moment of your life in the sight and company of an omniscient, omnipresent Creator."[26]

Worshiping God

To love Him is to know Him; to know Him is to worship Him. A truly biblical view of the self compels man to worship (Ps. 96:8). Once we capture even a partial understanding of the true character of God, the response is a mixture of awe, fear, joy, and delight.[27] The following passage from Kenneth Grahame's *The Wind in the Willows* represents an in-

25. C. S. Lewis, "Answers to Questions on Christianity," in *God in the Dock: Essays on Theology and Ethics,* ed. Walter Hooper (Grand Rapids: Eerdmans, 1970), p. 50.
26. J. I. Packer, *Knowing God* (Downers Grove, Ill.: InterVarsity, 1983).
27. For a theological and practical exploration of worship, see Ronald Allen and Gordon Borror, *Worship: Rediscovering the Missing Jewel* (Portland, Oreg.: Multnomah, 1982).

sightful understanding of the attitude of worship. Here, Mole and Rat encounter the "august presence":

> "Rat!" he found breath to whisper, shaking. "Are you afraid?"
>
> "Afraid?" murmured the Rat, his eyes shining with unutterable love. "Afraid of Him? O, never, never! And yet—and yet—O, Mole, I am afraid!"
>
> Then the two animals, crouching to the earth, bowed their heads and did worship.[28]

Since our view of the self must be God-centered, then so must our worship. God's holiness, power, and goodness strike the chord of reverence in the hearts of His creatures. Such an attitude of veneration is an expression of the true order of things: *God,* infinite, all-powerful, and sovereign; *man,* finite, limited, and dependent.

> Ascribe to the Lord, O families of the peoples,
> Ascribe to the Lord glory and strength.
> Ascribe to the Lord the glory of His name;
> Bring an offering, and come into His courts.
> Worship the Lord in holy attire;
> Tremble before Him, all the earth.
> Say among the nations, "The Lord reigns;
> Indeed, the world is firmly established,
> it will not be moved;
> He will judge the peoples with equity."
>
> (Ps. 96:7-10)

Worship is truly a human activity. It is "that exercise of the human spirit that confronts us with the mystery and marvel of God in whose presence the most appropriate and salutary response is adoring love."[29]

The expressions of worship are both public and private. In a public sense, praise, prayer, singing, proclamation, and the ordinances are the usual demonstrations of worship. But again, the focus of these activities must be the Person of God, not the worshiper or his actions. Even at a personal level, true worship can be found. The worship of an everyday presentation of ourselves to God ("your spiritual service of worship," Rom. 12:1) is manifested in the practical application of faith and love in daily living (Rom. 12:9-21).[30]

28. Kenneth Grahame, *The Wind in the Willows* (New York: Scribner's, 1908), p. 134.
29. Ralph P. Martin, *The Worship of God* (Grand Rapids: Eerdmans, 1982), p. 29.
30. See E. Kasemann, "Worship in Everyday Life: a Note on Romans 12," in *New Testament Questions for Today* (Philadelphia: Fortress, 1969), pp. 188-95.

THE RESPONSE TOWARD OTHERS

A biblical view of the self allows us to cherish what God cherishes. Martin Buber's classic book *I and Thou*[31] points out that we can relate to others in two ways. The first is to see others in an "I-It" relationship, that is, to relate to others as we would to an object. From this perspective, each person is significant only because he plays a functional role in our lives (the "grocer," the "mailman," the "sales clerk," etc.). Tragically, society's addiction to technology depersonalizes relationships and insulates individuals from each other. Many lives revolve around personalities experienced through television, videos, radio, compact discs, or other audio-visual media. This impersonal nature of daily living is a true example of the "I-It" relationship.

The second way to relate to others is in an "I-Thou" relationship. This is the mcre biblical approach. Each person we encounter is not an "It," but a "Thou"; a separate human being with thoughts and feelings like myself; a person with a significance that is inherent in his creation in God's image.

As a result of a biblical worldview of the self, we are in a better position to respond to those around us. Since we are confident of our place in the world and relationship to God, we now can turn our hearts to those around us. Many terms are found in the Bible to describe how we should respond to others: love (1 Pet. 4:8), deference (Rom. 12:10; Col. 3:12ff.), encouragement (Rom. 15:5), service (Gal. 5:13). There are times when we must confront, rebuke, or admonish (Luke 17:3; 2 Tim. 4:2; Titus 1:13; 2:15), but even when this is necessary the focus is upon the edification of the individual (Rom. 15:1-2; Gal. 6:1; 1 Thess. 5:11).

The Christian is free to respond to others in such a kind manner because of his self-view, which adopts God's perspective on others. He is able to see others through the eyes of God and value them as He does. The Christian will thus stand against all forms of prejudice or racial discrimination.[32] He believes that all people stand equal in the sight of God regardless of position in society, ethnic background, or physical attributes (Gal. 3:28).

We are to accept others because we have been accepted by God (Rom. 15:7). We are likewise to forgive others because we have been forgiven (Eph. 4:32). Our relationship to others may be summed up in the

31. Martin Buber, *I and Thou*, trans. Ronald Gregor Smith (Edinburgh: T. & T. Clark, 1937).
32. For a good discussion of the various approaches to the issue of racism, see Douglas M. Jones, "The Biblical Offense of Racism," *Antithesis* 1:1 (Jan/Feb 1990): 32-37.

word *humility.* The humility of Jesus Christ, who condescended to become a man, is the example for us to follow (Phil. 2:5-8). Such an attitude is described by the apostle Paul, "Do nothing from selfishness or empty conceit, but with humility of mind let each of you regard one another as more important than himself; do not merely look out for your own personal interests, but also for the interests of others" (Phil. 2:3-4).

Walter Wangerin, Jr., applies this biblical perspective with these poignant words:

> Every time you meet another human being you have the opportunity. It's a chance at holiness. For you will do one of two things, then. Either you will build him up, or tear him down . . . you will create, or you will destroy. . . . There are no useless, minor meetings. There are no dead-end jobs. There are no pointless lives. Swallow your sorrows, forget your grievances and all the hurt your poor life has sustained. Turn your face to the human before you and let her, for one pure moment, shine. Think her important, and then she will suspect that she is fashioned of God.[33]

THE RESPONSE TOWARD SELF

Having a view of myself is quite a paradox. I am both the subject and object of the observation. Yet once I adequately settle on an understanding of humanity in general, I am free to see myself as a part of the great works of art created by God. Many benefits accrue to those who sees himself or herself through the eyes of God, but we will highlight two here: *purpose* and *peace*.

Purpose: A Reason to Live

The most important personal benefit of knowing who I am is knowing why I am here. All life is potentially governed by two laws: the law of survival and the law of significance.[34] At the natural level, the animals of the wild follow the first law—survival is fundamental to existence. But humanity alone is also driven by the second law—the desire to find meaning and purpose, the motivation to contribute to humanity and life. When individuals equate love with sex, vocation with salary, and value with material possessions, they become less human and more like the lower animals.

As we discussed in chapter 3, nontheistic worldviews founder on the issue of personal meaning and purpose. The naturalist, for example,

33. Walter Wangerin, Jr., *Ragman and Other Cries of Faith* (San Francisco: Harper & Row, 1984), pp. 129-30.
34. Warren Bryan Martin, *A College of Character* (San Francisco: Jossey-Bass, 1984), p. 116.

would encourage us not to think about the question of purpose, or for that matter, about any of the other ultimate questions of life. Either the answers are unknowable or they are so disturbing that they would distract us from enjoying the here and now.

But the human restlessness present in every heart drives us to seek out a reason for our existence. Austrian psychiatrist Viktor Frankl survived the Nazi death camp, Auschwitz. During the terror of his imprisonment, he was struck by the fact that many who endured the death camp were not the most hardy in physical make-up but those who had an internal reason to live. Finding a purpose for life is not an act of faith, Frankl concludes, but a fact of human existence. He goes on further, "I think the meaning of our existence is not invented by ourselves, but rather detected."[35] This meaning is clearly found in a biblical worldview. We have been made *by* God and *for* God (Col. 1:16). True life is given by God to enjoy. True meaning is derived from the reality of God's special creation of me and His never-ending oversight of my life.

Even sociological studies demonstrate that "a worldview constructed around a belief in a Being who personally cares about human life and history may have provided more meaning and direction than a perspective of the world that does not allow for involvement of a personal God."[36] This of course does not mean that a biblical worldview is correct because it gives man a reason to live, but since it does meet the human need for meaning it must be seen as a viable option even by skeptics. The old maxim is appropriate: "Christianity is not true because it works, it works because it is true."

How does God's purpose for me translate into the decisions I make in my personal life? God's explicit will is for my holiness (Rom. 12:1-2; 1 Thess. 4:3), that is, for my character and will to be conformed to His. Once I set my mind to pursue this goal, other lifetime decisions take on a revised priority. I can now see them in the light of pleasing God. I will be motivated to adopt a biblical set of values rather than those of the people around me. The better I know Him, the easier my decisions will become. The result is a spiritual sensitivity that allows the decisions I make to be guided by an understanding of God's priorities.

35. Viktor E. Frankl, *Man's Search for Meaning*, trans. Ilse Lasch (New York: Pocket Books, 1963), p. 157.
36. Carol C. Molmar and Daniel W. Stuempfig, "Effects of World View on Purpose in Life," *The Journal of Psychology* 122:4, pp. 370.

Peace: A Freedom for Living

The distress present in modern society has caused a neurosis, both individually and socially. Anxiety permeates the lives of people who seek a relief from their restlessness by an addiction to success, sensuality, or drugs. Our generation is marked by disorder and disharmony, and the result is an alienation from God, others, and even myself.

The anxiety and restlessness of this age are removed by the presence of God, the God of peace (Judg. 6:24). The idea of peace, the Hebrew *shalom*, is a major biblical theme. Peace is the goal for every person, family (Gen. 13:8), and community (1 Sam. 20:42). Strife and disorder are signs of God's absence. Ultimately, when God makes all things new in the age to come, peace will reign (Is. 9:27; Zech. 9:9-10).

Jesus promised His disciples, "Peace I leave with you, My peace I give to you; not as the world gives, do I give to you. Let not your heart be troubled nor let it be fearful. . . . These things have I spoken to you, that in Me you might have peace. In the world you have tribulation, but take courage; I have overcome the world" (John 14:27; 16:33). When we come to Christ, we are restored to peace. We have peace with ourselves (Rom. 14:17; 15:13), peace with others (Gal. 5:22; Eph. 2:14-17; 4:3), and peace with God (Rom.5:1).

The future for the believer is secure. A glorious eternal life is guaranteed for all those who love the Lord. As a result, the present takes on a new dynamic. The difficulties of this life have a new meaning. I can endure suffering and deprivation now that I have a reason to live beyond my present circumstances. I am much like the bride-to-be, whose thoughts of her wedding dominate her thinking. She has a bounce in her step and a gleam in her eye as she thinks about the future. She can endure the irritations of daily life because of that wonderful event to come. The anticipation of the wedding affects the way she spends her time and money. For the Christian, the certainty of the future should serve as a powerful motivation to live and look beyond the circumstances of this life. A positive spirit and upbeat attitude reflect a genuine grasp of God's promises.

When my self-concept is God-centered and not self-centered, I have a different perspective on how I approach life. Self-centered philosophies are tantamont to idolatry.[37] Seeking to fulfill myself, my desires, and my pleasures is a never-ending craving for more which is also idolatrous (Eph. 5:5).

There is one aspect of transcendental self-perception that is correct biblically. A preoccupation with the needs of individual expression re-

37. Paul Vitz, *Psychology as Religion*, p. 91.

sults in an alienation from ultimate reality. However, ultimate reality is not the cosmic "It" of pantheism but the personal God of the Bible. The biblical agenda is not self-fulfillment but self-denial (Luke 9:23). This in no way is an eradication of my significance as a person, but an expression of that which is truly human. We must start with God, the Creator and Former of man, if we ever hope to be more than "mere men." Johnson concludes, "As our knowledge of [God] and his infinite, transcendent value increases, we will find that our esteem of ourselves as one of his beloved ones will grow as well."[38]

Now we must expand our circle of application and turn our gaze outward. A biblical worldview sets man is his proper place in the world and gives guidance for his relationships to other "works of art" in God's creation. Our next exploration will be the biblical view for the family.

CASE STUDY: What Is a Person?

Determining the biblical perspective of the self involves more than merely answering, "Who am I?" but also, "*What* am I?" In American culture, the developing crisis over the meaning of the self in terms of "personhood" dominates public moral and legal thinking. Why is this so? The answer centers on the societal view of individual rights. In the United States, a "person" has certain rights, a non-person does not.

The question is focused on issues related to the individual human being at the beginning and the end of life. At the beginning of life, issues such as contraception, in vitro fertilization, abortion, and fetal organ harvesting raise questions as to the nature of the unborn child. Life certainly begins at conception, but when does the fertilized ovum become a "person"? If the unborn child is not a person, then the child ("it") possesses no guarantee of "life, liberty and the pursuit of happiness." Performing any medical procedures, destructive or otherwise, is acceptable as long as it does not infringe on the rights of a "person."

The same question is asked in issues related to the end of an individual's life. Active or passive euthanasia is often seen as an option for one who is declared "legally dead" or who is kept alive "by means of respirators, food tubes, etc."[39] Is the individual a "person" deserving full rights, or, because of the lack of mental and physical activity, is the indi-

---

38. Johnson, "Self-Esteem," p. 234.
39. This does not address the issue of euthanasia for the sake of alleviating pain or hastening imminent death. This is the question of (aided or unaided) suicide and does not address the issue of the "personhood" of the patient.

vidual a "non-person" who may be "treated" as the family or medical authorities see fit?

Defining personhood is a quagmire into which few dare to jump. Some practitioners take a functional approach and compose elaborate lists of requirements that an individual must perform in order to be designated a "person."[40] The most common is that a "person" possesses self-consciousness, that is, that one must be aware of his own existence.

A most important practical question to be answered in these issues is *who* will decide the nature of personhood? If doctors, lawyers, and judges continue to decide as they have, the functional approach to personhood will dominate for utilitarian reasons. The possible chilling implications project a society that guarantees life for all except the unborn, elderly, and handicapped. A view of the self from below is rarely a pretty picture.

CASE STUDY: Worldviews and Animal Rights— Are Animals People Too?

The collision of worldviews is seen clearly in the modern conflict over animal rights. Recent activists claim there is no clear distinction between humanity and animals. To assert that humans have a right to use animals for their own benefit is labeled "specie-ism," a new type of bigotry.

An interesting twist occurs from the perspective of naturalism. Scientists have been at the forefront of animal research for the purpose of discovering truth about biological processes and saving human lives. However, the proponent of a naturalistic worldview must admit that the only empirical, observable differences between animals and humanity are of degree, not kind. Since animals can reason, feel pain, and behave socially, it is reasoned, why should humans exploit them for reasons solely to benefit humanity?

Transcendentalism arrives at a similar conclusion but relies upon different assumptions. Since man and animals, along with all of reality, share in the universal divine oneness, the exploitation of animals by man is considered the height of self-centered bigotry.

The issue is not simply sparked by a split between those who are for animals and those who are against. The divisive nature of the current

40. See for example, Mary Anne Warren, "On the Moral and Legal Status of Abortion," in *Moral Dilemmas: Readings in Ethics and Social Philosophy*, ed. Richard L. Purtill (Belmont, Calif.: Wadsworth, 1985), p. 167. Her list includes, among other things, consciousness, reasoning, activity, communication, and self-awareness.

movement is, in part, the result of a worldview conflict over the nature and place of humanity in creation. But even from a theistic perspective, the issue is not settled by an appeal to mankind's special place in God's creation. The deliberations must be carried out from a God-centered perspective. The question must be asked, What is God's purpose for His creative work? Specifically, what is God's purpose for the animals, and how does mankind help fulfill that purpose? Here, the Scriptures give guidance and set the agenda.

Since, however, the three major worldview groups disagree fundamentally about the nature of humanity and the animals, the conflict will continue unabated with the only victories coming in the most persuasive court decisions.

DISCUSSION QUESTIONS

1. "The worship of the self is the new idolatry." Explain this statement. Give several examples where this is illustrated in our society. How is this emphasis seen among Christians?
2. How do you think Ayn Rand would view Communism? From the brief quotation of her thought, speculate on her attitude toward religion. Explain.
3. Why are people so hesitant to accept personal responsibility for sin? How does this affect both the message and method of evangelism?
4. Think for a moment about the atrocities committed under the Nazi regime before and during World War II. How would the various approaches to explaining personal evil (diseased, determined, depraved) interpret these events?
5. How are the phrases "knowing God" and "worshiping God" a good summary of every individual's responsibility to God? How would the concept of "loving God" relate to these two?
6. Describe how a biblical view of the self leads one to respond to: (a) the poor; (b) the mentally and physically handicapped; (c) people of different ethnic backgrounds; and (d) the rich and famous. What is at the root of partiality and bigotry?

FURTHER READING

Aeschliman, Michael D. *The Restitution of Man* (Grand Rapids: Eerdmans, 1983).

Johnson, William A. *The Search for Transcendence* (New York: Harper & Row, 1974).

Lewis, C. S. *The Abolition of Man* (New York: Macmillan, 1960).

McDonald, H. D. *The Christian View of Man* (Westchester, Ill.: Crossway, 1981).

Myers, David G. *The Inflated Self: Human Illusion and the Biblical Call to Hope* (New York: Seabury, 1981).

Niebuhr, Reinhold. *The Nature and Destiny of Man,* vol. 1 (New York: Scribner's, 1964).

Packer, James I. *Knowing God* (Downers Grove, Ill.: InterVarsity, 1973).

————. *Knowing Man* (Westchester, Ill.: Crossway, 1979).

Vitz, Paul C. *Psychology as Religion: The Cult of Self-Worship* (Grand Rapids: Eerdmans, 1977).

Wagner, Maurice E. *The Sensation of Being Somebody: Building a Biblically Adequate Self-Concept* (Grand Rapids: Zondervan, 1975).

8

A VIEW FOR THE FAMILY

Chris Whittle, creator of "Channel One," observes that once we were a nation of parents with 2.5 children; now we are a nation of children with 2.5 parents.[1] Today's family is now characterized by what some have called the three Ds—divorce, day care, and dual incomes.[2] Old family values may still be promoted—with profound changes—by the Huxtable family on "The Cosby Show." But this is still a fantasy; in very few black (or other) families is the father a doctor, the mother a lawyer, and the children at such a high level of communication that conflicts are humorously resolved within twenty-two minutes (plus commercials). Many yearn for the elusive dream of a happy home and loving family, but they no longer know what an ideal family is.

1. Chris Whittle, *Tennessee Business Roundtable*, March 7, 1990 (Nashville).
2. Kerby Anderson and Bob McEnany, *Future Tense*, a forthcoming book to be published by Thomas Nelson, Nashville.

208 MAKING SENSE OF YOUR WORLD

THE TRADITIONAL FAMILY: BACK TO THE FUTURE

Americans who long for the "traditional family" are pursuing a dream that is all but extinct. In the first place, what we have called the *traditional family* has never existed in many non-Western cultures.[3] Although one of the few cultural universals is a kinship group, family structures are as varied as the cultures they represent.

In the second place, the "traditional family" warmly remembered by many Baby Boomers, and idealized on television shows such as "Father Knows Best" and "Ozzie and Harriet," is a recent development in American history. For most of our ancestors, family life included fathers and mothers working side-by-side in an agrarian setting (the bread grower and bread maker). The children contributed significant labor to the family unit. It has been only since the Industrial Revolution of the late nineteenth century that men go to an office or factory (the bread winner), leaving their wives at home (the homemaker), while the children spend the day at school.

Will the "traditional family" that the next generation warmly remembers be exemplified by "Stepfather Knows Best" and "Ozzie and Harry"? A cover story for *Newsweek* concludes, "Our families will continue to be different in the 21st century except in one way. They will give us sustenance and love as they always have."[4] But no basis whatsoever was given for such optimism.

What is a normal family? The experts disagree, and when polls are taken, the populace disagrees. The "traditional family" has a strong hold on the American imagination, but by 1988 fewer than twenty-seven percent of the United States population fit the so-called traditional model.[5]

Former Supreme Court Justice Potter Stewart once remarked that although we may not be able to define a family, we know one when we see it. But do we? The *Oxford English Dictionary* contains twenty definitions of *family*. Legal agencies operate with different meanings, some including or excluding those who regard themselves as "family." A State of California task force defined family by function, such as providing for the physical health and safety of its members, teaching social skills, and creating a retreat from external stresses.[6] In one survey, respondents over-

---

3. Robert L. Munroe and Ruth H. Munroe, *Cross-Cultural Human Development* (Monterey, Calif.: Wadsworth, 1975), pp. 7-25.
4. Jerrold K. Footlick, "What Happened to the Family?" in *Newsweek,* special edition: "The 21st Century Family," Winter/Spring 1990, p. 20.
5. Jean Seligmann, "Variations on a Theme," in *Newsweek*, special edition, Winter/Spring 1990, p. 39.
6. Footlick, "What Happened to the Family?", p. 18.

whelmingly rejected the definition "a group of people related by blood, marriage or adoption," and chose as their definition "a group who love and care for each other." Feminist Gloria Steinem declares, "Family is content, not form."[7] The freedoms loudly proclaimed by Steinem and others carry a price tag. Much like Oscar Wilde's description of a mackerel in the moonlight: it glitters, but it stinks.

THE TRANSITIONAL FAMILY: BACKWARD FROM THE PRESENT

Today, signs of changing attitudes within the family are everywhere. Historian James Hitchcock describes the process of moral worldview erosion within a culture:

> With regard to each previously held absolute a predictable pattern is followed—first unthinkable thoughts are expressed publicly, in the media and elsewhere, justified on the ground of free speech and the need to hear "all points of view." Then certain respectable people—clergy, professors, judges, etc.—announce that such ideas must be taken seriously, even if not approved. The "rigidity" of past beliefs is scored, to the point where those who hold to traditional opinions are made to feel slightly guilty. Finally a few respectable individuals proclaim publicly their acceptance of the new idea. Within an amazingly brief period of time what had been unthinkable becomes quite thinkable, then becomes a new orthodoxy. Those who hold to the old idea are quickly placed in the position of being eccentric and in need of justification.[8]

Hitchcock is correct; those who value traditional family structures in which moral absolutes reign are now on the defensive. The staggering fact is that most of these changes have taken place within half a generation. To view these transitions and their implications more clearly, we shall focus on the family in general, on marriage, on parenting, and then consider how different worldviews regard the family.

FAMILY

Anthropologists admit that although "the family has been the seedbed of socialization in all heretofore known cultures . . . the signs are now clear that the family is atrophying."[9] Some eagerly await presiding over the funeral of the family unit.

7. "Overheard," *Newsweek*, special edition, Winter/Spring 1990, p. 11.
8. James Hitchcock, "Competing Ethical Systems," *Imprimis* 120:4 (April 1981): 5.
9. E. Adamson Hoebel and Everett L. Frost, *Cultural and Social Anthropology* (New York: McGraw-Hill, 1976), p. 417.

An alternative approach many are adopting is to redefine the family. For example, in September of 1989 the New York State Court of Appeals maintained that the term *family* "should not be rigidly restricted" to husbands and wives, but should include "domestic partners." Thus the lines marking off the family are becoming blurred, and homosexual relationships may now claim whatever legal status the *family* affords.[10] This is not a new step; the Board of Supervisors of San Francisco had already taken steps to enact such measures.[11] However, "It is one thing when that argument proceeds from the mouth of a gay-rights activist; it is quite another when the highest court of New York and the governing board of a metropolitan area put their weight behind such distortion."[12] Those who opposed the measure were labeled "bigots."

American society is confused over what "the family" actually is. This is reflected in the fact that there is less domestic stability in our society than ever before.

MARRIAGE

In my office is a cartoon that pictures a couple before a marriage counselor. He asks them incredulously, "You are monogamous, heterosexual and faithful? How long have you been practicing this alternative lifestyle?" Humorous, yes; far-fetched, no. Marriage is in serious trouble. Since 1965 the divorce rate has doubled, and demographers project that half of all first marriages made today will end in divorce. Most divorced people remarry, but six out of ten second marriages will fail.[13] The concept of commitment to a spouse simply because one is married to him/her is rare.

Furthermore, "traditional" roles, which had at least been considered acceptable, are now targets for demolition. Feminists like Vivian Gornick claim that "being a housewife is an illegitimate profession . . . the choice to serve and be protected and plan toward being a family-maker is a choice that shouldn't be. The heart of radical feminism is to change that."[14] The role of the husband and the identity of the wife are no longer clearly defined.

10. Footlick, "What Happened to the Family?", p. 18.
11. The only thing that stopped its becoming law was a petition of twenty-seven thousand names that opposed it and thus required it to be decided by referendum. It was defeated by San Francisco voters by a margin of 50.5 percent to 49.5 percent. Mayor Art Agnos said, "We are going to come back with it again and again until it succeeds." See Robert Digitals, *World*, 18 November 1989, p. 12.
12. Timothy K. Jones, "Sort of Married," *Christianity Today*, 8 September 1989, p. 14.
13. Footlick, "What Happened to the Family?", p. 16.
14. Vivian Gornick, University of Illinois, *The Daily Illini*, 25 April 1981.

PARENTING

Parenting is also in upheaval, struggling for survival in the back-wash of divorce and materialism. Of all the children born in the decade of the eighties, one third will live in a stepfamily before they leave high school. The changing values and moral standards of today's children are far more reflective of the entertainment media than they are of the moral standards their parents would prefer them to adopt. Sexual self-discipline is no longer a value among our youth. As George Will describes their philosophy, "The good life is the glandular life."[15]

Some of the upheaval may be traced to demands placed on parents outside the home. The requirements for "success" in a materialistic society come into unavoidable conflict with the demands of family life, and thus the children become "hindrances to mobility and obstacles to total self-expression."[16] Although the ideal may be *Little House on the Prairie*,[17] the reality is *Little House on the Freeway*.[18] Kerby Anderson comments, "In a culture which values narcissism over compassion, business world success over parenting, children become villains instead of precious gifts from God."[19] Some experts are now advising that "we must take them away from families and communally raise them."[20] Solutions such as leaving children in day care can generate more trauma than help and constantly plague concerned parents.

WORLDVIEWS AND THE FAMILY

Why are these changes taking place? One reason is that as we become more aware of alternative worldviews, new values challenge those of the past. Hoebel and Frost offer the common diagnosis: "With advancing civilization, kinship recedes in relative importance."[21] Some anthropologists would add that we *should* evolve out of the need for families— let family become extinct—since (with the rise in divorce and child abuse) families no longer seem to be performing their societal functions well.

15. Cited in Carl F. H. Henry, *The Christian Mindset in a Secular Society* (Portland, Oreg.: Multnomah, 1984), p. 15.
16. Kerby Anderson, "Where's Dad?" syndicated column, January 15, 1985.
17. Laura Ingalls Wilder, *Little House on the Prairie* (New York: Harper & Row, 1953).
18. Tim Kimmel, *Little House on the Freeway* (Portland, Oreg.: Multnomah, 1987).
19. Kerby Anderson, "Where's Dad?"
20. Dr. Mary Jo Bane (professor at Wellesley College), quoted by the Associated Press in the *Tulsa World*, 21 August 1977.
21. Hoebel and Frost, *Cultural and Social Anthropology*, p. 210.

We have said that a worldview is both a view *of* the world and a view *for* the world. The three major worldviews we have discussed have implications for each one's view of the family—both for marriage and for parenting.

A *naturalist* worldview says all creatures evolved and that biological mating accounts for the very existence of the family in history. Animals tend to group in "families," and mankind did the same. Eventually, humans saw that families had social value, and marriage with parenting became an institution. But the family (and the love within the family) has no *intrinsic* value for the naturalist. Because there are no absolutes, any value placed on the family is tenuous and may differ from person to person.

Further, any standards of morality are merely traditional or sociological. Because all consequences arise within this life, mankind fears herpes more than he fears hell.[22] Man's sex life is reduced to "a series of stimulating encounters with biologically differing mates, events with no moral significance or religious answerability."[23]

For example, atheistic philosopher Bertrand Russell advocated only "terrestrial" reasons (i.e., reasons deriving from this life) for marital fidelity. Therefore he saw no problem with "a few temporary extramarital affairs"[24] within a permanent marriage. He stated very clearly, "Agnostics, as such, have no distinctive views about sexual morality."[25] His wife, however, felt differently. This is the naturalist's ethical dilemma: Where are the standards for the standards? Any priority placed on the family by an individual naturalist consists in values brought to his worldview, and not in values derived from his worldview.

Unlike the naturalist worldview, a *transcendental* worldview does not have any defined view of the family that necessarily follows from its premises. It is amorphous, and thus may take whatever form is dictated either by one's culture or by the individual. The result may range from the deification of family in oriental cultures to the desertion of family in Western communes.

Because "God" in this worldview is an impersonal force, there is no reason to promote an institution that focuses on developing personality and relationships. Thus, one of the key reasons for the existence of the traditional family is aborted.

22. Henry, *Christian Mindset*, p. 15.
23. Ibid.
24. Bertrand Russell, "What Is an Agnostic?" in *Bertrand Russell On God and Religion*, ed. Al Seckel (Buffalo, N.Y.: Prometheus, 1986), p. 26.
25. Ibid., p. 80.

Moral standards are again seen as more *descriptive* of my personal preference than *prescriptive* of moral absolutes. One university student told me, "Maybe Christianity is true for you, but don't force your morality on me." This attitude is extended by anthropologists into a larger question: Because more than half the societies of the world are polygamous,[26] who is to say Christians are right about monogamy? Indeed, the only absolute is that there are no absolutes, and "every man does that which is right in his own eyes" (Judg. 21:25, KJV). And what of Christianity? It is considered a threat to self-fulfillment, according to a growing vanguard of society.

By contrast, a *theistic* view of the family derives from the character of the personal God in whose image man was made. Family is the place where children are taught spiritual truth, where values and behavior are rooted in divine commands, and where family relationships are to model divine truth. These relationships are anchored outside of man and have eternal value. The remainder of this chapter shall focus on developing a biblical view of the family.

THE TRANSFORMED FAMILY: FORWARD TO "THE BEGINNING"

Carl F. H. Henry observes that today's secular *mind*-set rests as never before upon a nonbiblical *will*-set.[27] Sadly, this is true even within Christian circles. The sins of the culture have become the sins of the church—and this is seen no more clearly than in the eroding family. Christians believe what God says, but the ethical gap between our view *of* the family and our view *for* the family is growing wider.

Our culture has absorbed symbols of traditional idealism ("Father Knows Best") and transitional idealism ("The Cosby Show"). But God's authority offers biblical realism. The biblical view of the family is rooted in the Scriptures. There Christians find both descriptions *of* God-honoring families (and those that are not) and prescriptions *for* what God wants the family to be.

A BIBLICAL VIEW OF THE FAMILY

The Divine Metaphors in the Family

It is significant that God illustrates divine relationships from the family: Christ is the *Son,* God is the *Father,* we are *born* again, and be-

26. Hoebel and Frost, *Cultural and Social Anthropology*, p. 201.
27. Henry, *Christian Mindset*, p. 19.

come *children* and *sons*, *adopted* into His family, with *inheritance* and riches at our disposal. We are *disciplined* as beloved *sons*. Other family images include Christ as the *bridegroom* and the church as the *bride* of Christ.

God structured human relationships so that the family would serve as a domestic mirror to reflect our eternal relationship with Him. Of course, our understanding of His love will be limited—we are limited beings. I may describe the heat and light of the sun by pointing to the heat and light of a candle; but the reality is infinitely superior to the illustration. Likewise, when the Bible says that God is our loving Father, we must remember that human father-love does not begin to compare with the depths of divine Father-love.

But God did not use family illustrations haphazardly. These pictures show what God intended the family to be. This becomes clear as we examine the direct biblical references to the family.

The Creative Prototype for the Family

The Creator had a blueprint in mind when He built the Christian home. The blueprint toward which Scripture turns for guidance in marriage relationships is found in the creation ordinances, in which God dealt with man as he came from His hand in a state of integrity. Both Jesus (Matt. 19:3-9; Mark 10:3-9) and Paul (Eph. 5:31) appeal to Genesis 2 as the definitive word regarding what God intended marriage to be *before* it became marred by sin.[28] We need to reexamine the blueprint and remodel our homes.

In Genesis 1:27 the fact of man's creation is given; Genesis 2:18-25 offers further detail.[29] Everything God created received His benediction (Gen. 1:4, 10, 12, 18, 21, 25, 31). The first malediction in the Bible is found in Genesis 2:18—it is *not good* that man should be alone. God had placed man in a perfect environment where he enjoyed absolute Divine communion. However, Adam was lacking because God created him to be in *two* relationships: communion with God (Eccles. 3:11) and communion with other human beings.

But not just any kind of communion with other human beings would meet man's need. Companionship is God's design, which includes both

28. See John Murray, *Principles of Conduct* (Grand Rapids: Eerdmans, 1957), pp. 27-81, for a thorough discussion.
29. K. A. Kitchen, *Ancient Orient and the Old Testament* (Downers Grove, Ill.: InterVarsity, 1966), p. 117.

comradeship and sexual partnership.[30] Adam recognized the woman as his true counterpart—bone of his bone, flesh of his flesh (Gen. 2:23).

The narrative continues, "For this cause"—that is, because of the unique oneness in a husband/wife relationship—a man shall leave his parents (marriage is exclusive) and cleave to his wife (marriage is permanent), and the two shall be "one flesh" (marriage is intimate).[31] Although not a formal definition, Genesis 2:24 offers the clearest description of marriage we have in the Bible. Husbands and wives are to be "one"— physically, emotionally, intellectually, and spiritually.

God imposed both order and priorities on human relationships. God's structure for relationships did not begin after the Fall of man but with the institution of marriage (1 Cor. 11:8-9; 1 Tim. 2:13).[32]

A BIBLICAL VIEW FOR THE FAMILY

God's Blueprint for Marriage

God placed priorities upon relationships. First, our eternal relationship is with God—apparently there will be no marriage in heaven. This does not deny the validity of marriage, or make it God's Band-Aid for loneliness in this world. More likely it reflects man's inability to invest his emotions and passions in more than one being; in heaven, this limitation will be removed and the very best of love relationships will be enhanced and multiplied by as many beings as populate heaven. In other words, the marriage relationship will not be diminished; all other relationships will be enhanced. The marriage of Christ and the church will be a reality, so the need for its prophetic picture will disappear. Even so, the basis for all horizontal relationships is our vertical, eternal relationship with God. "We love, because He first loved us" (1 John 4:19).

Second, our permanent earthly relationship is with our spouse and takes priority over all other earthly relationships. Imagine two circles touching each other at their perimeters—the level of acquaintanceship. As those two circles become more and more entwined—much like orbs in an eclipse—there is greater and greater oneness. Marriage is a covenant toward oneness, and when it is broken by divorce God is deeply offended

---

30. God's design was one of *complementarity* (man with woman) rather than one of *identity* (man with man).

31. "Flesh" is a metaphor at times for the totality of a person (Gen. 6:17). In other words, marriage is the closest companionship possible.

32. Susan T. Foh, *Women and the Word of God* (Philipsburg, N.J.: Presby. & Ref., 1979), pp. 61-69.

(Mal. 2:14-16).[33] Idolatry—the heinous Old Testament sin—is God's spiritual analogy for adultery. God's goal for marriage was, and is, that husbands and wives experience the deepest human companionship possible.

This is directly opposed to modern trends. Analysts predict that we are moving from the "Me" decade (the 80s) into the "My" decade (the 90s). Husbands are not to hold their wives back—or let their wives hold them back—from total fulfillment, even if their life goals exclude their mates. Today's creedal statements are: "I'm worth it; I've gotta be me; I'm going to grab the success I deserve!" The biblical portrait is drastically different. Our marriages should be an earthly "wedding album" that pictures the future divine union of Christ with His church.

Third, our temporary earthly relationship is with our children; one day they leave our home to establish their own marriages. One major goal for parenting is to teach children about God's blueprint for marriage so that they may build a God-honoring marriage—their own permanent earthly relationship. (All other relationships follow in decreasing priority.)

In the perfect environment of Eden, God made extensive lush provision for man and gave only one prohibition. The couple was not to eat the fruit of the tree of knowledge of good and evil. Satan approached Eve. All of God's positive provision was ignored as Satan focused upon God's single prohibition and reinterpreted God's motives for His command (Gen. 3:5). After Satan enticed her, Adam joined in the sin by partaking of the fruit of the tree under her leadership. The phrase "with her" (Gen. 3:6) carries a nuance that has implications for marital roles: Adam allowed Eve to take "headship" and lead him, which resulted in sin (1 Tim. 2:14).[34] The roles of man and woman were reversed in Adam's disobedience.

Genesis 3:16 records the result of this tragedy. Because of sin, there would now be tension between husbands and wives as they strive toward oneness. This tension was not God's punishment upon man; rather, Genesis 3:16 was God's warning of what would happen with two fallen people in a marriage relationship. In other words, The "battle of the sexes" began.

Fallen people fall short of God's ideal for oneness. Therefore, God gave guidelines to reclaim the ideal He had designed for the first couple.

33. Note that God's relationship to a husband depends at least partially upon how he treats his wife (1 Pet. 3:7).
34. Umberto Cassuto, *From Adam to Noah*, trans. Israel Abrahams (Jerusalem: Magnes, 1961), p. 148.

For the husband, the Bible offers two explicit guidelines for how he is to exercise his headship. One comes from Paul and the other from Peter.

Guidelines for Husbands

a. Love your wife. Because a wife is commanded to "submit, the symmetrical command for a husband would be, "Rule your wife." Instead, husbands are commanded to love their wives (Eph. 5:25).

Many misunderstand what love is because modern usage is vague: I love Jesus, I love my wife, I love my dog, I love mint chocolate/chocolate chip ice cream (I really do!). Fortunately, the Bible does not simply give a generic command to love; it gives guidelines for how genuine marital love is to be expressed. The divine analogy of Christ with the church (from Ephesians 5—and we will add a final point from the Song of Solomon) is descriptive of the *kind* of love husbands are to have to bring about oneness.

First, Christ's love for the church is *self-sacrificing*. Many have noticed the divine analogy: when Christ "gave Himself up" for the church (Eph. 5:25), He died for her. Thus a husband is to love his wife enough to be willing to die for her. Although this is true, we should remember that death takes one grand decision, and then the act is over. Christ also ever lives for His bride (Rom. 8:26-34; Heb. 7:25). Likewise, husbands are to "give themselves up" in daily decisions to live for their wives. A husband who says he would die for his wife should be willing to put his love into action in smaller ways as well.

Second, Christ's love for the church is *unconditional*. Although His goal is that the church should be without spot and unblemished (Eph. 5:26-27), we were not all that spiritually "attractive" when Christ died for us (Rom. 5:8, 10). Christ's unconditional love would embrace the church, whether or not she had gained weight, or had gray hair, or continued in irritating habits (if I may take a bit of license with these expressions). Husbands are to incarnate unconditional love.

The third and fourth may be taken together: Christ's love is *volitional* and *continuous*. The present imperative verb indicates that husbands are to "keep on loving" their wives. Love is an action that includes man's volition. This does not discount the emotional element of love at all; it simply suggests that decisions can govern emotions, which is an important lesson for a generation that views divorce as a form of spring cleaning. Husbands are to choose—and choose continuously—to behave in loving ways toward their wives.

Fifth and finally, the husband's love for his wife is to be *romantic* love. Romantic love is not infatuation, in which the mind is in neutral and passion reigns. Infatuation has a vision that sees in the other person what we *think* is there—but it is easily self-deceived; it is akin to being in love with love. Infatuation causes a man to forget that, while he sees his wife occasionally at her worst, he usually sees other women only at their best—whether at work or at church. In contrast, true romantic love is realistic; the mind is both in control and focused on creative ways to express love to one's spouse. The pattern for romantic behavior is partially seen in the Song of Solomon, wherein a portrait is painted of the beauty of sexual, romantic love (e.g., 5:1*b*, "Drink and imbibe deeply, O lovers!"). A survey of the Song of Solomon reveals that Solomon enhanced romantic love in three ways. First, he made the Shulamite feel *security* in her position as his chosen bride (1:5–2:2). Second, there was constant *communication* as love was expressed verbally. Third, the husband's *giving attitude* contributed to the mood of romance and desire. The wise husband will give special attention to creative ways to romance his wife.

There is still one crucial element missing from the husband's relationship to his spouse, and this is supplied by Peter.

b. Understand your wife. "Women! Nobody can understand them!" True. Nobody can exhaustively understand any other human being, regardless of gender. But Peter (who was married) supplemented Paul's command to love one's wife when he commanded husbands to "live with your wife in an understanding way" (1 Pet. 3:7). Three implications flow from this command. First, men are not to abuse their position of headship over their wife's *weaker* (submissive) role.[35] Second, akin to the command to love, this command involves a *choice* husbands make when responding to domestic circumstances. Instead of responding sharply or with sarcasm, husbands are purposefully to honor their wives ("grant her honor") in ways that encourage and build. Third, fulfilling this command involves time spent in *communication*, which is a key ingredient in developing biblical oneness. If husbands do not obey this responsibility, there will be serious consequences: their prayers may be hindered. In other words, the husband's horizontal relationship with his wife affects his vertical relationship with his Lord (see Matt. 5:22-23).

But the wife is not passive in home-building. Whether or not the husband responds to God's guidance, God has also given the wife principles she can practice to help remodel her marriage.

35. The verse continues "as with a weaker vessel, since she is a woman." It is interesting that a simile is used; she is not explicitly said to be a weaker vessel, but the husband is to grant consideration as though she were. Furthermore, whatever "weakness" may be in view is likely related to the position a wife has in submission to her husband. The entire context is dealing with submission due to position (2:12-13, 18; 3:1, 5). Because she is in a weaker position, the husband is not to abuse his role as head of the family but is to live considerately with her in all things.

Guidelines for Wives

After the Fall, God told Eve, "Your desire shall be for your husband, and he shall rule over you." This is not a description of something that will make life easier for the woman (or else it would be grossly out of place in this context of judgment). Actually her desire will be to dominate her husband; she will struggle in her role as a submissive wife. The Edenic judgment was *not* that the husband now *began* to rule; it simply indicated that headship no longer came easily for either spouse.[36] A paraphrase of the verse might be, *"Your inclination shall be to dominate your husband, but his proper role is to be your head."*[37] Therefore God gave guidelines to help wives build toward deeper intimacy with their husbands.

a. Submit to your husband. Within the context of Ephesians 5:18-33 is the command to be filled with the Spirit (v. 18). This imperative is modified by four participles that describe some ways in which Spirit-filled behavior is manifested. The fourth of these is "being subject to one another in the fear of Christ" (v. 21). Apparently the apostle was concerned lest mutual subjection be both misunderstood and/or distorted, and so he offered specific authority relationships, balanced by corresponding commands for those in a position of responsibility. The structure is as follows:

Headship	*Don't Abuse Headship*
Wives submit (5:22-24) . . .[38]	and husbands love (5:25-31)
Children obey (6:1-3) . . .	and parents do not provoke (6:4)
Slaves be obedient (6:5-8) . . .	and masters rule kindly (6:9)

It is important to note that submission is not absolute but qualified. First, the verb is not causative *(not* "husbands, make your wives submit") but reflexive: submission is a voluntary, self-imposed relationship of a wife to her husband. Second, submission is a husband/wife relationship, not necessarily a male/female relationship. Every command for wives to submit to husbands in the Bible is exclusive; they are to submit to *their own* husbands, not to other men. Third, submission is an atti-

---

36. Genesis 4:7 contains exactly the same construction as 3:16. See Cassuto, *From Adam to Noah*, p. 165-66; Foh, *Women and the Word*, pp. 68-69.

37. The paraphase expresses the nuances of three words: "desire" (in this case, a natural inclination that is not healthy), "for" (not longing for, but the direction toward which the "desire" will be aimed), and "shall rule" (the proper rule that will reestablish creation roles; not a rule that is certain but one that rightly should happen).

38. Verse 22 contains no verb but is dependent upon the preceding verse to supply the verb: "be subject."

220 MAKING SENSE OF YOUR WORLD

tude.[39] It is related in Ephesians 5:33 to "respect" for her husband. First Peter 3:4-5 describes it as a "gentle and quiet spirit," which may win an unsaved husband. We also may make a distinction between *submission* and *obedience*—ordinarily the two overlap, but at times they may not. Although there may be limits to obedience, there are no limits to submission.[40]

b. Love your husband. Surprisingly, the command to love one's husband is not given as the complement to the husband's obligation to love his wife in Ephesians 5. However, Titus 2:4 commands older women in the church to encourage the younger women "to love their husbands." This love is again an act of the will and is to be manifested in loving behavior, as she "rules" her home well. As with the husband's love, this love is to be unconditional. One husband reacted, "It's very humbling to know there is another person who knows what a rat you are, but still accepts and loves you anyway."

God's blueprint for the family does not end with the marriage relationship. Although marriage is mankind's permanent earthly relationship, our temporary earthly bond is with our children, the fruit of the marriage union.

God's Blueprint for Parenting

The challenges marriage is facing may be matched by the task Christian parents face. Christian homes are feeling the impact as the values of a biblical worldview collide with our secular culture. Two major challenges come from outside the family.

First, technology has outrun the ethics that manage the technology. This has resulted in parents having historically unprecedented choices available. Geoffrey Cowley observes, "For the first time in history, people are deciding, rather than wondering, what kind of children they will bear. . . . The whole definition of normal could well be changed. The issue becomes not the ability of the child to be happy but rather our ability to be happy with the child."[41] If today's parents are unable to meet these challenges, how can their children develop the ethical structure for the decisions they will be forced to make?

---

39. This is in contrast to those who believe submission means that the wife is intrinsically inferior to the husband. Note the implications of this line of reasoning if it were applied to the Trinity (1 Cor. 11:3).

40. If a husband tells his wife to do what is explicitly contrary to God's Word, she cannot obey him, but her attitude can still be submissive and not rebellious. Further, a submissive wife still has biblical responsibilities toward her husband, such as speaking the truth to him in love (Eph. 4), confronting him when he is in sin (Matt. 18:15), and so on.

41. Geoffrey Cowley, "Made to Order Babies," *Newsweek*, special edition, Winter/Spring 1990, p. 94.

A second external challenge comes from education: one major assumption public education makes is that there are absolutely no absolutes. Almost anything else can be taught to our children (or taught to their teachers) with public sanction. For example, Beverly Galyean is a teacher of hundreds of public school teachers (from her federally funded Los Angeles school program). She states her philosophy of education as follows: "Once we begin to see that we are all God, that we all have the attributes of God, then I think the whole purpose of human life is to reown the Godlikeness within us; the perfect love, the perfect wisdom, the perfect understanding, the perfect intelligence, and when we do that, we create back to that old, the essential oneness which is consciousness. So my whole view is very much based on that idea."[42] This is nothing more than the transcendental worldview, expressed in terms that are really quite old (see Gen. 3:5).

Other challenges face parents. Children are maturing earlier than ever physically and later than ever emotionally.[43] Secular authorities are alarmed because this difference is "evident in all areas of youthful development: sex, love, marriage, education and work."[44]

Peer influences are often blatantly anti-Christian. The Christian teen who lives in a home governed by biblical principles often finds his or her outside life continually in conflict with those home values, which produces further stress. The most common way teenagers cope with stress is to put on headphones and escape into music. However, the escape to music tends to compound the problem of teenage stress because of five major themes that dominate today's teenage music: (1) sex, (2) drugs, (3) rebellion, (4) false religion, and (5) Satan.[45]

Informed Christian parents are concerned. Carl F. H. Henry rightly observes, "Training children in the Way is a matter of parental duty. The rebellious child in your own home who on occasion is tempted to tell you to go to the eschatological unmentionable may be the most important potential leader you will ever direct into the service of Christ."[46] A child is a parent's greatest missionary enterprise. All other goals are temporal, but a child's relationship to Christ is eternal.

As Christian parents, we want our children to be redeemed, and then to think thoughts consistent with and conducive toward holy living.

---

42. Frances Adeny, "Educators Look East," *SCP Journal* (Winter 1981-82): 29, cited in Erwin Lutzer and John F. DeVries, *Satan's "Evangelistic" Strategy for This New Age* (Wheaton, Ill.: Victor, 1989), p. 137.
43. Kenneth L. Woodward, "Young Beyond Their Years," *Newsweek*, special edition, p. 55.
44. Ibid.
45. Lutzer and DeVries, *New Age*, pp. 139, 141.
46. Henry, *Christian Mindset*, p. 18.

We also desire that our children develop biblical wisdom, the Old Testament education principle that demonstrates skill in the art of living. As we attempt to move our children from dependence (upon parents) to independence (from parents), we want them to obey God when we are no longer around. Our desire is that they seek heavenly things first, and then put earthly concerns in their proper place (Matt. 6:33).

To accomplish these goals, Scripture again offers explicit and implicit responsibilities that parents owe their children and children owe their parents.

Guidelines for Parents

a. Love. Children are to be viewed by their parents not as a burden but a blessing (Psalm 127). The nurture parents give is to be gentle and tender (1 Thess. 2:7). No child should feel he or she has to earn parental love (contrast Gen. 25:28). Enacting this principle involves spending time with our children. Charles Francis Adams, nineteenth-century political figure and diplomat, kept a diary. One day he entered, ''Went fishing with my son today—a day wasted.'' His son, Brook Adams, also kept a diary that is still in existence. On the same day he made this entry: ''Went fishing with my father—the most wonderful day of my life!''[47] What the father saw as a waste the son saw as an investment. Being a loving parent takes time.

Furthermore, unconditional love will not permit favoritism of one child over another, nor will it withhold love if a child does not meet certain behavior norms or talent expectations (see Gen. 25:28). It will not treat a child's personal problems as insignificant. When an earthly father incarnates heavenly love, the child is drawn that much closer to the heavenly Father.

b. Training. Unconditional love does not, however, mean there are no expectations from the child. Jesus said, ''If you love me, you will keep my commandments.'' Parents are to train their children in the skill of living (Prov. 22:6). A father is measured for spiritual leadership in part by the godly control he exercises within his home (1 Tim. 3:4-5). Overindulgent parents can harm a child when withholding discipline that is needed to help the child mature. The tragic lives of Absalom (2 Sam. 14-18) and Adonijah (1 Kings 1) serve as negative case studies: apparently David loved his sons, but because he did not discipline them they rebelled against him and against God.

Even in discipline, however, unconditional love will attempt to distinguish between those times when a child is simply being childish (which

47. *Family Happiness Is Homemade* 11:9 (September 1987).

will be outgrown) and willful childishness (which may not be outgrown)—and will respond accordingly.

Children are to be brought up in the nurture (discipline that regulates character) and instruction (training by the Word) of the Lord (Eph. 6:4). This includes encouragement, teaching, exhortation, and discipline.[48] Much of disciplining is common sense; withholding appropriate punishment (Prov. 23:13), equivocating limits (1 Kings 1), and not clarifying expectations may produce improper behavior and insecurity in a child (Eph. 6:4; Col. 3:21).

Deuteronomy 6:6-9 offers guidelines for parental instruction. First, God's words are to be engraved on the hearts of the parents—they are steeped in Scripture and model it ("shall be on your heart," v. 6). The passage proceeds to suggest *how* parents are to teach: there should be opportunities for formal instruction ("teach them") and informal instruction ("talk of them," v. 7). Also *where* to teach and *when* to teach are suggested—at all places where opportunites are present, and at all times. Life is the laboratory in which parents are to instruct their children in wisdom.[49]

c. Modeling. The most effective lessons are more "caught than taught." This was certainly true of the disciples as they observed the priorities of Jesus. Likewise, children are more apt to observe what their parents *do* than to listen to what they *say*. While trying to comfort a young girl who had just wrecked her mother's car, I assured her that when her mother arrived, she would be more pleased that her daughter was safe than concerned about a car. However, as soon as the mother arrived, she never looked at the girl but screeched, "Look at what you did to my car!" No matter how much the mother might have protested later that she loves her daughter, the girl will not believe her, because in the moment of testing the mother did not model godly parental love or priorities.

Second Timothy suggests two deterrents to apostasy in the life of Timothy. The second one is familiar: the Scriptures (2 Tim. 3:16; "sacred writings" in v. 15), which are inspired and profitable for teaching and training (vv. 16-17). The first deterrent, however, may not be as readily noticed: the godly life of the teacher establishes the credibility of the teaching ("knowing from whom you have learned them," v. 14). Although the reference may be to Paul, it is more likely that Lois and Eu-

48. Prov. 13:24; 19:18; 20:30; 23:13-14; 29:15; 2 Thess. 2:11; Heb. 12:7.
49. One friend in the military has been posted to a location where he is separated for a year from his family. This creative man is sending back monthly video tapes of guitar lessons for his sons, and devotions for his family.

nice, the two godly women who reared Timothy, are in mind. Parents' lives must match their lips.

Guidelines for Children

By definition, children vary in their ability to understand what the Bible says. As they mature, however, they bear greater responsibility and accountability for their choices, including how they treat their parents. The Bible does not hesitate to give clear instructions, which children are expected to obey.

a. Honor. The "first commandment with a promise" was given in the Old Testament (Ex. 20:12) and repeated in the New Testament (Eph. 6:2). The Hebrew concept of "honor" includes more than just *love* for one's parents; it means to *cherish* one's parents. The Bible uses as a gauge of a decadent society whether or not parents are cherished by their children (Ex. 21:15, 17; Matt. 10:31; Rom. 1:30).

b. Learn. Second, children (when young) are to embrace the instruction of their parents; and when children are older they are to listen to their parents' wise counsel (Prov. 1:8ff.; 17:6). Our day is characterized by the worship of youth; age is considered a disease to be avoided. Yet the Bible describes the wisdom of age as a treasure to be cherished.

c. Obey. Children are told clearly to obey their parents "in the Lord, for this is right" (Eph. 6:1; Col. 3:20). Second Timothy 3:2 includes in its description of apostasy that children will be "disobedient to parents." Indeed, a child's rebellion can disqualify the father from ministry (1 Tim. 3:4-5, 12; see also 1 Sam. 3 and 8).

d. Care. As advances in medicine extend the average lifespan (and Baby Boomers age), the population demographics of the United States will change drastically. Whereas the population used to resemble a pyramid, at present it resembles a barrel. In the next decades it will resemble a hot air balloon.[50] Even "traditional" families will change: the Census Bureau says that within the next decade four generation families will be the norm. The costs for medical care for the aged are escalating, and the Social Security system is less than secure.

One passage (which is often misunderstood) specifically addresses this mandate. Children are to care for their widowed mothers. If a child does not, he or she "has denied the faith, and is worse than an unbeliever" (1 Tim. 5:3-5, 8). This biblical command may become far more rele-

---

50. In 1960, 55 percent of the population was in the workforce, and 9.3 percent was retired. By 2030, 57.4 percent will be in the workforce, yet those who are retired will number almost 21 percent. See Melinda Beck, "The Geezer Boom," *Newsweek*, special edition, Winter/Spring 1990, pp. 62-66.

vant to Christian families and to the church than it has been in recent decades.[51]

CONCLUSION

Almost forty years ago, R. Redfield was prophetic in observing that man used to be bound by the moral order, but now follows the technical order in which "men are bound by things, or are themselves things."[52] This cultural trend has escalated. Christians are to be salt and light in their society. There are few areas of personal need and pain that touch individuals as much as the family. A solid Christian family, anchored in biblical principles, can have tremendous impact as a witnessing force in the community.

As Christians face the next generation, we need to be rooted "in the beginning" with our principles firmly set. Then when our worldview collides with our culture we may faithfully say, "As for me and my house, we will serve the Lord" (Josh. 24:15).

CASE STUDY: Love and Infatuation

This chapter has suggested that romantic love is not "emotions gone out of control." It is rooted in the mind and in the will. Romantic love is not *infatuation,* in which the mind is in neutral and passion reigns. Infatuation has a vision that sees in the other person what we *think* is there—but it is easily self-deceived; infatuation is akin to being in love with love. The two approaches can be analyzed by comparing and contrasting the following examples.

The television blared away. The theme of the network special was simply "love." The host (ironically, David Nelson of "Ozzie and Harriet" fame) asked the lead singer for the visiting rock band questions about love, because the singer sang so much about it. The rock star—with tight black leather pants, no shirt, and beautiful blond hair reaching below his waist—mumbled that "love is something that just hits you."

The special guest was an elderly man considered well-qualified to speak about love and marriage. His credentials? He had been married and divorced more than any American male: an incredible seventeen times.

---

51. Many questions will have to be addressed by Christians. Will stepchildren feel the same obligation to care for their step-parents when such parents get old?

52. R. Redfield, *The Primitive World and Its Transformations* (Ithaca, N.Y.: Cornell U., 1953), p. 21.

In response to Nelson's questions he said, "Love can't be defined. It just comes over you. But when it does, you always know it!" In other words, love is exclusively *feelings*.

Consider another perspective, which comes from Charles Williams and G. K. Chesterton, summarized by Rodney Clapp:

> Romantic love is not above abuse. Anything experienced by imperfect creatures is bound to be flawed in the process. [Williams] saw three principal misperceptions: (1) the assumption that romantic love lasts forever, when in fact it nearly always passes with time; (2) the assumption that the glory we now behold only in particular persons does not reside in all; and (3) the assumption that romantic love is sufficient in itself, while God and God alone is. Williams did not approve a romantic love unchecked by the intellect. . . . Once romantic love occurs, it "desires and demands the full exercise of the intellect for its exploration."
>
> It is indisputably wise, when we fall in love, to back off occasionally and ask sober questions—perhaps in consultation with a friend or pastor. Romantic love can be immature or sick, just as some parents develop a sick love for their children and "smother" them with affection. Rationally examining our feelings and drives can help us determine if they are part of a deep and true romantic love, or something such as masochism or worse. . . .
>
> Chesterton considered the wonder of one woman enough for a single lifetime. "Keeping to one woman is a small price to pay for so much as seeing one woman," he said. "To complain that I could only be married once was like complaining that I had only been born once. It was incommensurate with the terrible excitement of which one was talking. It showed, not an exaggerated sensibility to sex, but a curious insensibility to it."[53]

CASE STUDY: *Challenges for the Changing Family*

The dream of a generation ago was captured in the ditty "First comes love, then comes marriage, then comes Martha with the baby carriage." For some, the dream has become a nightmare. Bill and Martha divorced, with Martha taking custody of their three children. Bill began a homosexual relationship with Jim, and the couple adopted a son who now calls his "parents" Daddy and Poppa.

Martha met Eric (who had children by a former marriage) and they married, which gave her three children a stepbrother, a stepsister, a step-

53. Rodney Clapp, "What Hollywood Doesn't Know About Romantic Love," *Christianity Today*, 3 February 1984, pp. 31, 32.

father, two sets of "step-grandparents," plus the prevous relatives on their father's side.

Eric and Martha desired children, and when they were unable to have them they decided to have Martha impregnated by artificial insemination. While Martha was pregnant, tests showed that the baby had Huntington's disease which, although always fatal, is usually dormant until after age forty. Eric and Martha must decide whether *some* life is better than *none*. If they keep the baby (who will be the only one without a step-parent), at age eighteen he will be able legally to have the identity of his "real" father—the one who donated the sperm, that is.

Babies can be born through a surrogate mother, an embryo transfer, or from an artificial womb. Lesbian and homosexual couples may now legally adopt children. The traditional definitions of "Daddy" and "Mommy" no longer describe many who rear children.

DISCUSSION QUESTIONS

1. Describe the changes in society that you can pick out in your own town. How have these changes affected your family?
2. Discuss: Does the Bible give more good examples or bad examples of godly families within its pages? Why do you think this is so?
3. Discuss how the Christian family can be used as an example of "salt and light" (Matthew 5:16) in your community.
4. Turn to 1 Corinthians 13 and list at least five things or actions love will do. Give an illustration for each of the five: (1) in a husband/wife relationship, and (2) in a child/parent relationship.
5. Where is the earliest place in the Bible that we find God's blueprint for family living? How do you explain biblical examples of polygamy and divorce in light of God's blueprint?
6. For a family project, get a copy of today's newspaper. Have your family scan it for every article that affects (directly or indirectly) God's blueprint for the family. Discuss whether or not any teachings of the Bible apply to the articles, and then pray together about what you can do to keep your family strong.

FURTHER READING

Adams, Jay E. *Christian Living in the Home*. Phillipsburg, N.J.: Presby. & Ref., 1972.

————. *Marriage, Divorce, and Remarriage in the Bible*. Grand Rapids: Baker, 1980.

Crabb, Larry. *The Marriage Builder*. Grand Rapids: Zondervan, 1982.

Hurley, James. *Man and Woman in Biblical Perspective*. Grand Rapids: Zondervan, 1981.

Kesler, Jay; Ronald A. Beers; and LaVonne Neff, eds. *Parents & Children*. Wheaton, Ill.: Victor, 1986.

Kesler, Jay, and Ronald A. Beers, eds. *Parents & Teenagers*. Wheaton, Ill.: Victor, 1984.

Mason, Mike. *The Mystery of Marriage*. Portland, Oreg.: Multnomah, 1985.

Newsweek, special edition. "The 21st Century Family." Winter/Spring 1990.

————. "The New Teens—What Makes Them Different." Summer/Fall 1990.

Petersen, J. Allan. *The Myth of the Greener Grass*. Wheaton, Ill.: Tyndale House, 1983.

9

A VIEW FOR THE CHURCH

Christians are related to a Person, but also to a People. The Bible knows nothing of "private" religion; "no one can be reconciled to God without being reconciled to the people of God among whom his experience of God's grace immediately sets him."[1] Unfortunately, while individual Christians may be respected for their faithfulness and moral integrity (such as Billy Graham or Mother Theresa), few people have the same high regard for the Body of Christ. Often people object that "the church is full of hypocrites," which allows the critic to commit the fallacy of generalization (what may be true of some of the parts is true of the whole) and dismiss Christianity altogether.

The public no longer ascribes credibility to the church. Further, as the sins of the culture become the sins of the church, the credibility gap

1. Bruce Milne, *Know the Truth* (Downers Grove, Ill.: InterVarsity, 1982), pp. 209-10.

widens. The church is no longer a place of integrity in the eyes of the non-Christian world. Financial "huckstering" has long been a target for late-night comedians. The televangelist scandals of the late 1980s and continuing media stereotypes of Christian preachers have eroded the confidence of many. Young Christians are disillusioned. Many people wonder if the church hinders more than it helps.

What has happened to the church today? Are its message and its goals out of touch with our technological society? Is the church no longer necessary? Before we answer these questions, we must ask how modern culture has touched the lives of the people who make up the church.

THE CHURCH IN A CHANGING WORLD: A VIEW OF THE PRESENT

THE PULPIT AND THE PEW: CHANGES

It is axiomatic that cultures undergo change. In a broad sense, theology is application of the truth of God's Word to the culture in which it is ministered. Ideally, Christians adjust, adapt, and apply biblical truth in light of these changes. When a culture becomes increasingly secular, the task is more difficult. In today's moral and social turmoil, the church has functioned less like an anchor giving stability and strength in the midst of a hurricane, and more like a spider spinning a web on the hands of a clock. Although the church cannot change its message or its goals, three specific areas of change illustrate how the church must adapt its strategy to minister to a new culture.

First, the *sphere of ministry* has changed. We no longer live in a monolithic society with a single ethical system; today's culture is pluralistic, both in morality and religion. "In God We Trust" symbolized the faith of a former generation, but now is simply a slogan. Scientific explanations account for things that had been viewed as evidence of the supernatural. Through technology man is now able to solve many of his own problems that once were matters of faith and prayer; the tendency is to rely on immediate solutions for all our concerns. Today if a woman is barren she takes a fertility pill instead of praying. Others search for chemical imbalance as an explanation for sinful behavior. As a result, there is an inclination to put trust in the visible, the here and now.[2]

Second, the *person in the pew* has changed. The attitudes of our cultural environment have affected the individuals within the church. One

2. Fertility treatments can produce results, and chemical imbalances do occur. The focus here is on an encroaching mindset. See Millard Erickson, *Christian Theology* (Grand Rapids: Baker, 1985), p. 899.

anthropologist sermonizes, "The price of man's development of technology, of the standardization of the pattern of living, and of the drive to economic equality among men has been very high. The accelerated pace, the rise of cynicism, the worship of conformity, the commercialization of happiness, and the awesome horror of new weapons of war are some of the shadows cast by civilization in the twentieth century."[3] Individuals in the pew find themselves in the backwash of many cultural trends.

These trends have caused many to reexamine both the authority and the relevance of traditional church teachings. In past generations, churchgoers were caught up in the same (sometimes irrelevant) theological debates hammered out in seminaries (limited atonement, God's sovereignty and man's free will, tongues, etc); today, many are wondering why Stephanie cannot be the pastor of a church. Still others ask what is so wrong with the New Age movement, or if homosexuality (or simply its abuse) is a sin. Taking firm and unmovable positions on any issue is considered bigotry by our culture (in which intolerance is not tolerated), and this makes many Christians uncomfortable.

Some trends are beyond the control of most church members. There is simply less time today to devote to activities outside the home. In 1973 the average American had 26.2 hours per week of leisure time; by 1988 this had dropped to 16.6 hours per week.[4] People are understandably less willing to become involved in church programs that require much time. For many, church is now a place to "come to" rather than a vital worshiping community.

As we saw in chapter 8, the "traditional" family is not the "normative" family. The church is no longer filled with two-parent homes. Now singles, re-singles, and particularly single parents and working women, all of whom have unique needs, fill the pews.

Finally, the *nature of pastoring* has changed. First and foremost, the credibility gap between what the pastor says and how he lives is increasingly suspect. The clergy no longer command respect for the integrity of their position.

Other changes affect pastoral effectiveness. Preaching used to be more didactic; today it must be conversational, relational, and include self-disclosure. The pastor used to "shepherd"; now strategic planning is

---

3. Walter A. Fairservis, in Foreword to Raymond Firth, *Human Types: An Introduction to Social Anthropology* (New York: Mentor, 1958), p. 1.
4. Steven McKinley, "Caring for the Cocooned," *Leadership* (Winter 1990), p. 28.

central to many ministries.[5] Pastoral counseling used to be isolated to crisis circumstances within a family; today many pastors could become full-time counselors.

Jim Petersen identifies three forces in society that have greatly impacted the life of the church: relativism ("there are no absolutes, of truth or of morals"), privatization ("what I do is my own business"), and individualism ("the center of my fulfillment is *me*").[6] The task of the church, on the other hand, is grounded in God's absolute truth, is corporate, and is God-centered.

What should be the priorities of a church that strives to minister in and to a changing world? Different answers have been suggested, depending upon the worldview of the respondent.

THE CHURCH AND WORLDVIEWS

For a *naturalist* the Christian church is, at best, a group of people who may do helpful social work but who delude themselves, and then encourage each other in their corporate delusion that they have a personal relationship with a Supreme Being.

At worst, some naturalists consider the church a threat because of its biblical roots and values. One credo of naturalism, the *Humanist Manifesto II*, proclaims, "Humans are responsible for what we are or will become. No deity will save us; we must save ourselves."[7] In this view the church is a negative and distracting influence which retards man's social and moral evolution. Paul Kurtz and Edwin H. Wilson assert that "traditional theism, especially faith in the prayer-hearing God, assumed to love and care for persons, to hear and understand their prayers, and to be able to do something about them, is an unproved and outmoded faith. Salvationism, based on mere affirmations, still appears as harmful, diverting people with false hopes of heaven and hereafter. Reasonable minds look to other means for survival."[8]

For a *transcendentalist* also, the church serves at best a horizontal function. Any ideology that promotes cosmic oneness may be stirred into the spiritual melting-pot with other religions. Because transcendentalism

---

5. David Fisher, "A New Context in Ministry," *Leadership* (Winter 1990), pp. 24-25. Further contrasts are available in Lyle Schaller, "The Changing Caregiver," *Leadership* (Winter 1990), pp. 26-28.

6. Jim Petersen, "The Eclipse of the Gospel," *Discipleship Journal* 55 (1990):12.

7. *Humanist Manifesto II* (Buffalo: Prometheus, 1973), p. 16. See also *Case Study: Hypocrites in the Church*, at the end of this chapter.

8. Paul Kurtz and Edwin H. Wilson, Preface to *Humanist Manifesto II* (Buffalo, N.Y.: Prometheus, 1973), p. 13.

maintains that there are no absolutes and truth is relative, then everything that divides, such as a religion which affirms absolutes and seeks to maintain doctrinal purity, is to be jettisoned. Thus the biblical church is regarded as an enemy of transcendentalism.

A *theist* who believes God has revealed Himself in the Bible and has given guidelines for corporate life as well as individual life regards the church as the agent through which five crucial needs are met: the function of worship (upward), the functions of nurture and edification (inward), and the functions of evangelism and social concern (outward). Indeed, the church is the extension of Christ in this world. These perspectives are rooted in the biblical view of the church, to which we now turn.

THE MEANING OF THE CHURCH: A VIEW OF THE CHURCH

DEFINITION OF THE CHURCH

The original meaning of the word "church" (*ekklesia*) was "assembly."[9] Although the root idea is "called out," the emphasis of the word is more accurately "called together." The concept is an old one: in classical Greek the word referred to a group of people assembled together for a purpose, often business or political meetings (Acts 19:32, 39, 41). It came to be used of an assembly of Christians.

Biblically, some aspects of Christ's relationship to the church remain mysterious (Eph. 5:32). However, two Christological illustrations demonstrate the most important functions of the church. These two prominent metaphors are "the bride of Christ" (2 Cor. 11:2-3; Eph. 5:21-32; Rev. 19:6-9, 21:9) and "the Body of Christ" (Rom. 12:5; 1 Cor. 12:12-27; Eph. 1:22-23; 2:16; 4:25; 5:23, 30; Col. 2:19, 3:15). As the bride of Christ, the church is to submit to Christ and to remain pure for her husband. The focus of this metaphor is single-minded devotion to Jesus Christ alone, forsaking all other claims on our allegiance.

As the Body of Christ, the church is to demonstrate her union with Christ, to judiciously exercise spiritual gifts, and to grow spiritually.[10] The focus of this metaphor is upon the headship of Christ. Clowney

9. See K. L. Schmidt, "Ekklesia," in *Theological Dictionary of the New Testament*, ed. Gerhard Kittel and Gerhard Friedrich, 10 vols (Grand Rapids: Eerdmans, 1978) 3:501-36.
10. For discussions of both metaphors see J. Oliver Buswell, *A Systematic Theology of the Christian Religion* (Grand Rapids: Zondervan, 1963), 2:217-26. Acts 1:1 fits well with the "body" metaphor: it implies that the book of Acts is a record of what Christ *continues* to do and teach through the church just like Luke's gospel is a record of what Christ *began* to do and teach in His physical body while on earth.

states, "Neither the individual nor the group is primary in the church, because Christ is primary."[11]

Theologically, "the Church includes all persons anywhere in the world who are savingly related to Christ."[12] Corporately, the church is composed of a group of people who are resident aliens in this world, who maintain heavenly citizenship, and thus have a strong bond of fellowship with other resident aliens.[13]

The Jews had a common prayer, "God I thank you that I was born a man and not a woman, a freeman and not a slave, a Jew and not a gentile." In contrast to this, Paul proclaimed that "there is neither Jew nor Greek, there is neither slave nor free man, there is neither male nor female; for you are all one in Christ Jesus" (Gal. 3:28). Only on the basis of Christ's work can cultural barriers be hurdled and so diverse a group be brought together to build up one another in love.[14] For this reason Christian fellowship between believers is rich and immediate, even in cross-cultural settings.

BEGINNINGS OF THE CHURCH

Jesus anticipated the beginning of the church and gave Peter its "keys" (Matt. 16:18). He told the disciples to remain in Jerusalem for the coming baptism of the Spirit (Acts 1:4-5). The church began when the Spirit came upon the Christians on the Day of Pentecost. First, Jesus seems to refer to the church as future (Matt. 16:18). Second, Luke does not mention *ekklesia* at all in the gospel, but mentions it twenty-four times in Acts. Third, the function of Christ as Head and the ministry of spiritual gifts awaited His resurrection and ascension respectively (Eph. 1:20, 4:7-12).

Yet there is a sense in which the church is a unique continuation of God's people of all ages. Through his bold witness at Pentecost, Peter

11. Edmund Clowney, *The Doctrine of the Church* (Philadelphia: Presby. & Ref., 1969), p. 48.

12. Erickson, *Christian Theology*, p. 1034. Erickson continues, "It also includes all who *have lived* and been part of his body, and all who *will live* and be part of his body" (italics added). Many extend the definition of the church to include Israel in the Old Testament. *The Westminster Confession* states, "The catholic or universal Church, which is invisible, consists of the whole number of the elect, that *have been*, *are*, or *shall be* gathered into one, under Christ the head thereof" (*The Westminster Confession of Faith* [Richmond, Va.: The Board of Christian Education, Presbyterian Church of the United States, 1963], xxvii.1 [italics added]). We regard the church as fitting a separate program from the promises God made to Israel, and therefore this chapter will focus on the New Testament church. See the discussion in Charles Ryrie, *Basic Theology* (Wheaton, Ill: Victor, 1986), pp. 399-401.

13. Francis Lyall, *Slaves, Citizens, Sons: Legal Metaphors in the Epistles* (Grand Rapids: Zondervan, 1984), pp. 47-66.

14. John apparently disciplined a first century church dictator who "loves to be first" above other Christians. Diotrephes also exalted himself above Christ. See *proteuon*, used of Christ in Col. 1:18, compared with *philoproteuon*, used of Diotrephes in 3 John 9.

exercised the "keys" to open the door of faith to the Jews (Acts 2), later to the Samaritans (Acts 8, the "Samaritan Pentecost"), and finally to the Gentiles (Acts 10-11, the "Gentile Pentecost"). Consequently, the church now includes all nations and peoples in one Body (Eph. 2-3).

DESCRIPTION OF THE CHURCH

There is one church, and there are also individual churches that make up the church. Three considerations support this conclusion. First, the majority of usages of *ekklesia* in the New Testament refer to a local church.[15] Second, though many churches within a city met in homes,[16] Paul addressed the church (singular, corporate) of any city to which he wrote.[17] John employed the same practice in his brief epistles to the seven churches of Asia Minor (Rev. 2-3). Sometimes the term was used of all believers in a city (Acts 8:1), and sometimes of believers in a broad geographical area (Acts 9:31). Third, even though groups of varying sizes were included within the churches, Scripture is very clear that there is one unified Body and one baptism (Eph. 4:4-5). Jesus did not say, "I will build my churches," but, "I will build my church" (Matt. 16:18). In fact, one focus of Jesus' high priestly prayer was that believers would be united (John 17:21-22). The basis of such unity is the work of Christ on the cross, making diverse groups into one Body (1 Cor. 12:12-27).

This means that all Christians, everywhere, are a part of one another. Of course, there is a distinction between the visible church (local believers who gather together) and the universal church (all Christians collectively).[18] But all believers have the same mission and message. The church is not fragmented. Rather, "the individual congregation, or group of believers in a specific place, is never regarded as only a part or component of the whole church. The church is not a sum or composite of the individual local groups. Instead, the whole is found in each place."[19]

DIFFERENCES AMONG CHURCHES

Some have objected that because there are so many different denominations, and only one of them can be right, how do you know which one, if any, is right? Does the existence of groups of Christians who may

15. Erickson, p. 1033.
16. Rom. 16:5; 1 Cor.16:19. See particularly the singular in 1 Cor. 1:2 and 2 Cor. 1:1.
17. Galatians was not written to a city, but to a cluster of cities in a Roman province (1:2, "to the churches of Galatia").
18. This includes all who have been baptized by the Holy Spirit into the Body of Christ (1 Cor. 12:13).
19. Erickson, p. 1033.

disagree with each other argue against the truth of Christianity? The major differences in areas of doctrine and church structure are obvious to those outside the church. The answer to this common objection requires both an historical perspective and some insight into the limitations of fallen man.

Doctrine

First, some denominations exist not because they teach some things as true which others teach as false, but because they emphasize certain doctrines or practices differently from other churches. Second, where there are true doctrinal disagreements, most churches agree with each other on about 95 percent of their doctrine. Third, this huge area of central agreement is astounding in light of the fact that we are formulating doctrine about the infinite God with finite minds, and we are sinful people who sometimes distort truth, whether or not we are aware of doing so. Because of human mental and moral limitations, one might expect far more doctrinal disagreement among Christians than actually exists.

Where Christians do disagree they must do so in a spirit of love and concern and must not allow conflicts to become personal. Whenever possible, Christians should join forces and work together. Not only does this offer a good testimony before the world, it demonstrates good stewardship to avoid duplicating efforts both on the mission field and at home (John 13:34-35).

Structure and Leadership

While the church is a growing *organism* (Eph. 4:16), it is also an *organization,* which requires structure for full effectiveness. The New Testament gives ample evidence for various structures that arose to meet immediate needs: the "deacons" of Acts 6, the elders and deacons of the pastoral epistles,[20] and various substructures that helped individual congregations function more efficiently (1 Tim. 5:3-22). From these hints have arisen various forms by which the functions of the church are carried out. Historically, the three most prominent structures are congregational, presbyterian, and episcopal.

Congregational. The chief emphasis in this structure is placed on the local congregation, which elects officers (Acts 6:3-5), ordains ministers, exercises discipline (Matt. 18:17), and is independent of church councils and denominational agencies. While apostolic authority was exercised within the early church, the apostles were foundational (Eph. 2:20) and

20. See Titus 1:5-9 and 1 Tim. 3:1-13.

appointed no successors for after their death. Rather, Christ only is the head of the church (Col. 1:18), and all believers are individual priests (1 Pet. 2:9). Historical support for this form is found in the first century church manual, the *Didache*.[21] Today baptist, congregational, and independent churches reflect this sort of organization.

Presbyterian. Presbyterians would agree with congregationalists that overseers and elders (Gk. *presbyters*) are one and the same. One term describes who they are (presbyters or elders) while the other describes what they do (overseers).[22] Rather than guidance by congregational vote, the elders of a local church oversee the affairs of that church (Acts 15:1-29; Heb. 13:17; 1 Thess. 5:12-13). Further, the elders are subject to the larger "presbytery" (a collection of congregations) which is in turn subject to the "synods" (regional gatherings of presbyteries) and then to the "general assembly" (the denominational gathering).

Although synods and councils may err (in contrast to the inerrancy position of Catholicism), they do adjudicate church matters. The *Westminster Confession* states:

> It belongeth to synods and councils, ministerially, to determine controversies of faith, and cases of conscience; to set down rules and directions for the better ordering of the public worship of God, and government of his Church; to receive complaints in cases of mal-administration, and authoritatively to determine the same: which decrees and determinations, if consonant to the word of God, are to be received with reverence and submission.[23]

Presbyterian, Reformed, and some Lutheran churches adopt this form of organization. The "Plymouth Brethren" function under a simplified presbyterian structure.

Episcopal. The episcopal form distinguishes between elders and bishops, the latter being authoritative over the elders. As the apostles were God's leaders for the New Testament church (overseeing and appointing elders, Acts 14:23), so bishops today exercise the same apostolic function. This ministry includes ordination and pastoral appointment (Acts 6:6, 14:21-23; 1 Tim. 4:14; Titus 1:5). Episcopalian, Methodist (with

---

21. Leon Morris, "Church Government," in *Baker's Dictionary of Theology*, ed. Everett F. Harrison (Grand Rapids: Baker, 1960), pp. 126-27.

22. The terms "elder" and "bishop" are used interchangeably (Titus 1:5 and 7; Acts 20:17 and 28).

23. *Westminster Confession*, xxxiii.2. Acts 16:4 is cited as scriptural support.

some "presbyterian" modifications), and Anglican churches follow this pattern.[24]

If one were to use governmental terms, the episcopalian form is closest to a *monarchy,* the presbyterian form much like an *oligarchy,* and the congregational like a *democracy.* No one questions whether or not God has used all of these forms to accomplish His purposes in the world, and no one questions that, at least in some periods of church history, each has been abused. All of these structures were found quite early in the life of the church.

Two crucial issues touch the structure of the church. The first relates to function *vs.* form. *Function* refers to the biblical goals of the church, while *form* refers to how (in terms of structure and programs) those goals are accomplished. Logically, function creates form.[25] The crucial issue for any local church is not what form its programs take, but whether or not it fulfills the function for which God instituted the church.

The second issue is leadership. The qualifications by which Scripture describes elders and deacons are to be taken seriously. These qualities are not necessarily related to popularity or success but to godly character (1 Tim. 3; Titus 1). They do not describe what leaders are to do but rather what they are to be. God clearly requires that Christian leaders be men of integrity and honor, whom even those outside the church will respect and admire (1 Tim. 3:7).

When these two issues are in biblical balance, the goals for the church will be in proper perspective. But what are the goals for the church? We will consider the task for the future as we examine three major goals in the next section.

THE MISSION OF THE CHURCH: A VIEW FOR THE FUTURE

The church can be seen in action in many spheres of our complex culture. Campus ministries, groups of Christian professionals or businessmen, Christian colleges, and missions organizations fulfill different aspects of the church's ministry. These parachurch organizations, which

---

24. The Roman Catholic church is a variation of this form of government, with the addition of the papacy and the strong priority given to church tradition over Scripture. This discussion has focused upon the Protestant church. We should also note that some groups such as Quakers advocate no form of government.

25. Forms of evangelism, worship, discipleship, and personal ministry may need to change in order to accomplish the same goals. A common problem for many churches is that once forms have been created, they tend to become indestructible. See Jim Petersen, "The Eclipse of the Gospel," *Discipleship Journal* 55 (1990), p. 12.

are recent in origin, derive their purpose and function from the local church.

God created the church to accomplish three main goals: first, *intimacy* with God; second, *community* with believers; third, *mission* to the world.[26] These remain constant as the function of the church into the future, regardless of the forms used to reach these goals.

INTIMACY WITH GOD (UPWARD)

The goal of individuals within the worshiping church is the same as that of the apostle Paul: "That I may know Him" (Phil. 3:10). The worship of the church promotes experiential and intellectual knowledge of Jesus Christ.

Worship

Worship is not defined in the Bible. Different words are used to translate concepts we associate with worship,[27] and they seem to cluster around two ideas: *internal* feelings of reverence, and *external* prostration before Jesus. Both are reactions to being in the presence of a holy God.

Experiences and feelings by themselves, however, do not constitute worship. When the Israelites worked up substantial feelings in their "worship" services and even covered God's altar with their tears, they were not necessarily worshiping God (Mal. 2:13). Rather, worship of God must be done in Spirit and in truth (John 4:24). This includes the teaching role of the church.

Teaching

God the Spirit has given His truth to the church for her instruction and learning. One of the primary functions of the corporate meeting of believers is to receive instruction in God's Word (Acts 6:4; Eph. 4:11-13; 2 Tim. 3:14–4:2). The church is to teach its worshipers to be both hearers and doers of Scripture (James 1:22).

When both worship and teaching are a vital part of the church, Christians are strengthened to cope with earthly challenges. Their eyes are not on the world but on Christ (Heb. 12:2), and their mission as His ambassadors takes priority over all else (2 Cor. 5:15-21).

---

26. Wayne Jacobsen, "Caring for the Overextended," *Leadership* (Winter 1990), p. 33.
27. *Leiturgia, latreuo, proskuneo, sebomai, threskeia*. For a helpful discussion of each see Terry Miethe, *The New Christian's Guide to Following Jesus* (Minneapolis: Bethany, 1982), p. 69.

COMMUNITY AMONG BELIEVERS (INWARD)

The most visible pictures of the communion of believers are the two ordinances[28] of the church: the initiatory rite of *baptism* and the continuing rite of the *Lord's Supper*. Baptism is the means by which believers are publicly associated with Christ and identified with His Body, the church.[29] It is a one-time action that speaks of a decision to accept Jesus Christ as Savior, and is an outward indication of an inward change. All believers are to be obedient to this command and example of the Lord (Matt. 28:19; Acts 2:37-38).

The second ordinance is the Lord's Supper. Jesus commanded believers to partake of the symbolic bread and cup in order to remember the Lord's death until He comes (Matt. 26:26-28; 1 Cor. 11:23-29). This continuous activity represents the ongoing "feeding" upon Christ as believers participate together in true "communion."

There are also other ways the communion of believers may be expressed besides the ordinances. Christians are to meet together regularly for fellowship and worship (Heb. 10:25). The early Christians met at least on a weekly basis (1 Cor. 16:2; Acts 20:7), sometimes more often than that (Acts 2:46), to "stimulate one another to love and good deeds" and to encourage each other (Heb. 10:24-25). A significant part of this communion was mutual bearing of burdens (Gal. 6:2). Sometimes the bearing of burdens was financial (Acts 4:32-35; 11:29; James 2:8, 15-16); at other times this responsibility included confrontation and church discipline (Matt. 18:15-17; 1 Cor. 5:1-5; Gal. 6:1).

The reason for this family intimacy is that believers are members of one another (1 Cor. 12:12-27). Such involvement fulfills God's commandment for servanthood (Phil. 2:1-4), which Jesus said is the defining characteristic of Christian greatness (Mark 10:43-45).

John White points out that as a Christian I have no free will to choose who my brothers and sisters are, or whether or not I will be committed to them. "They belong to us and we to them. We have no control over the fact that we are to love, care and be responsible for them."[30] I owe Christ everything; He demands that my indebtedness to Him be transferred to my new family, the family of God. Some Christians may attract me; others may seem repugnant, and the feeling may be reciprocal.

28. Some prefer the term "sacrament." From its original usage, it connotes something of the idea of mystery (it was used in Latin to translate the Greek *mysterion*). Therefore, those groups that view the ordinances as more than a "remembrance" of Christ tend to use the term "sacrament."
29. For clear examples of association/identification, see Mark 10:38-39 and 1 Cor. 12:13.
30. John White, *The Fight* (Downers Grove, Ill.: InterVarsity, 1976), p. 130.

Even so, "You are not to confine yourself to the favorite few. You are committed to the freaks and oddballs of the lunatic fringe as well as to those Christians about whom you feel highly critical. You belong to people whose views you disagree with."[31]

The basis of Christian fellowship (*koinonia*) is not found within the Christian or his brother; the basis is found in Christ alone. As J. Y. Campbell explained, "The primary idea expressed by *koinonos* and its cognates is not that of association with another person or persons, but that of participation in something in which others also participate."[32] The biblical idea of fellowship is not the comraderie of a social club but keeping Christ central to all thoughts and activities. The fellowship of the church includes the sharing of joys and sorrows (1 Cor. 12:26). Hurt is reduced by being shared; joy is increased by being shared.[33]

There is great freedom here. If the Body of Christ functions as God intended, then we belong to a body of people who should always love and accept us whether or not we are attractive or successful, because their commitment to us is not based on their admiration for us but on Christ's Person and work.[34] This does not happen naturally, but supernaturally. To the degree that Christ is "the Head" of individual Christians, the corporate Body of Christ will follow its Head and will function as a body. And the proper functioning of the Body of Christ (inward ministry) will have immediate results in one of the other tasks of the church, witnessing (outward ministry).

MISSION TO THE WORLD (OUTWARD)

The task of the church is to make disciples (Matt. 28:18-20). Jesus said that those who follow Him are to be His "witnesses" (Acts 1:8). This mandate is rooted in the authority of our Lord, and is encouraged by His continuing presence with His witnesses ("I am with you always, even to the end of the age," Matt. 28:20).

On the individual level, the idea of being a witness has become confused with questions of techniques and methods.

Some people "witness" by carrying leatherbound Bibles, other by giving tracts to service station attendants or leaving literature in public toilets. Many sport bumper stickers ranging from the ancient fish symbol to

---

31. Ibid.
32. J. Y. Campbell, "KOINONIA and Its Cognates in the NT," *Journal of Biblical Literature* 51(1932): 353, cited by Clowney in *The Church*, p. 51.
33. Erickson, p. 1056.
34. White, *The Fight*, p. 132.

242 MAKING SENSE OF YOUR WORLD

"Honk if you love Jesus." Yet others erect roadside billboards. . . . Some older postreformation groups witness by their dress. Amish and Mennonite men of certain groups do not wear ties or shave their beards, feeling that it would be worldly to do so.[35]

Some well-meaning groups teach methods of gospel presentation by "flow chart" or by surveys whose results will never be tabulated. But this is to make abnormal and complex what God intended to be simple. "Witnessing and projecting an image are not the same thing."[36] As a witness a Christian is someone who is "truthful about what he has seen, heard, or personally experienced"[37] about Jesus Christ. He is to be genuine and not overconfident that he knows the answers to every objection that might be raised. "The task of a witness is not to convert people nor to 'clinch a deal' but to supply them with the data by means of which the Holy Spirit brings conviction to them."[38] Therefore he must respond honestly to questions from a biblical worldview, for he can do no less.

An effective Christian witness is able both to articulate and defend his faith (1 Pet. 3:15) and to incarnate its truth through a consistent Christian life. Christians have been granted the ministry of reconciliation and serve as ambassadors of Christ. Because Christ makes His appeal to the unsaved through individual Christians, the believer's walk must match his talk so that the gospel is not hindered (2 Cor. 5:15-21).

On the corporate level, the fellowship of believers is one of the most effective "tools" for Christian witness.

> The church that convinces men that there is a God in heaven is a church that manifests what only a heavenly God can do, that is, to unite human beings in heavenly love. . . . There is nothing on earth which convinces men about heaven or that awakens their craving for it like the discovery of Christian brothers who love one another.[39]

Even though unbelievers rarely if ever entered the meetings of the early church (1 Cor. 14:23 only hints at the possibility), Jesus was quite specific about the external witness of the church: "By this all men will know that you are My disciples, if you have love for one another" (John 13:35). This served as the church's only advertising campaign in the first century and has continued to be the most effective one it has ever had.

35. Ibid., pp. 62-63.
36. Ibid., p. 66.
37. Ibid., p. 61.
38. Ibid., p. 75.
39. Ibid., pp. 149-150.

God instituted the family and the church to meet our horizontal needs of fulfillment and loneliness. To the people who long for intimacy with others, we say that the Good Shepherd knows His sheep personally (John 10:27), not just by computer code.

The church is to be characterized by openness to all. Distinctions that may matter to government and society are unimportant as individuals stand together under Christ. Whether those differences be racial ("neither Jew nor Greek"), economic and social ("neither slave nor free man"), or gender-related ("neither male nor female"), the fact is that "you are all one in Christ Jesus" (Gal. 3:28). When Christians truly "do nothing from selfishness or empty conceit, but with humility of mind let each of you regard one another as more important than himself" (Phil. 2:3), there is a feeling of belonging and acceptance that is contagious and winsome to people who are hurting deeply.

CONCLUSION

Individually, Christians are not doing well. As a brief perusal of most Christian bookstores will attest, many more books are oriented toward helping Christians cope with personal problems than ever before. In the first century, Christians were concerned about how to impact their world. Today, Christians seem more concerned about how the world has impacted them.

Corporately, the church is not doing well. I remember the incredible optimism evangelicals had in 1980, anticipating our greatest ever impact over the next decade. That decade is now history. During the last week of 1989, two television networks offered specials summarizing the highlights of the previous decade. The only attention evangelicals received on those hour-long shows was three spots highlighting scandals involving Christian leaders. This was the media summary of the evangelical legacy.

The church has the best news of all for the world. Jesus Christ offers hope for the hopeless. We freely admit that we are sinners; we identify with Isaiah in our intense awareness of both personal and public sin (Isa. 6:1-6). But we proclaim with joy that we are sinners who have been redeemed by the grace of God through faith in our Lord Jesus Christ. Hours before He was arrested and crucified, Jesus prayed for the future church. Of all the things He could have mentioned, He really prayed only for one thing—unity (John 17:20-23). His reason was not just that believers would meet the needs of each other (though this is important) but "that the world may believe . . . [and] know that Thou didst send Me" (John 17:21, 23).

As we seek to obey the Lord corporately and individually, we are to be salt and light in our society (Matt 5:13-16). Although salt enhances the taste of foods (Job 6:6), the function of a preservative is in view. The believer is to be an agent in the world that helps delay moral decay by living a consistent Christian life. The danger is in losing one's saltiness. Technically this is impossible, for sodium chloride is not like a battery that can eventually lose its charge. The point, however, is that foreign elements can be added to salt; it is then no longer useful. The danger for the Christian is that we will become double-minded. With so much of the world in us that we cannot enjoy Christ, and so much of Christ in us that we cannot enjoy the world, we become totally ineffective and unstable (James 1:8).

Light is another common metaphor in the Bible, found twenty-one times in John's gospel alone. Collectively, believers are to be a spiritual beacon in the world. Individually, we are to serve as lights in the world (Phil. 2:15), not because of our intrinsic glow but because of our connectedness with the unique Light (John 8:12), Jesus Christ (Eph. 5:8; see Rev. 2:5).

Both of these metaphors make the point that for the church and its impact on the world, actions do speak louder than words. We are to fulfill our upward, inward, and outward ministries faithfully, adapting our methods, though not our message, to the changing needs of our culture. We are to function as salt and light, both individually (as members of a local church) and corporately (as "the church"), so that as a watching world observes our good works our Father will be glorified (Matt. 5:16).

CASE STUDY: The German Brethren Church[40]

In Nazi Germany the Brethren church was commanded by Hitler to unite with all other religious groups. Half the Brethren church accepted Hitler's dictum; the other half refused. Those who submitted had easier lives over the next few years than did their former associates, although their doctrinal sharpness and spiritual vitality eroded. The second group remained spiritually vital, but most families lost at least one member to the concentration camps.

After the war was over, the two groups of Christian brothers faced each other again. There were deep emotions on both sides. What would

---

40. Adapted from Francis Schaeffer, *The Church at the End of the Twentieth Century* (Downers Grove, Ill.: InterVarsity, 1970), pp. 150-51.

they do? The elders of the two groups met at a specified time in a quiet place. The participant who described the meeting had suffered deeply; his father had gone to the concentration camp, and his mother had been dragged away from him. The issues before the two groups, unity and for-giveness, reached deep into individual emotions.

The men decided to set aside several days during which each did nothing except search his own heart concerning his own failures and the commands of Christ. Then they met together again. What happened?

The man responded, "We were just one."

CASE STUDY: Hypocrites in the Church

Is the church its own worst enemy? Decades ago philosopher Ber-trand Russell offered this diatribe against Christianity:

> You find as you look round the world that every single bit of progress in humane feeling, every improvement in the criminal law, every step towards the diminution of war, . . . every mitigation of slavery, every moral progress that there has been in the world, has been consistently op-posed by the organized churches of the world. I say quite deliberately that the Christian religion, as organized in its churches, has been and still is the principal *enemy of moral progress* in the world.[41]

Recently the challenge has taken a more popular form: "Don't talk to me about Christianity. I went to church long enough to know that the church is full of hypocrites." This charge might not always be made openly, but the erosion of public confidence in institutions, especially re-ligious institutions, has resulted in a "worst case" interpretation of the Christian church.

While it is true that the church is full of sinners, and that the church is not *empty* of hypocrites, does it follow that the church is *full* of hypo-crites?[42] Are its goals and programs morally bankrupt? Are the problems so severe that the church is no longer effective?

Consider the case of John Prin. He did not grow up in church, and came to Christ from a smorgasbord background filled with drugs, suicidal depression, and infidelity. He describes his introduction to the local church.

41. Bertrand Russell, "Why I Am Not a Christian," in *Bertrand Russell on God and Religion*, ed. Al Seckel (Buffalo, N.Y.: Prometheus, 1986), pp. 69-70 (italics added).
42. R. C. Sproul, *Reason to Believe* (Grand Rapids: Zondervan, 1978), chapter 5.

To my surprise, I found total acceptance at church even though I was sinful and imperfect. Fellow Christians listened, advised, and encouraged me and my wife (who accepted the Lord three months [later] . . .) to grow into the people God wanted us to be. No finger-wagging. No shocked expressions. There was only the demonstration that the church is his body, commissioned to do his work, "to have love for one another" (John 13:35).[43]

Prin receives social, intellectual, and spiritual nourishment from his local church. He adds, "My church is now the first place I turn to for help. It is where I laugh more than anywhere else, and where the meaning of a life in Christ becomes clear."[44]

But, Prin states, his church is not merely a place where he receives personal help. Practical evidence of Christ's love is being manifested through outreach programs: day care for children and elderly, programs for the mentally handicapped, help for refugees, free clothing and food, a counseling center, and a summer camp.

These programs, financed by church members and staffed by volunteers, exist for only one purpose: to bring God's loving Spirit to as many hurting people as possible. Just as I experienced. Just as Jesus did when he walked this earth.[45]

DISCUSSION QUESTIONS

1. If you had an unsaved friend and wanted to show him the Body of Christ in action, where would you take him? To a worship service, an all-church picnic, or a church basketball game? Why?
2. What are the ordinances of the church, and how do they contribute to the ongoing life of a local church?
3. Describe the inward, outward, and upward ministries of the church.
4. What does it mean for Christians to function as salt and light in this world? What are some ways in which we have failed in our task? What can we do, as individuals and as local churches, to close the "credibility gap" and fulfill this responsibility?
5. If, on a personal level, you simply do not like an individual in your church, what is your responsibility toward him or her? (See Eph. 4:11–5:1.)

43. John Prin, "My Higher Power Has a Name & a Body," *Christianity Today*, 24 September 1990, p. 24.
44. Ibid., p. 25.
45. Ibid.

6. Read the following passages and list specific responsibilities God has given Christians toward each other: Philippians 2:1-4; Galatians 6:1-5; Ephesians 4:11–5:1; Romans 14:1–15:13; 1 Corinthians 12:12-31.

FURTHER READING

Allen, Ronald B. and Gordon Borror. *Worship: Rediscovering the Missing Jewel.* Portland, Oreg.: Multnomah, 1982.

Beasley-Murray, G. R. *Baptism in the New Testament.* Grand Rapids: Eerdmans, 1962.

Coleman, Robert E. *The Master Plan of Discipleship.* Old Tappan, N.J.: Revell, 1987.

Erickson, Millard. *Christian Theology*, vol. 3. Grand Rapids: Baker, 1985. Pp. 1025-1148.

Kane, J. Herbert. *Understanding Christian Missions.* Grand Rapids: Baker, 1974.

Martin, Ralph P. *Worship in the Early Church.* Grand Rapids: Eerdmans, 1964.

Peters, George. *A Biblical Theology of Missions.* Chicago: Moody, 1973.

————. *Saturation Evangelism.* Grand Rapids: Zondervan, 1970.

Saucy, Robert L. *The Church in God's Program.* Chicago: Moody, 1972.

Schaeffer, Francis A.. *The Church at the End of the 20th Century.* Downers Grove, Ill.: InterVarsity, 1970.

Strauch, Alexander. *Biblical Eldership.* Littleton, Colo.: Lewis & Roth, 1986.

10

A VIEW FOR THE WORLD

LIVING IN TWO WORLDS

The 1985 scene is now famous: forty-five rock musicians linking arms and swaying to the steady rhythm of the song "We Are the World," a piece which expressed universal solidarity. Bob Geldof, a performer with the British rock group Boom Town Rats, organized the event after seeing television reports of the devastating drought in parts of Africa. Famine, disease, and death ravaged the population, particularly that of Ethiopia, and little was being done to help them.

Geldof captured two gatherings of rock musicians in several albums and videos. The grand finale on July 13, 1985, was "Live Aid," the seventeen-hour, cross-Atlantic concert featuring 63 bands. More than one billion people in 150 countries watched the extravaganza by television. The proceeds from these events, which grew into the hundreds of millions of dollars, provided food, medicine, and supplies for the needy in Ethiopia and other countries.

The global awareness that these events captured is a remarkable reminder that the world is no longer out there—it is right here. The plight of people halfway around the globe has become as important as the concerns of our next door neighbor. But it does not stop there. The fashionable "we are the world" mentality extends beyond the human needs of starvation and disease. For many, it includes rescuing dogs and cats from biomedical research, snail darters (fish) from dam-building, the air and rivers from pollution, and the land from development.

Amid the popular clamor to "save the world," what does a biblical worldview have to say? In other words, What is a biblical worldview in this context? The term *world* is generally used with a dual focus: the natural world and the social world. The Bible also refers to the "world" (Greek, *kosmos*) in these two ways.[1] The first is the *kosmos* of the created, physical realm (Matt. 24:21). This is the natural world—the world of mountains, seas, plants, and animals. The second is the *kosmos* of the created, personal realm (Matt. 4:8; John 3:16). This is the social world—the world of people, cultures, and societies.

Applying a biblical perspective to the broader concerns in the world has not always been an integral part of Christian thinking. A biblical worldview is usually applied to personal regeneration, personal decision-making, family, and church. Any reference to the world is usually a plea for evangelism and missions. For many, the social world and the natural world seem extraneous to the personal religion of the Christian. How does the Bible address these concerns? We shall look in turn at a biblical view for the world from the perspective of the natural world, and then from the perspective of the social world.

THE NATURAL WORLD

Responding to the needs of the natural realm seems to be the purview of rock stars and "whole-earth" activists. Hollywood personalities invest their talents and dollars to preserve the environment and save the animals. Environmental organizations force campaigning politicians to

---

1. The complexities of the various meanings of *kosmos* are explored by Hermann Sasse in *Theological Dictionary of the New Testament*, ed. Gerhard Kittel and Gerhard Friedrich, 10 vols. (Grand Rapids: Eerdmans, 1964-76), 3:868-98.

take a stand on ecological issues and promise government funds for preservation and clean-up. Membership and financial support for groups such as Greenpeace USA and the World Wildlife Fund are some of the biggest gainers among non-profit organizations. The ecological bandwagon takes on riders at a dizzying rate. What in the world has caused this environmental clamor?

THE ENVIRONMENTAL SITUATION

First we must try to make sense out of all the current claims. To gain a perspective, the present concern for ecological integrity is a relatively recent phenomenon. Thirty years ago there were no environmental institutes or popular movements to preserve nature. In 1972, twenty-one countries sponsored some form of environmental protection agency. Now, more than 160 nations have some governmental arm to monitor environmental concerns.

Ecological awareness, at least as we are experiencing it today, began to develop in the early sixties as part of a larger concern for humanity and the global quality of life. As technology began to dominate the social life of Americans, the producing, using, and discarding of products seriously affected the natural environment. As a result, many conclude that the current state of affairs is a crisis, with ''nature'' as the hostage in danger of extinction.

Actually defining the environmental situation is difficult. The natural world may be divided into four interrelated spheres: air, water, plants, and animals. The interruption of the natural environmental processes results in any number of ecological crises. Man's intervention with technology and industry has produced many concerns about the future of planet earth. Air and water pollution threaten the basic sources of nourishment for life. The elimination of many species of animals for commercial purposes affects the biological cycle in ways that are yet to be measured. The destruction of forests, especially the tropical forests of South America, damages the earth's ability to replenish oxygen in the atmosphere. Further concerns arise from offshore oil drilling, the use of pesticides, and the frantic rate of residential and commercial development.

An even graver problem is seen when the combination of several of these factors is considered from a global perspective. The release into the air of carbon dioxide (from burning fossil fuels), chlorofluorocarbons (from refrigerators, air conditioners, and aerosol spray cans), and methane gas (from coal mining, livestock, and landfills) forms a barrier trapping the sun's heat in the earth's atmosphere. This phenomenon, known as the "greenhouse effect," could result in global warming, rising sea levels, changing climates, and even temperatures too high to sustain human life.

Many scientists argue that the concerns over global warming are misguided and unfounded. Yet, the potential effects, in theory, are frightening. The growing atmospheric bilge certainly will have some impact on the environment. By the time the ultimate effects of the global greenhouse are determined, it may be too late for responsible action.

When we survey the array of environmental dysfunctions, the most sobering thought is that they are the result of humanity's willful decision to exploit nature. Little regard has been given to the effect certain activities will have on the environment. Further, a naive belief pervades Western society that if a crisis endangers human existence, science will find a way to overcome the problem. The underlying attitude toward the natural world is indifference—we use anything that is "not-man" to increase our comfort and quality of life.

ROOTS OF INDIFFERENCE

Such a view toward the environment is a long way from the world-views that see nature as divine or at least a partner in the cycle of life. Many experts point to Christianity as the culprit in the ecological crisis. Lynn White, professor emeritus of history at UCLA, claims that Western society's destructive attitude toward nature lies in the Judeo-Christian tradition: "By destroying pagan animism, Christianity made it possible to exploit nature in a mood of indifference to the feelings of natural objects."[2] White considers science and technology so "tinctured with orthodox Christian arrogance toward nature"[3] that there is little hope for our environment in the present.

Even though many share White's conclusions,[4] his analysis is seriously flawed. Animism's worship of nature had long subsided before many cultures adopted an indifference to the environment. Ecological problems also threaten non-Western societies where the Judeo-Christian tradition has little influence.

However, the attack on a supposed Christian view of nature is not limited to those outside the faith. Christian writer Wesley Granberg-

2. Quoted by Paul R. Ehrlich, Anne H. Ehrlich, and John P. Holdren, *Ecoscience: Population, Resources, Environment* (San Francisco: W. H. Freeman, 1977), p. 809.

3. Ibid., p. 810.

4. See, for example, Arnold Toynbee, "The Religious Background of the Present Environmental Crisis," in *Ecology and Religion in History*, ed. D. and E. Springs (New York: Harper & Row, 1974).

Michaelson charges, "Western Christianity has been quick to stress humanity's role to 'rule and subdue' the earth, providing a godly rationale for the onslaught of modern technology and offering few if any safeguards against the desecration of the earth."[5]

Admittedly, Christian response to environmental issues has been slow, limited, and for the most part obscured by the secular response. There seem to be at least two reasons for this.

The first is found in the spirit of the times leading up to the modern ecological heyday. Spiritual and doctrinal issues overwhelmed any social agenda, and Christians were so theologically preoccupied with man's relationship to God and far-reaching (eternal) spiritual concerns that the natural (temporal) world was ignored. A new heaven and earth are promised in the Bible, so why devote time and energy to a world that will be destroyed?

Second, the recent association of environmental movements with certain streams of transcendental thought, particularly the New Age movement, makes evangelicals uneasy. New Agers preach that we must save the universe because we are all a part of the single fabric of existence. To preserve the environment is to preserve ourselves. Some see a New Age conspiracy in certain responses to ecological concerns,[6] and the result is that many evangelicals shy away from environmental pursuits to avoid the New Age label.

In spite of the late start, many evangelicals are responding to environmental matters. The rationale, urged on by the seriousness of the ecological condition, is found in a careful understanding of the scriptural perspective of God's purpose for man and the earth.

A BIBLICAL PERSPECTIVE

A biblical worldview certainly does not present an attitude of indifference toward the natural world. The many passages that describe God's concern and care for His creation are difficult to ignore. From a biblical perspective, the earth belongs to the Lord and is the physical sign of His glory and power (Pss. 19:1; 24:1; Rom. 1:19-21). Living things are dependent upon God for "the breath of life" (Gen. 6:17; 7:15), while the sea, land, and trees are said to offer praise to their Creator (Ps. 96). Psalm 8 is God's invitation to wonder at what He has made: "O Lord, our Lord,

5. Wesley Granberg-Michaelson, ed., *Tending the Garden: Essays on the Gospel and the Earth* (Grand Rapids: Eerdmans, 1987), p. 2.
6. Constance Cumby, *The Hidden Dangers of the Rainbow: The New Age Movement and Our Coming Age of Barbarism* (Shreveport, La.: Huntington House, 1983), pp. 155ff.

how majestic is Thy name in all the earth, who hast displayed Thy splendor above the heavens!'' (Ps. 8:1).

The psalmist continues by proclaiming that man has been appointed by God "to rule over the works of Thy hands" because "Thou hast put all things under his feet" (Ps. 8:6). Indeed, the physical world is created "for" mankind (Gen. 1:28; 2:7ff.) but not for the purpose of exploitation. Man was given the mandate to "cultivate and keep" the garden (Gen. 2:15), not to worship or abuse it. Man's "dominion" over the earth is *derived*, that is, he cares for the earth by the authority of God and should treat it as God would.

However, some are not convinced that environmental concerns are necessary for the Christian agenda. Is it not true, they argue, that the physical world is subject to decay and will be transformed when God re-creates a new heaven and earth? If so, then why worry about the environment? It will all be changed by God anyway.

The argument may seem persuasive, yet it falls apart when we apply it to other aspects of God's creation. For example, why take care of our physical bodies? Why exercise or eat the right foods? After all, our bodies will be transformed at the resurrection. Admittedly, the differences between the natural world and our natural bodies are great; yet, an attitude of indifference toward a natural creation of God cannot be justified at any level.

Imagine a prominent artist creating a work of art "for" a group of people he dearly loved. How would the recipients respond to the gift? Would they not care for the work of art as the precious gift that it was? Further, consider if the art was necessary for the very survival of the group and its posterity. Would they not make painstaking efforts to preserve, protect, and enjoy the work?

While Christians may be guilty of focusing attention only upon spiritual matters, it is often forgotten that all creation is included in God's plan of redemption (Rom. 8:18-25). The Lord has total claim of the world: He created and will redeem the physical realm. Christians, of all people, should raise the loudest voices against the abuses foisted upon God's creation.

What may surprise many is that Christians have not been silent. Thousands are motivated to respond to ecological problems on the basis of theological principles and biblical injunctions. For example, the Christian Nature Federation recently began operations in southern California. The organization seeks to re-establish within the natural sciences "the Christian worldview which acknowledges a transcendent, personal, caring God who created the natural world out of nothing, who is sovereign over the affairs of men, and who provides redemption from the effects of the Fall through the Savior, Jesus Christ.''[7]

The AuSable Institute, located in Michigan, is a resource for Christians to learn about their relationship to the environment. The philosophy of the AuSable Institute is to ''confess that God is owner of all. Humankind is not the owner of that over which it has authority. Human authority is more that of trustee than owner. The scope of this trust is global. Since all creatures depend on the earth for life, health, and fulfillment, stewardship is the responsible use and care of creation. This is a clear and repeated testimony of Scripture.''[8]

The AuSable Institute brings together scientists, theologians, church leaders, and students to discuss biblical stewardship of the environment. The forum is new for many evangelicals, but most are finding the dialogue to correlate easily with a renewed evangelical concern on public issues.

A CHRISTIAN RESPONSE

A biblical worldview demands some response to environmental issues. Several principles must guide.

First, humanity does take the prominent place in God's plan for His creation. Redemption history is the single thread weaving together God's revelation in the Scriptures. However, we cannot ignore the fact that environmental dysfunctions are the result of man's sin in two developing contexts. Initially, the natural world was subject to corruption because of man's fall (Gen. 3:17-19; Rom. 8:19-22). Current exploitation of the environment arises from man's arrogance and indifference toward God's work.

Second, man's prominence in God's plan in no way justifies an indifference to environmental concerns. Certainly given the biblical passages and themes noted above, God has a high view of His creative work. We must seek to have God's perspective on the natural world.

Third, science and technology cannot completely answer the environmental questions or solve ecological dilemmas. They are tools or, at best, servants to be guided by the moral decisions of humanity. Science did not cause the ecological problems we now have, man's exploitative attitude toward the environment and his misuse of technology is the root

7. Quoted in *World*, 28 October 1989, p. 16.
8. Quoted in Granberg-Michaelson, *Tending the Garden*, p. vii.

cause. Whatever course of action is taken by humanity will also arise from moral considerations.

Fourth, whatever approach we take toward environmental issues must arise from a biblical view of the natural world, not cultural or societal trends. For too long Christians have reacted to public issues with undisguised surprise and emotion. Christians should have been demanding a biblical approach to the environment long before it became fashionable to do so.

A time is coming when God will renew His handiwork. The groanings of creation will never be allayed by mankind's efforts, but tending the garden God has given us can provide a world that preserves the witness to His glory. The old saying is quite true: "We do not inherit the earth from our parents, we borrow it from our children."

THE SOCIAL WORLD

The natural world seems passive to man. It responds to man's initiatives; it declares God's glory and serves as a constant witness to God's power and presence. Man's confrontation with the created world of nature should be one of reverent, nurturing stewardship. The natural world does not cause wars, it does not tempt man to sin, nor does it pressure him to conform.

Confronting the social world is more problematic: it fights back. The world of people, with its social pressures and conflicting values, frequently sets the agenda for Christian response. Within the social world, Christians have the unique dilemma of living in two different realms: the realm of God and the realm of the world. The guidelines for living in God's realm are spelled out in Scripture. However, the realm of the world follows the rhythm of an uncertain drummer. Most often it places social demands upon each person to live in such a way that fosters harmony and happiness. Sometimes those social demands conflict with the biblical design. How should Christians apply a biblical worldview to the pressures of the social world?

CHILDREN OF OUR CULTURE

As we briefly discussed in the first chapter, we are all products of our culture, our immediate social world. In the social environment in which we are reared, a whole world of values and accepted behaviors is taught and confirmed. Society determines and conserves what is good and bad, what is right and wrong, and what is beautiful and ugly. These values may be received from an external authority (i.e., the Bible), or they may be self-derived (i.e., social customs, mores, etc.), but they are always present and serve to conform the members of the society to similar patterns of believing and behaving.

The social world includes many avenues of personal expression and relationships. The intangible patterns of cultural behavior seen in daily interactions, family life, and community values are the soul of one's culture. These elements of life shape the thinking and valuing of the members of the society. The expression of these values is usually seen in the creative arenas of a society: art, music, and literature. The proliferation and existence of various kinds of entertainment both express and shape the values of a people. The more formal institutions of society, such as the educational systems and economic structures, determine on a broad scale how the society functions as an integrated whole and how personal needs are met.

The most unique facet of culture is the government. Government alone has the authority to determine behavior (by making laws) and to enforce adherence to that behavior (by punishing lawbreakers). Many of the problems related to modern government are not explicitly addressed in the Bible. For example, the Bible does not commend democracy over autocracy or socialism over communism. However, biblical teachings have led many to favor one form of government over another.[9] What the Bible does dictate is that the purpose of government is to restrain evil and preserve order (Rom. 13:1-7; 1 Pet. 2:13-14). The many forms of government in biblical times, which were present as a background to the writing of Scripture, indicate God's concern for justice over structure.

The social world is neither a friend nor an enemy of God. Biblically, human society is not in itself evil, that is, there is nothing inherently evil about customs, government, art, or literature. However, the Bible speaks often of the "world" as evil and antagonistic to the reign of God. This is true for two reasons. First, society is made up of humans, and humans by nature are depraved (Jer. 17:9; Rom. 3:10-11; Eph. 2:1-3). Therefore, the reality of evil in the heart of every person spoils the aggregate of social structures as well.

Second, beyond man's personal evil is the reality of the spiritual world that influences social systems. Satan is called "the god of this age" (2 Cor. 4:4) and "the ruler of the kingdom of the air" (Eph. 2:2) who continually works to bend the course of the world toward his direction

9. See, for example, the essays and bibliographies in Richard John Neuhaus and Michael Cromartie, eds., *Piety and Politics: Evangelicals and Fundamentalists Confront the World* (Washington, D.C.: Ethics and Public Policy Center, 1987); also Ronald H. Nash, *Poverty and Wealth: The Christian Debate Over Capitalism* (Westchester, Ill.: Crossway, 1986).

(Eph. 6:12). The apostle John states emphatically that "the whole world lies in the power of the evil one" (1 John 5:19), and James warns Christians to avoid sympathetic association with the world (James 1:27; 4:4). Theologian Robert Webber concludes, "Satan works through the structures of society to distort, pervert and disfigure that which is good. No part of the created order can escape the influence and power of Satan."[10]

Does this mean the social world is totally godless? Are there any aspects of the social world God has salvaged for His purposes? Should Christians ever involve themselves in the affairs of the social world or should they write it off as destined for destruction?

ISSUES OF OUR CULTURE

There is no question that Christians are to guide their lives by the authority of God mediated through the Scriptures. Questions arise, however, when the Christian must "go public." Do the biblical mandates for godliness and moral purity apply only to the Christian's personal life, or should they be extended to all of society? This conflict between private and public morality is at the heart of the Christian's dilemma.

Should Christians (and their churches) concern themselves with social issues? Many contemporary evangelicals have answered yes. The current evangelical social agenda is to confront "the tide of moral decline in American culture."[11] Key moral and public concerns in the immediate American society include the following:

Life/Death Issues
Abortion
Euthanasia
Capital punishment

Individual Rights Issues
Women ("equal rights")
Homosexuals ("personal rights")
Minorities ("civil rights")
Poor ("welfare rights")

Public Education Issues
School prayer
Teaching creation/evolution
Teaching sex education

10. Robert Webber, *The Church in the World* (Grand Rapids: Zondervan, 1986), p. 27.
11. James Davidson Hunter, *Evangelicalism: The Coming Generation* (Chicago: U. of Chicago, 1987), p. 125.

National Defense Issues
    Nuclear weapons/power
    Military spending

These do not include the many issues involved in the broader questions of economic and governmental reform. There is little agreement in American culture concerning the "right" position on each of the above issues. Many evangelical writers are attempting to address these and many other issues from a biblical perspective for the purpose of setting out a biblical response. But even evangelical Christians disagree on what view is the "right" (i.e., "biblical") view and what agenda the Christian should follow.[12] Declarations have attempted to address social issues with a united Christian front (for example, "A Declaration of Evangelical Social Concern" of November 1973 and "The Oxford Declaration on Christian Faith and Economics" of January 1990), but mobilization of Christians has been fragmented and inconsistent.

ATTITUDES TOWARD OUR CULTURE

A biblical worldview may lead one to a specific position on an issue, but should a Christian work to conform society to this moral stance? If so, by what means should one's culture be changed? Historically, the answer has been worked out from three different perspectives with differing agendas: separation, reconciliation, and transformation.[13]

Separation: The Christian Avoiding the World

From a separatistic perspective, the "world" is fundamentally antagonistic to God and the spiritual realm. There is no hope for its transformation, and therefore engaging society or the government in any form of interaction is futile for the Christian. Christians are to live by the norms of God's kingdom, as described in the Scriptures. Secular society is to be ignored. Although Christians cannot always escape some influence of the world, they must respond to the call " 'Come out from their midst and be separate, says the Lord" (2 Cor. 6:17). Christians are "aliens and strang-

---

12. A survey of contemporary books and periodicals by evangelicals demonstrates the diversity of thought. For the views of "the coming generation" of evangelicals, see Hunter, *Evangelicalism*, pp. 130-54.

13. Webber points out that these three approaches follow a chronological development of church history. The separation approach was reflected in the early church; the reconciliation approach has antecedents in early Constantinianism; and the transformation approach is rooted in Augustine and elaborated in the early medieval period. It is interesting to note that all three approaches were utilized by the Reformers: the Anabaptists, Luther, and Calvin respectively. See Robert Webber, *The Church in the World*, p. 81.

ers'' (1 Pet. 2:11) in this present world, which is epitomized by spiritual darkness and evil (1 John 2:15-16; 5:19).

How this separation from the world is carried out has varied. Some physically disassociate themselves from the influence of the world, as did the medieval monks, the modern Amish, and similar traditions. Because a complete physical separation is difficult in contemporary society, some groups take a social and philosophical approach to "coming out from among them." While maintaining employment in the "world," the rest of the individual's life revolves around the local church. Government and society are attacked from the pulpit and in daily conversation as being "godless" and "anti-Christian." In many cases, alternate institutions are set up to shield the Christian from social interaction with the world. The only accepted engagement with secular society is for the purpose of evangelism.

A somewhat similar separatistic approach to cultural engagement dominated the agenda of post-Depression fundamentalists. Armed with the expectation of Christ's imminent return, fundamentalist Christians focused on personal evangelism, usually ignoring involvement in social issues. Christianity was counter-cultural in the extreme, not a part of culture.

This view of Christianity and the world grows steadily weaker. With minor exceptions, most mainline and fundamental evangelicals agree that interaction with the world is not only inevitable but necessary to accomplish the will of God. The gospel of Jesus Christ has social implications, as do God's calls for justice and compassion on the part of social institutions.

However, the separatist approach does have positive features. It gives a helpful insight into the distinction between God's will and the ways of the world. The antagonism is real, not imagined. Further, many who have practiced a separatistic approach have demonstrated that the secular pressures to conformity can be overcome.

On the other hand, the separatist approach is somewhat impractical in its application to daily life. Although some persons may be able to withdraw from worldly influences, most Christians have neither the resources nor the opportunity to disengage completely from the world. Then, of course, there is always the problem of degree: where are we to draw the line in the separation? Further, the separatist approach runs counter to the pattern of godly servants in the Bible who were very much *in* the world but not *of* the world. Joseph, Nehemiah, and Daniel are but a few such examples of outstanding individuals who are highly praised for their application of godly principles to their social world.

Reconciliation: The Christian Befriending the World

The mention of Joseph, Nehemiah, and Daniel reminds us of the biblical accounts of those who maintained a commitment to God's principles while spending most of their lives in what believers today would consider "secular" service. This social and spiritual détente recognizes the superiority of God's law while acknowledging the legitimate place and authority of social institutions.

The reconciliation approach appeals to Paul's affirmation that Christians are to obey the governing authorities and be in subjection to them (Rom. 13:1). Paul follows this admonition with the pronouncement that all authority (including social authority mediated through the government) is established by God. In light of the social and political context in which Paul wrote these words, his command is even more striking. Lest there be any doubt concerning the authorities that were to be respected, Peter adjures Christians to "honor the king" (1 Pet. 2:17).

The reconciliation approach is not a capitulation to secular society but rather the recognition of the biblical role that social structures play in God's plan. Thus, at most points, what the government ordains, God ordains (Rom. 13:2). Government may be God's servant (Rom. 13:4), not His enemy. It is the necessary means by which order and peace are preserved among men.

However, because the Christian lives in two realms, conflict is inevitable. There are limits to the obedience a Christian must exercise toward social authorities. When such an authority conflicts with a command of God, Christians have no other option but to "obey God rather than men" (Acts 5:29). Biblical examples of such conflicts clearly represent the pattern to follow (Dan. 3:6; Acts 4:5). Today it is illegal in some countries for Christians to worship and evangelize; yet, like the apostle Peter, many continue to "break the law" in order to obey the higher authority of God's law.

Those involved with the Operation Rescue program appeal to this conflict as the rationale for their obstruction of abortion clinics. The secular law permits abortion, they argue, but God's law does not. Therefore, they feel justified breaking the immoral worldly law in order to promote the law of God. It is debatable whether or not this reasoning is a correct application of the principle of appealing to a higher authority;[14] nevertheless, their approach is one form of reconciliation.

---

14. For differing perspectives on the legitimacy of the Operation Rescue agenda see Randall Terry, *Operation Rescue* (Springdale, Pa.: Whitaker House, 1988) and J. M. Connors, "Operation Rescue" *America* (29 April 1989), 160:400-402.

Most evangelical groups would fall into this category. The moral agenda of the reconciliation approach is not to change or "Christianize" the structure of society or government, but rather to ensure that morality and justice prevail. How morality and justice are advanced in society is currently worked out with different programs among Christians. On the one hand, the fundamentalist right seeks for a return to "traditional values" and less government involvement in the affairs of everyday life. Politically, the fundamentalists lobby for "laws promoting morality," that is, laws against abortion, illegal drugs, pornography; laws for school prayer and the like. The most obvious example of this approach is the now-defunct Moral Majority[15] (see the second case study at the end of this chapter).

On the other hand, the evangelical radical left equates a moral government with a system that ensures justice for all people, help for the poor and needy, and care for the ill. They argue for *more* government involvement in the affairs of everyday life to carry out the biblical mandate to meet the needs of our brothers. They claim that our current system has resulted in the exploitation of many who cannot afford health care, job training, and adequate housing. The moral failure of individuals (including Christians) who ignore these needs places the burden upon a "government of the people" to promote biblical justice in society. This approach is advanced by such groups as Evangelicals for Social Action and periodicals such as *The Other Side* and *Sojourners*.[16]

A reconciliation approach that shuns political involvement is the resurgence of the Anabaptist tradition. Championed by John Howard Yoder of the University of Notre Dame and James William McClendon of Berkeley's Graduate Theological Union, the new Anabaptist agenda urges the church to allow the Christian community to mold social ethics.[17] The life of Jesus is the pattern for all Christians to follow. Neither He nor His followers possessed genuine political authority, yet Jesus and the Christian movement were agents of radical social change.

Jesus acknowledged the believer's responsibility to governing authorities ("Render unto Caesar . . ."), but also forged a path of nonvio-

15. For a full description of the agenda for the fundamentalist right, see Jerry Falwell, Ed Dobson, and Ed Hindson, eds., *The Fundamentalist Phenomenon: The Resurgence of Conservative Christianity* (New York: Doubleday, 1981).

16. Good sources for an exposition of the evangelical radical left are the periodicals mentioned above and Ronald J. Sider, *Rich Christians in an Age of Hunger*, 2d ed. (Downers Grove, Ill.: InterVarsity, 1984); and Jim Wallis, ed., *The Rise of Christian Conscience* (San Francisco: Harper & Row, 1987).

17. See John Howard Yoder, *The Politics of Jesus* (Grand Rapids: Eerdmans, 1972); *The Priestly Kingdom: Social Ethics as Gospel* (Notre Dame, Ind.: U. of Notre Dame, 1986); and James William McClendon, Jr., *Ethics: Systematic Theology* (Nashville: Abingdon, 1986).

lence and peacemaking. In this way, Christians intimidate worldly powers by the sheer force of their moral authority. For example, Queen Mary feared the prayers of John Knox more than the fire power of the Spanish Armada. Entire nations have been influenced toward social change by the nonviolent approaches of Dietrich Bonhoeffer, Martin Luther King, Jr., Mother Teresa, Dorothy Day, John Wesley, and a host of other "social activists."

Christians are to recognize that their social ethics and agenda are "peculiar" in the eyes of the world and will be the object of scorn and even attack, yet the Lord Himself will vindicate a godly, uncompromising confrontation with the social world. The Anabaptist approach will engage society with nonpolitical, nonviolent means of overcoming discrimination, pornography, abortion, and other outward manifestations of moral disease. The life-changing message of the gospel must be at the heart of any efforts of social change.[18]

Whether fundamentalist right, radical left, or Anabaptist, the reconciliation approach accepts God's authority as primary while acknowledging the biblical legitimacy of secular social institutions. A pluralistic society is not only accepted but expected. In many ways, modern society is a great deal like the pluralism of the first century when Christianity was born. The Christian community, however, will not allow the prevailing social ethos to dictate the church's agenda for spreading the truth of God into society.

The most difficult problem faced by the reconciliation approach is, again, where to draw the line. There is a wide range of possible areas of agreement and disagreement in the application of this view. Some Christians will adopt a laissez faire attitude toward social issues while at the same time seeking to be good citizens and Christians. Others zealously involve themselves in political or social action groups in order to call secular society into account for its unbiblical tendencies.

Transformation: The Christian Renewing the World

The zealous involvement of some Christians mentioned above is an extreme position for the reconciliation approach but characteristic for those who adopt the transformation approach. The goal of the transformationists is to bring the "secular world" into obedience to the "sacred realm" of God. For the transformationist, there is no distinction between sacred and secular. All is God's. Some elements of God's reign have re-

18. For an excellent exploration of the practical application of the Anabaptist approach, see Stanley Hauerwas and William H. Willimon, *Resident Aliens: Life in the Christian Colony* (Nashville: Abingdon, 1989).

jected Him and continue in a state of rebellion, but the Lord is still the authority in all affairs of life.

The work of Christ, it is believed, is more than merely a spiritual pardon for sin, but it is "cosmic in scope."[19] Christians are to involve themselves in the process whereby all creation "will be set free from its slavery to corruption into the freedom of the glory of the children of God" (Rom. 8:21). Then, and only then, will Christ "have first place in everything" (Col. 1:13-18). The very structure of society must be re-formed under the lordship of Jesus Christ. All civil magistrates must bow the knee to God who grants them authority.

Unlike the reconciliationists, those who hold to a transformation approach have no room for a legitimate pluralistic society. All authorities are commanded by God to "worship the Lord with reverence . . . [and] do homage to the Son" (Ps. 2:11, 12). Therefore, all aspects of society —government, economics, law, education—must be under the singular authority of God's law. There is no latitude for alternate views.

How this transformation is accomplished is not always clear. Different representations of this approach have been seen historically, for example, in the Holy Roman Empire and in some of the early Puritan societies. In these cases, the state bowed to the dictates of the church. There was not a state-church, rather there was a church-state. The law of God (as understood by the church leaders of the time) determined the moral foundation for civil legislation.

The most obvious form of modern transformational thought is seen in the theonomist movement. Theonomy (from *theos*, "God," and *nomos*, "law"; also known as Christian reconstructionism) seeks a radical reform of American society to bring it into conformity to God's laws. "God's law" is defined as the moral and civil teachings of the Old Testament. This excludes those aspects of the ceremonial law that were specifically fulfilled by Christ or abrogated by the New Testament.[20] In other words, the civil law code of ancient Israel is accepted as the God-ordained pattern for a biblical view of society and government.

The transformationist approach will always be fraught with questions. At the heart of the problem is the idea of superimposing the Old Testament law onto modern society. Was God's specific legislation for Israel intended to be the only acceptable pattern of civil government? Not

19. Richard Mouw, *When the Kings Come Marching In* (Grand Rapids: Eerdmans, 1983), p. 63.
20. For a full explanation of the teachings of theonomy, see the writings of R. J. Rushdoony, Gary North, and Greg Bahnsen. The most succinct description of the application of theonomy can be found in Greg Bahnsen, *Theonomy in Christian Ethics*, 2d ed. (Phillipsburg, N.J.: Presby. & Ref., 1984).

everyone agrees that the Old Testament civil law should be enforced in modern society. Theonomists often criticize those who disagree by claiming that they "only accept part of the Bible as valid for our age,"[21] an unusual charge because even theonomists do not live by the details of the Mosaic law. When the Bible does describe guidelines for government, the form it outlines is a totalitarian state governed by rulers in a family succession (Deut. 17:14-20). Such a form is arguably unworkable in modern Western society.

In addition, the distinctions made by theonomists among the civil, moral, and ceremonial laws of the Old Testament are somewhat artificial. These distinctions may be helpful in categorizing the various spheres of application of the law for Israel, but to use such nonbiblical categories as a means for accepting some for today (civil and moral) and rejecting others (ceremonial) is inappropriate.

There will always be difficulty in understanding the discontinuities between the Old Covenant and the New. However, the New Testament is clear that the law served as a "tutor" until Christ came (Gal. 3:18-19, 23-25). Jesus Christ came and fulfilled the whole law (Matt. 5:17-19), not merely the ceremonial aspects of Israel's ordinances. Jesus is "the end of the law" to all who believe (Rom. 10:4).

What can be accepted by all is: the lordship of Jesus Christ over all the earth; the sole source of morality located in the revelation of God; and the legitimacy of civil authority as a servant of God. The Christian faces the challenge of holiness in the personal sphere and wholeness in the public square.

CHALLENGE OF OUR CULTURE

Our day is besieged with moral and social difficulties. Abortion and pornography are allowed by the government; how should the Christian respond? The judicial system is riddled with inequities; should a prophetic voice be raised? Prejudice and discrimination against minorities continues; should Christians take a stand?

Everyday life oozes with unbiblical and antitheistic values: the sensuality and violence of television and other forms of media; the "God-neutral" approach to learning in public education; the societal partiality toward the rich, the powerful, and the young; the pragmatic ethics that justify lying and cheating in the pursuit of "having it all." How does the Christian determine the correct response?

---

21. Kevin L. Clauson, "The Christian America Response to Theonomy" in *God and Politics*, p. 64. Clauson is not a theonomist but is sympathetic with this aspect of their teaching.

The three approaches described in this chapter all reflect a biblical response to the pressures of the world. Separation will one day be a reality; social institutions will one day be reconciled to God's standards; and the world will one day be transformed. Until the perfect has come, however, Christians are left with the responsibility to make a difference. A biblical worldview will not allow a passive approach toward the social world. Francis Schaeffer reminded us that Jesus Christ is Lord of all: "He is our Lord, not just in religious things and not just in cultural things . . . but in our intellectual lives, and in business, and in our relation to society, and in our attitude toward the moral breakdown of our culture."[22] Although we do not have an abiding city on earth, we do have duties that constrain us. Writer Madeleine L'Engle admits, "It is impossible to listen to the Gospel week after week and turn my back on the social issues confronting me."[23]

The goal is to be Christ-centered in all things. For this reason, Christians cannot sit by idly as culture squeezes the soul and mind out of its people. Carl Henry sums it up best, "The divine mandate is to beam light, sprinkle salt, and knead leaven into an otherwise hopeless world."[24] Social engagement must take place at every level of the Christian life. Let's look at several examples: our work life, media and entertainment, and public social issues.

The Working Life

The Christian's greatest intensity of time and involvement with the world is usually found in the workplace. The role of work in society has been changing. The alienation of one's work from the family and neighborhood reflects a tremendous shift in the social life of America. At the personal level, although we remain convinced that our work is an important element of a meaningful human experience, the paycheck usually becomes the focus of our significance.

For the Christian, *how* one works is more important than *what* one does. Referring to the work of servants, Paul admonished: "Whatever you do, do your work heartily, as for the Lord rather than for men; knowing that from the Lord you will receive the reward of the inheritance. It is the Lord whom you serve" (Col. 3:23-24). Excellence, integrity, and honesty should be the marks of the Christian's work.

22. Francis A. Schaeffer, *The Great Evangelical Disaster* (Westchester, Ill.: Crossway, 1984), p. 39.
23. Madeleine L'Engle, "What May I Expect from My Church," in *Churches on the Wrong Road*, ed. Stanley Atkins and Theodore McConnell (Chicago: Regnery, 1986), p. 260.
24. Carl F. H. Henry, "The New Coalitions," *Christianity Today*, 17 November 1989, p. 26.

Unfortunately, many employers are more concerned with profits than with any other aspect of their business. The bottom line determines the direction of the company and personnel decisions. The company uses people to produce things or services.

Biblically, companies have the responsibility to practice sound financial principles and hold employees accountable for the quality of their work. People are far more important than products, programs, or projects. Because this is true, the work of a company should be designed to produce and develop the people who are employed. However, not all employers see the development of their employees as even a peripheral goal of their operations. If an employer is abusive and takes advantage of employees, the worker still has a responsibility before God to work with integrity (1 Pet. 2:18-20).

The Christian worker will also be concerned about the spiritual status of those with whom he works. Meeting the social, physical, and spiritual needs of those around him is a priority as he seeks to implement a biblical worldview in the work place. Excellent resources are available for the Christian who desires to explore a biblical perspective of work.[25]

Media and Entertainment

Western society is driven by its entertainment. Personal schedules, public functions, and even government and church programs conform to the entertainment itinerary. Entertainers are arguably the most powerful and well-paid individuals in our culture.

The Christian dilemma arises from both the content and value of the current types of entertainment in the media. Television, radio, and movies constitute the major means of media entertainment. This is not to exclude sporting events, games, concerts, literature, or other types of entertainment, but the emphasis here is on entertainment in media that is readily available and passively enjoyed.

Unfortunately, a great deal of media entertainment is both wicked and worthless. A biblical worldview calls for the Christian to guard what he sees, thinks, and hears. The psalmist echoes this admonition when he declares: "I will set no worthless thing before my eyes" (Ps. 101:3). "Worthless" is the Hebrew *belial*, a term that indicates both degradation

25. Among these are: Calvin Redekop and Urie A. Bender, *What Am I? What Am I?: Searching for Meaning in Your Work* (Grand Rapids: Zondervan, 1988); Richard C. Chewning, John W. Eby, and Shirley J. Roels, *Business Through the Eyes of Faith* (San Francisco: Harper & Row, 1990); John A. Bernbaum and Simon M. Steer, *Why Work? Careers and Employment in Biblical Perspective* (Grand Rapids: Baker, 1986); and Judith Allen Shelley, *Not Just a Job: Serving Christ in Your Work* (Downers Grove, Ill.: InterVarsity, 1985).

as well as worthlessness.[26] The designation, "children of Belial," occurs sixteen times in the Old Testament in reference to people who were "wicked and good for nothing." The term "Belial" eventually became a personal reference for Satan. It is no wonder that when Paul charges Christians not to allow the wickedness of the world to influence them, he asks "What harmony has Christ with Belial?" (2 Cor. 6:15).

Obviously, Christians should avoid all forms of entertainment that appeal to prurient interests. Movies, television programs, and songs that flaunt sensuality and promiscuity are never appropriate for the Christian. Fleeing immorality is always the best and wisest course of action. This is not merely a prudish view of morality but a recognition that the vivid imagery of entertainment heavily influences values and can desensitize our moral convictions.

But even beyond avoiding the obvious immoral forms of entertainment, Christians are called to discern that which is *excellent* (Phil. 1:9-11). Not everything that is harmful is necessarily evil. The writer of Hebrews admonishes believers to "lay aside every encumbrance . . . and run with endurance the race that is set before us" (Heb. 12:1). The "encumbrance" described is not necessarily that which is evil or sinful, but rather that which "hinders the runner." Habits, hobbies, avocations, and other activities that are substitutes for biblical responsibilities or that compromise spiritual values obviously weigh down those running the race. A biblical worldview forces the Christian to think just as seriously about his leisure time as he does about his prayer time.

Christians must honor that which is good and true, and this may involve speaking out against forms of entertainment that are immoral or antibiblical. At the same time recognizing that non-Christians will disagree, the follower of Christ has no alternative but to stand up for that which is right. This is not advocating censorship, rather it is a proclamation of truth that must serve as the moral conscience of society.

MORALITY IN OUR CULTURE

The "salt and light" venue of the Christian's confrontation with the world is most clearly seen when dealing with issues of public morality. Abortion, pornography, discrimination, and a host of other moral questions are not the problem but rather *symptoms* of a greater problem. The problem is rooted in a conflict of worldviews: *Who* is the authority? Is it

26. See Philip E. Hughes, *The Second Epistle to the Corinthians*. New International Commentary on the New Testament (Grand Rapids: Eerdmans, 1962), pp. 248-52.

God or is it ourselves? The challenge to God's standards cannot be met merely by turning moral issues into political positions.

Christians must speak from a base of moral authority and personal compassion. They should be marked by a desire for justice, a drive toward righteousness, and a concern for the individual. True transformation can take place in society from the inside out. Attacking social problems at the root may do more than legislative reform to stem the further growth of immorality. For example, if Christians targeted the causes for widespread abortion and helped to relieve the social and economic hardships that often lead a woman to choose abortion, many of the pro-choice utilitarian arguments would be voided. The sheer moral authority of an uncompromising stand on principles, coupled with a sincere understanding and compassion, would make an impact on society that would be difficult to overcome.

The Bible lays out principles to guide human relationships. How these relate to forms of government and a social agenda is not always clear. But what is clear is that Christians are called to care for the needs of the poor (James 2:15-16; 1 John 3:17-18) and to do good to all (Gal. 6:10). Loving one's neighbor includes loving those who have different beliefs and backgrounds (Luke 10:25-37). Like the apostle Paul, we must seek wisdom in relating to outsiders (Col. 4:5-6), even going as far as accommodating their lifeview (1 Cor. 9:19-23) in order to communicate the word of truth to them. Naive isolationism and social withdrawal cannot fulfill the biblical mandate to influence the world. Christians must visibly stand out as those who walk after different goals for different reasons. Richard John Neuhaus delivers this challenge: "There should be a Christian distinctiveness, a Christian way of being out of sync, a Christian uncomfortableness, which we feel and which others feel about us, with all of the positions one can take in the political, cultural, and ideological debates in our society."[27]

The work of Jesus Christ provides the basis for the Christian's response to the world. Now, the natural world rots, rusts, and decays; the social world corrupts, fights, and dies. What began through His death and resurrection shall continue until He returns. Jesus reminded His followers of their ultimate hope: "In the world you will have tribulation, but take courage; I have overcome the world" (John 16:33).

---

27. Richard John Neuhaus, "Advancing the Rose of Religion in Public Life," in *Christian Allies in a Secular Age*, ed. Kevin Perrotta and John C. Blattner (Ann Arbor, Mich.: Servant, 1987), p. 50.

CASE STUDY: Saving the World—Ecology and Worldviews

The hoopla surrounding the twentieth anniversary of the first Earth Day on April 22, 1990, kicked off what has been called the "Decade of the Environment." The many rallies, media events, coins, stamps, shirts, and bumper stickers underline the concerted effort put forth to save the earth from continued man-made vandalization. Different approaches to many issues often result from different worldview starting points. However, the public response to environmental problems presents a case in which unified action can arise from differing worldviews.

The theistic mandate to care for the world God created and entrusted to humanity serves as the basis for a pro-active Christian response. As discussed earlier in this chapter, the derived authority mankind possesses over the environment will not allow for the exploitation of nature for the benefit of mankind's comfort.

From a naturalistic worldview, the urgency to respond to the environmental crisis is based on the pragmatic concern for the survival of the human race. From a utilitarian ethic, if the exploitation of the environment continues, we could be responsible for the destruction of planet earth.

The rise of environmental consciousness also coincides with the growing influence of popular transcendental thought. Although a connection between the two may not be a cause-effect, there is no doubt that ecological concerns are an integral part of the New Age worldview. If humanity is one with the environment, the need to care for the earth is obvious. Less mystical is the call by some in the educational wing of environmental activism for a new "ecological ethic" by which decisions governing environmental issues can be guided. The foundation for such an ethic would be opposed to both the ethics of naturalism (i.e., humanism) and theism.[28] Even though such a "moral ecology" is not strictly transcendental in nature, it adds support to a New Age, whole-earth interpretation of life.

Many factors contribute to the new-found emphasis on ecological care and protection. The most obvious is the need to deal with the current ecological mess: burgeoning landfills, polluted lakes, smog-filled air, and nuclear waste disposal. Whatever the reason for the ecological crisis, the call to respond and preserve the environment cuts across worldview biases.

28. For example, see Paul R. Ehrlich et al, *Ecoscience*, p. 811.

CASE STUDY: Religion and Politics—The Recent Resurgence

Christian political engagement rose to prominence in the 1980s. The most visible movement came from the fundamentalist Christian right. Of the many organizations raising political dust during this time, Jerry Falwell's Moral Majority, Robert Grant's Christian Voice, and Ed McAteer's Religious Roundtable were the most well-known. All were formed about the same time (1979-80), and the political agenda for each group aimed at two targets: Congress and the electorate. Raising the level of moral awareness in the lawmaking process was accomplished by lobbying members of Congress and mobilizing a conservative American constituency. Lawmakers were called into account for their congressional voting records. Congressional members who failed to support "traditional" family values were targeted by watch-dog arms of the organizations and became objects of negative campaigning.

In spite of the separatistic tenor of much of the rhetoric, these organizations included many non-Christians among their ranks. Jerry Falwell clearly delineated this policy when he stated the purpose of the Moral Majority: "to serve as a special interest group providing a voice for a return to moral sanity in these United States. Moral Majority is a political organization and is not based on theological considerations."[29] Joining forces with conservative Jews, Catholics, and secularists, the fundamental right emerged as a powerful political force during the eighties. Other similar organizations surfaced during the decade and rode the crest of conservative support. Most were more limited in their concerns, such as the Christian Action Council, Concerned Women of America, and the National Federation of Decency, to name a few. These organizaions raised millions to finance mass-mailings, research, education, and lobbying efforts.

The backlash from less conservative Americans was expected. New organizations arose to counter the religious right. People for the American Way and Americans for Common Sense were just two groups that joined with the American Civil Liberties Union and the National Organization for Women to promote a program of individual choice in moral decisions. Because the 1980s was a decade of relative peace and prosperity, the clashes between the right and the left seemed more recreational than meaningful. Only the abortion issue raised genuine emotional responses from both sides.

29. Jerry Falwell, "Future-Word: An Agenda for the Eighties," in *The Fundamentalist Phenomenon*, p. 188.

Now that the Moral Majority has ceased operations the future of the religious right's agenda is uncertain. The fall of several televangelists has potentially reduced the "superstar" mentality of American Christians for a while, and it seems possible that new Christian political activity will arise from the grassroots level.

DISCUSSION QUESTIONS

1. The "USA for Africa" (Bob Geldof) and other similar benefits raised great sums of money to provide relief for drought victims. What do you think were the various motivations for the many people involved in those programs? Why were Christians not at the forefront of those benevolent activities? Do such relief initiatives "fit" with a biblical worldview?
2. What are the major environmental needs in your part of the country? Are you motivated to become active in environmental concerns? Why or why not?
3. How would each of the three approaches to Christian social engagement in this chapter confront the following issues: abortion, civil rights for minorities, school prayer, teaching creation/evolution in public schools, military spending?
4. Writer Madeleine L'Engle claimed: "It is impossible to listen to the Gospel week after week and turn my back on the social issues confronting me." In your opinion, what aspects of the gospel message led her to make such a statement? Do you agree or disagree? Why? What "social issues" are particularly related to the message of the gospel?

FURTHER READING

The Natural World:

Dyrness, William. *Let the Earth Rejoice: A Biblical Theology of Holistic Mission*. Westchester, Ill.: Crossway, 1983.

Elsdon, Ron. *Bent World: A Christian Response to the Environmental Crisis*. Downers Grove, Ill.: InterVarsity, 1981.

Granberg-Michaelson, Wesley. *A Worldly Spirituality: The Call to Take Care of the Earth*. San Francisco: Harper & Row, 1984.

———. *Tending the Garden: Essays on the Gospel and the Earth*. Grand Rapids: Eerdmans, 1987.

Wilkinson, Loren. *Earthkeeping: Christian Stewardship of Natural Resources*. Grand Rapids: Eerdmans, 1980.

Wright, Richard T. *Biology Through the Eyes of Faith*. San Francisco: Harper & Row, 1989. See especially chapter 9, "Stewards of Creation."

The Social World:

Cerillo, Augustus, Jr., and Murray W. Dempster, eds. *Salt and Light: Evangelical Political Thought in Modern America*. Grand Rapids: Baker, 1989.

Davis, John Jefferson. *Evangelical Ethics: Issues Facing the Church Today*. Phillipsburg, N.J.: Presby. & Ref., 1985.

Hauerwas, Stanley, and William H. Willimon. *Resident Aliens: Life in the Christian Colony*. Nashville: Abingdon, 1989.

Mouw, J. Richard. *When the Kings Come Marching In*. Grand Rapids: Eerdmans, 1983.

Nash, Ronald. *Social Justice and the Christian Church*. Lanham, Md.: University Press of America, 1990.

Neuhaus, Richard John. *The Naked Public Square*. 2d ed. Grand Rapids: Eerdmans, 1986.

Niebuhr, Richard H. *Christ and Culture*. New York: Harper & Row, 1951.

Noll, Mark A. *One Nation Under God: Christian Faith and Political Action in America*. New York: Harper & Row, 1989.

Smith, Gary Scott, ed. *God and Politics: Four Views on the Reformation of Civil Government*. Phillipsburg, N.J.: Presby. & Ref., 1989.

Webber, Robert E. *The Church in the World*. Grand Rapids: Zondervan, 1986.

Wolterstorff, Nicholas. *Until Justice and Peace Embrace*. Grand Rapids: Eerdmans, 1983.

INDEX OF SCRIPTURES

EXTRABIBLICAL REFERENCES

INDEX OF PERSONS

INDEX OF SUBJECTS